PHILOSOPHY, POLITICS, AUTONOMY

ODÉON

JOSUÉ V. HARARI AND VINCENT DESCOMBES
General Editors

HERMENEUTICS AS POLITICS
Stanley Rosen

FAREWELL TO MATTERS OF PRINCIPLE
Philosophical Studies
Odo Marquard

WILLIAM SHAKESPEARE: A Theater of Envy
Rene Girard

IN DEFENSE OF THE ACCIDENTAL
Odo Marquard

PHILOSOPHY, POLITICS, AUTONOMY
Cornelius Castoriadis

Philosophy, Politics, Autonomy

CORNELIUS CASTORIADIS

Edited by
David Ames Curtis

New York Oxford
OXFORD UNIVERSITY PRESS
1991

Oxford University Press

Oxford New York Toronto
Delhi Bombay Calcutta Madras Karachi
Petaling Jaya Singapore Hong Kong Tokyo
Nairobi Dar es Salaam Cape Town
Melbourne Auckland

and associated companies in
Berlin Ibaden

Published by Oxford University Press, Inc.,
200 Madison Avenue, New York, New York 10016

Library of Congress Cataloging-in-Publication Data
Castoriadis, Cornelius.
Philosophy, politics, autonomy : essays in political philosophy /
Cornelius Castoriadis ; edited by David Ames Curtis.
p. cm. — (Odéon)
Some of the essays have been translated from French by the editor.
Includes bibliographical references and index.
ISBN 0-19-506962-5 (cloth). — ISBN 0-19-506963-3 (pbk.)
1. Political science—Philosophy.
I. Curtis, David Ames. II. Title.
JA71.C33 1992
320'.01—dc20 91-8980

1 3 5 7 9 8 6 4 2

Printed in the United States of America
on acid-free paper

Foreword

Only of late has the Anglophone reading public become aware of Cornelius Castoriadis and his five decades of work. Despite the pioneering efforts of the British journal *Solidarity* to translate Castoriadis' writings, efforts continued at one time by *Telos* and now by *Thesis Eleven*, it was only in 1984, with the publication of *Crossroads in the Labyrinth*, that Castoriadis' distinctive thought became accessible to a broad English-speaking audience. That first book-length translation, which contained articles from the previous decade, was followed by the publication of *The Imaginary Institution of Society* in 1987 and two volumes of his *Political and Social Writings* in 1988; the writings found in these latter translations, however, date from the mid-1940s through the mid-1970s. The publication of the present volume will be the first time that Castoriadis' essays are published in English in book form in a timely fashion.

What makes this situation so striking is that there are so few living, active writers of Cornelius Castoriadis' experience and breadth of vision. To recap briefly the path he has traveled,[1] Castoriadis, born in

1. For an in-depth biographical/intellectual history, see Castoriadis' General Introduction to the first volume of his *Political and Social Writings*, tr. David Ames Curtis, 2 vols. (Minneapolis: University of Minnesota, 1988) and my Foreword, also found in this first volume. A constantly updated supplement to the bibliography which appears in the Appendixes to that volume is available through: Agora International, 27 rue Froidevaux, 75014 Paris, France.

1922 in Constantinople, began his political life at age fifteen years as a member of the Greek Communist Youth, formed an opposition group within the Greek Communist Party (1941) after the German occupation, joined the Trotskyists (1942) when he became convinced that the Communists were unreformable, and spent much of the rest of the war dodging both Stalinist agents and the Gestapo. Leaving Greece for France, he joined the Trotskyist Fourth International in Paris, where his unwelcome attack on the Fourth's "unconditional defense of the Soviet Union" led him and others to form an opposition group, Socialisme ou Barbarie. Basing their criticism on people's actual aspirations toward autonomy in the form of workers' self-management, they developed an intransigent critique of Russia and other Stalinist regimes as new social formations, neither traditionally capitalist nor socialist. The group broke with the Fourth (1948) to become eventually the most influential source for a non-Communist Left in France as well as the forerunner to the ideas and actions of the May 1968 student rebellion. Editor of the journal *Socialisme ou Barbarie,* Castoriadis authored its principal texts (1949–1966). He retired from his day job as an economist at the Organization for Economic Cooperation and Development (1970) and became a practicing psychoanalyst (1974) as well as a Director of Studies at the Ecole des Hautes Etudes en Sciences Sociales (1979). He is now recognized as one of Europe's foremost political and social thinkers. That he addresses in the present collection such a wide variety of topics and disciplines as philosophy, politics, and history, both ancient and modern, economics, ecology, contemporary political and social thought, aesthetics, the philosophy of science, and psychoanalysis is an indication of the breadth of his vision.

In the articles, lectures, and conference discussions that follow, we discover Castoriadis the essayist and engaged writer.[2] Employing his

2. More than half of these writings originally appeared in English, a language he speaks fluently; I have edited them mainly with an eye toward correcting printer's errors, standardizing terminology and clarifying a few ambiguous phrases. With one exception, I translated the rest. As mentioned in note 17 of my Foreword to the first volume of Castoriadis's *Political and Social Writings* (Minneapolis: University of Minnesota Press, 1988), pp. xxi–xxii, the nonsexist—if still grating—use of "s/he" and "his/her" is employed when translating and editing Castoriadis's contemporary writings; he, too, now generally employs "nonsexist" language.

vast erudition, his fine sense of purpose and proportion, and his sharp wit, he goes straight to the heart of the issues he addresses, placing the aspiration for individual and collective autonomy at the center of his concerns. These essays represent not discussions about specific political and social events, nor a discourse designed to erect or resurrect a "social theory," nor even philosophical speculations about the nature of "the political." These essays are actual philosophical and political attempts, through example and participation, to contribute to the ongoing historical movements that foster people's creative assertion of their autonomy.

Where does this self-implicating human creation that is individual and collective autonomy come from? Like all creation, Castoriadis would say, it comes from nowhere (*ex nihilo*); we cannot reduce it to anterior "causes" or attribute it to an invariant "human nature." However, creation does not occur without any means (*cum nihilo*) or out of all context (*in nihilo*). In fact—and this is the principal thesis presented and defended in this book—the beginnings of autonomy as a social-historically effective project can be dated and located. It began in Greece and took place in the Greek *poleis* from the eighth to the fifth century B.C., to be repeated in another form in the *bürger* cities that arose at the end of the Middle Ages in Western Europe. This project of autonomy is expressed in the simultaneous, but not identical, creation (and then recreation) of philosophy and politics as the reflective questioning of instituted traditions and the attempt to alter these traditions and institutions through conscious collective action.

Here misunderstandings may arise. When someone speaks of ancient Greece or "European culture" today, the habitual reaction is often to shout "Imperialism!", "Eurocentrism!", and "Down with Western Civilization!"—as a Stanford University student's sign in fact proclaimed during a protest in favor of replacing the school's mandatory introductory course in European culture with a broader study of world cultures. Philosophy and politics began in Greece? What a narrow view! What about "Eastern Philosophy"? And did not Greek "democracy" mean slavery for many as well as the disenfranchisement of women?

For Castoriadis, philosophy is not synonymous with speculation about the world, its origins, its meaning. It is the reflective questioning of socially instituted representations, including those instituted with the help of philosophical reflection. His bold claim is that reflection itself as well as effective judging and choosing are historical in character and have their origin in ancient Greece. Thus there is, for example, no oriental "philosophy," this being an anachronistic use of the Greek term. What Greek philosophy makes possible, he argues, is not (religiously) instituted ideas and beliefs along with interminable commentary thereupon, but dozens of contending schools of thought. Thus too, politics as self-responsible conscious collective action to alter a society's institutions is also a Greek creation, one that not only implies but also presupposes the establishment of a public space open to all who assert themselves as free and consider themselves and each other as equals. As this is a *project,* autonomous political activity aims not at a ready-made system requiring no further changes, but rather at the inauguration and continual renewal of a reflective and willed effort to reshape our institutions to our recognized needs and desires in such a way that the project of individual and collective autonomy is itself fostered and reinforced. What is interesting about the Greek *poleis,* Castoriadis argues, is not a Greek "model" of democracy and politics (which we would somehow now be asked to endorse or to reject), but the ongoing instituting activity it fostered for four centuries. Moreover, philosophy implies politics and vice versa, for philosophy as the reflective challenge to inherited thought cannot exist without the assertion of a political will that this be possible, and politics cannot consciously transform existing institutions unless these institutions themselves can be put explicitly into question.

Far from being a sanctification of "Western values"—even those of dialogue and questioning for their own sake—the thrust of Castoriadis' argument, then, is that it is only to the extent that we are willing and able to put our values into question, *knowing why and for what purpose we are doing so,* that we can continue the West's unique project of autonomy. Autonomy is not merely "self-institution." The latter is always occurring in society, most often in the form of *heteronomy,* the "self-occultation" of this self-instituting process, its imputation to an extrasocial, supranatural source. It was because the Greeks had no sacred books that this project could come into being in the first place. It was because the reassertion of autonomy in Western

European cities was expressed in an effort at self-rule, free from Church dictates and State power, that lucid philosophical questioning could effectively be reborn.

This being the thrust of Castoriadis' argument, the priority he assigns to ancient Greece as the birthplace of philosophy, politics, and the project of autonomy appears not as a "romantic" glance backward or a pious "defense" of "Western values," but as an elucidation of their unique meaning, which implies and involves a critical continuation of this very project. As he argues in "The Greek *Polis* and the Creation of Democracy," the problem for those who wish to flatten out history and make the Greeks just another people is that history itself as impartial "historiography" along with "the reasoned investigation of other cultures and the reflection upon them" are also Greek inventions. This is the "minute" but absolutely "decisive point" that advocates of the flattening approach have missed. It is only when we acknowledge and come to appreciate the true uniqueness of the Greco-Western tradition that we realize the significant contribution an impartial understanding of other cultures *qua* other cultures offers for the project of autonomy, this effort to question our own representations and to transform our institutions. To adopt for a moment the coarse categories of course catalogues, coming to terms with and assuming the legacy of "Western Civilization" does not stand in contradiction to, but serves precisely as the presupposition for, the study of "world cultures" as well as the possible critical and genuine reception of them.[3] Likewise, an awareness of other cultures is necessary for us to be able to criticize and to alter our own. Here we can sense the aspiration for autonomy that is implicit in this talk of world cultures. Yet this aspiration often now not only dares not speak its name but denies its own existence.

Autonomy is not the only "social imaginary signification" of the modern West. The other main cultural meaning guiding our lives is what Castoriadis calls "the unlimited expansion of 'rational' mastery." Such pseudorational mastery has been implemented most notably in capitalism and totalitarianism but also in our technoscientific attitude

---

3. Should the point need making, "Greek" and "European" in Castoriadis' vocabulary designate cultural formations, not geographical locations, or "racial types."

toward, and transformation of, nature and society (now accompanied by the prospect of worldwide ecological destruction). With the waxing of the project of total control has come the waning of the project of autonomy. As with the *choice* Castoriadis formulated of "socialism or barbarism," the battle between autonomy and heteronomy—between the assertion of autonomy and that which today erodes its very existence—is not one of an external opposition but of two intimately connected options, unfolding together as they alter themselves and each other. To respond fully to the challenge of and the challenges to autonomy, in the domain of philosophy as well as in the political realm, is of the greatest import today. These essays invite us to assume precisely that responsibility, in our thought and in our action.

December 1989 David Ames Curtis

Contents

PHILOSOPHY, POLITICS, AUTONOMY

—1—

Intellectuals and History

An old philosophical habit: I feel obliged to begin by dwelling upon the terms in which the question is posed. First of all, the term "history." I do not understand by it merely history-already-made but also history-in-the-making and history-to-be-made.

In this sense, history is essentially creation—creation *and* destruction. Creation signifies something entirely different from the objective indeterminacy or the subjective unforeseeability of events and of the course of history. It is ridiculous to say, for example, that the advent of tragedy was unforeseeable, and it is stupid to see in *St. Matthew's Passion* an effect of the indeterminacy of history.

History is the domain in which human beings create ontological forms—history and society themselves being the first of these forms. Creation does not necessarily—nor even generally—signify "good" creation or the creation of "positive values." Auschwitz and the Gulag are creations just as much as the Parthenon and the *Principia Mathe-*

Speech given to the "Intellectuals and History" round-table discussion at the International Conference of Intellectuals and Artists in Valencia (June 16, 1987), commemorating the fiftieth anniversary of the 1937 Congress of Antifascist Writers in Valencia. Published as "Les Intellectuels et l'histoire" in *Lettre Internationale,* 15 (December 1987), pp. 14–16, reprinted in *Le Monde Morcelé. Les Carrefours du labyrinthe* III (Paris: Seuil, 1990), pp. 103–11, and translated as "Intellectuals and History," tr. David Ames Curtis, *Salmagundi,* 80 (Fall 1988), pp. 161–69.

matica. But among the creations in our history, Greco-Western history, there is one that we judge positively and take credit for: putting things into question, criticizing them, requiring a *logon didonai*—accounting for something and giving a reason for it—which is the presupposition for both philosophy and politics.

Now, *this* is a fundamental human posture—and, at the outset, it is in no way universally given. It implies that there is no extrahuman authority responsible, in the last instance, for what occurs in history, that there are no true causes or author of history. In other words, it means that history is not made by God or by *physis* or by "laws" of any kind. It is because they did not believe in such extrahistorical determinations (besides the ultimate limit of *Ananke*) that the Greeks were able to create democracy and philosophy.

We ourselves resume, reaffirm, and will to prolong this creation. We are and will to be in a tradition of radical criticism, which also implies both responsibility (we cannot put the blame on an omnipotent God, etc.) and self-limitation (we cannot invoke any extrahistorical norm for our conduct, which nevertheless must be provided with norms). As a result, we situate ourselves as critical actors in relation to what is, what could and should be, and even what has been. We can contribute to the character of "what is" so that it may be otherwise. We cannot change what has been, but we can change how we gaze upon it—and this gazing is an essential ingredient of our present attitudes (even if it is most often done unconsciously). In particular, we do not grant, in a first approximation, any philosophical privilege to historical reality, past or present. Past and present are nothing other than masses of brute facts (or empirical subject matter) except insofar as they have been critically reevaluated by us. Since we are downstream from this past and since it therefore has been able to enter into the presuppositions of what we think and what we are, we may say, as a second approximation, that this past acquires a sort of transcendental importance, for our knowledge and criticism of it form a part of our self-reflective activity. And this is so not only because it clearly shows the relativity of the present, through our knowledge of other epochs, but also because it allows us to glimpse the relativity of actual history, through reflection upon other histories that were actually possible, even if they have not been realized.

Second, the term "intellectual." I have never liked it or accepted it, for reasons that are at once aesthetic: the miserable and defensive arrogance implied therein, and logical: Who is not an intellectual? Without entering into basic questions of biophysiology, let us observe that if one intends by the term "intellectual" someone who works almost exclusively with his head and nearly not at all with his hands, one leaves out people whom one would clearly want to include (sculptors and other categories of artists), and one includes people who certainly were not intended thereby (computer specialists, bankers and brokers, etc.).

It is unclear why a talented Egyptologist or mathematician who wanted to know nothing outside their respective disciplines would particularly interest us here. From this remark one might conclude that, for purposes of the present discussion, we ought to include all those who, irrespective of their profession, try to go beyond their sphere of specialization and actively interest themselves in what is going on in society. But this is, and ought to be, the very definition of the democratic citizen, irrespective of his occupation. (And let us note that this is the exact opposite of Plato's definition of justice: minding one's own business and not getting mixed up in everyone else's—which is not at all surprising, since one of Plato's aims is to show that democratic societies are unjust.)

I will not try to respond to this question here. My remarks are aimed at those who, by their use of speech and through their explicit formulation of general ideas, have been able or are now able to attempt to have an influence on how their society evolves and on the course of history. The list is immense, and the questions raised by their words and deeds are endless. Therefore, I will also confine myself to a brief discussion of three points.

The first concerns two different kinds of relationship between the thinker and the political community, as exemplified in the radical opposition between Socrates, the philosopher in the city, and Plato, the philosopher who wants to be above the city. The second relates to a tendency that began to take hold of philosophers during a certain phase of history—namely, the tendency to rationalize the real, that is, to legitimate it. The era that is just now coming to a close has witnessed some particularly grievous instances of this tendency, with the fellow-travelers of Stalinism of course, but also, in an "empirically" different but philosophically equivalent fashion, with Heidegger and Nazism. I will conclude on a third point: the question raised by the relationship between, on the one hand, the criticism and the vision of the philosopher-citizen and, on the other, the fact that, from the standpoint of a project of autonomy and democracy, the great majority of men and women living in society are the source of creation, the principal bearers of the instituting imaginary, and that they should become the active subjects of an explicit politics.

Socrates and Plato

In Greece, the philosopher was, during a long initial period, just as much a citizen as a philosopher. It is for this reason too that he was sometimes called upon to "give laws," either to his city or to another one. Solon offers the most celebrated example of this role played by the philosopher-citizen. But still in 443 B.C., when the Athenians established in Italy a pan-Hellenic colony called Thurioi, it was Protagoras whom they asked to establish a set of laws.

The last in this line—the last great one, at any rate—is Socrates. Socrates is a philosopher, but he is also a citizen. He discusses matters with all his fellow citizens in the agora. He has a family and children. He takes part in three military expeditions. He takes up the supreme magistracy, and he is the epistates of the prytaneis (president of the Republic for a day) at perhaps the most tragic moment in the history of the Athenian democracy: the day of the trial of the victorious generals of the battle of Arginusae, when, as president of the people's assembly, he braves the furious crowd and refuses to initiate illegal proceedings against these generals. Similarly, a few years later he will refuse to obey the order of the Thirty Tyrants to arrest a citizen illegally.

His trial and conviction are a tragedy in the proper sense of the term. It would be inane to search for the innocent and the guilty here. Certainly the *demos* of 399 B.C. is no longer that of the sixth or the fifth centuries, and certainly too, the city could have continued to accept Socrates as it had accepted him for decades. But we must also understand that Socrates's practices transgress the limit of what, strictly speaking, a democracy can tolerate.

Democracy is the regime founded explicitly upon *doxa,* opinion, the confrontation of opinions, the formation of a common opinion. The refutation of another's opinions is more than permitted and legitimate there; it is the very breath of public life. But Socrates does not limit himself to showing that this or that *doxa* is erroneous, nor does he offer a *doxa* of his own in its stead. He shows that all *doxae* are erroneous, and still more, that those who defend these *doxae* do not know what they are talking about. Now, no life in society, and no political regime—democracy least of all—can continue to exist based upon the hypothesis that all its participants live in a world of incoherent mirages—which is precisely what Socrates is constantly demonstrating.

The city certainly should have accepted even this; it had done so for a long time, with Socrates as well as with others. But Socrates himself knew perfectly well that sooner or later he would have to account for his practices. He did not need anyone to prepare his apology, he said, because he had spent his life reflecting upon the apology he would offer, were he ever accused. And Socrates not only accepts the judgment of the tribunal made up of his fellow citizens; his speech in the *Crito,* which is so often taken as a moralizing and edifying harangue, is a magnificent development of the fundamental Greek idea that the individual is formed by the city: *polis andra didaskei,* it is the city that educates the man, as Simonides wrote. Socrates knows that he was brought up by Athens and that he could not have been so brought up anywhere else.

It is hard to think of a disciple who has, in practice, betrayed the spirit of his master more than Plato. Plato withdraws from the city, and it is at its gates that he establishes a school for his chosen disciples. One knows of no military campaign in which he would have participated. One knows not of a family he would have reared. He furnishes to the city that raised him and made him what he is none of those things that every citizen owes it: neither military service nor children nor acceptance of public responsibilities. He calumniates Athens to the most extreme degree, and, thanks to his immense genius as a stage director, a rhetorician, a Sophist, and a demagogue, he will succeed in imposing, for centuries to come, an image of the politicians of Athens—Themistocles and Pericles—as demagogues, of its thinkers as "Sophists" (in the sense imposed by him), its poets as corruptors of the city, and its people as a vile herd given over to their passions and illusions. He knowingly falsifies history—and in this domain he is the first inventor of Stalinist methods. If one knew the history of Athens only through Plato (from the third book of the *Laws*) one would know nothing of the battle of Salamis, the victory of Themistocles and of that despicable *demos* of oarsmen.[1]

What he wants to do is to establish a city removed from time and history, governed not by its own people but by "philosophers." But he is also—contrary to all of previous Greek experience, where the philosophers have shown an exemplary *phronesis,* a wisdom in their actions—the first to display that basic ineptitude which has, since then, so often characterized philosophers and intellectuals when faced with political reality. He wants to be the counselor to the prince, in fact a tyrant—this has never stopped since—and he fails miserably because he, the subtle psychologist and admirable portraitist, cannot tell apples from oranges and takes Dionysius the Younger, tyrant of Syracuse, for a potential philosopher-king—as, twenty-three centuries later, Heidegger will take Hitler and Nazism for the incarnations of the spirit [*esprit*] of the German people and of historical resistance against the reign of technique. It is Plato who inaugurates the era of philosophers who wriggle out of the city, but who, as possessors of the truth, want to dictate to it laws while completely ignoring people's instituting creativity and, at the same time being politically impotent, have as their supreme ambition to become counselors to the prince.

The Adoration of the *Fait Accompli*

Nevertheless, Plato is not at the source of this other deplorable aspect of the activity of intellectuals when confronted with history: the rationalization of the real, that is to say, the legitimation of the powers-that-be. And for good reason. In Greece, at least, adoration of the *fait accompli* is unknown and impossible as an attitude of the mind [*esprit*]. We must move ahead to the Stoics to begin to find its first seeds. Though it is impossible for us to discuss its origins here and now, it is

1. Pierre Vidal-Naquet has reminded me of this last point during friendly conversations.

evident that, after an enormous detour, this attitude harks back to the archaic and traditional phases of human history, when the institutions given at each time were considered sacred, and accomplishes the amazing feat of putting philosophy, born as an integral part of putting the established order in question, into the service of the conservation of this very order.

However, it is impossible not to see that Christianity, from its very inception, was the explicit creator of the spiritual, affective, and existential postures that will, for eighteen centuries and more, provide a basis for the sanctification of the powers-that-be. The dictum, "Render unto Caesar the things which be Caesar's," can only be interpreted along with the statement that "There is no power but of God: the powers that be are ordained of God." The true Christian kingdom is not of this world and, moreover, the history of this world, by becoming the history of Salvation, is immediately sanctified in its existence and in its "direction," that is to say, in its essential "sense."[2] Exploiting for its own ends the Greek philosophical *instrumentarium*, Christianity will furnish, for fifteen centuries, the conditions required for acceptance of the "real," such as it is—up to Descartes's "Better to change oneself than the order of the world" and, obviously, to the literal apotheosis of reality in the Hegelian system ("All that is real is rational"). Despite appearances, it is this same universe—an essentially theological, apolitical, acritical universe—to which belong both Nietzsche, when he proclaims the "innocence of becoming," and Heidegger, when he presents history as *Ereignis* and *Geschick*, advent of Being and donation/destination of and through the latter.

Let us be done with this ecclesiastical, academic, and literary "respectuosity." Let us finally speak of syphilis in this family, of which half the members are clearly suffering in general paralysis. We should take by the ear the theologian, the Hegelian, the Nietzschean, the Heideggerian, bring them to Kolyma in Siberia, to Auschwitz, into a Russian psychiatric hospital, into the torture chambers of the Argentine police, and require that they explain, on the spot and without subterfuges, the meaning of the expressions "There is no power but of

2. Translator's Note: In French, the word "sens" means both "direction" and "meaning" or "sense."

God," "All that is real is rational," "the innocence of becoming," or "releasement toward things."[3]

But we encounter the most extraordinary *mélange* when the intellectual, in a supreme *tour de force,* succeeds in tying the critique of reality to the adoration of force and power. This *tour de force* becomes elementary once a "revolutionary power" arises somewhere or other. Then begins the golden age of fellow-travelers, who were able to afford the luxury of an apparently intransigent opposition to a part of reality—reality "at home"—by paying for it with the glorification of another part of this same reality—over there, elsewhere, in Russia, in China, in Cuba, in Algeria, in Vietnam, or, if worst came to worst, in Albania. Rare are those among the great names in the Western intelligentsia who have not, at some moment between 1920 and 1970, made this "sacrifice of conscience," sometimes (the least often) in the most infantile kind of credulity, other times (most often) with the most paltry sort of trickery. Sartre, stating in a menacing tone: "You cannot discuss what Stalin is doing, since he alone has the information that explains his motives," will remain, no doubt, the most instructive specimen of the intellectual's tendency to look ridiculous.

Faced with this debauchery of pious perversity and of fraudulent use of reason, we must forcefully state the following, deeply buried evident truth: *reality possesses no privilege,* neither philosophical nor normative; the past has no more value than the present, and the latter exists not as model but as material. The past history of the world is in no

---

3. Translator's Note: I have followed the actual English translation of the German phrase, "Die Gelassenheit zu den Dingen." (Martin Heidegger, "Memorial Address," in *Discourse on Thinking,* tr. John M. Anderson and E. Hans Freund [New York: Harper and Row, 1966], p. 54. The original German title of this book is *Gelassenheit.*) The French translation reads: "l'âme égale en présence des choses," which could be translated as "the soul unruffled in the presence of things."

Author's Note: Cf. *ibid.,* p. 52, where Heidegger says, "No single man, no group of men, . . . no merely human organization [?!] is up to the task of taking in hand the governance of our atomic age." [Translator's Note: Translation slightly altered to accommodate both French and English translations.] And: "We are to do nothing but wait" ("Conversation on a Country Path," *ibid.,* p. 62). [Translator's Note: This "Conversation" between a "scientist," a "scholar," and a "teacher" was noted down in writing by Heidegger circa 1944–45, i.e., at the end of the Nazi regime in Germany. The statement quoted here is made by the "teacher" who expounds upon the meaning of "releasement."]

way sanctified—and it might be rather that it is damned, for it has shunted aside other, effectively possible histories. These latter have as much importance for the mind [*esprit*]—and perhaps more value for our practical attitudes—than "real" history. Our daily paper does not contain, as Hegel believed, "our morning realist prayer" but rather our daily surrealist farce. More than ever, perhaps, this is so today. If something should appear in the present year, it should create in us, initially and until there is proof to the contrary, the strong presumption that it incarnates stupidity, ugliness, maleficence, and vulgarity.

The Citizen

Certainly, to restore, to restitute, to reinstitute an authentic task for the intellectual in history is, first of all and above all, to restore, restitute, and reinstitute his/her critical function. Because history is always both creation and destruction at once, and because creation (like destruction) concerns the sublime as much as the monstruous, elucidation and criticism are, more than anybody else's, in the custody of those who, by occupation and by position, can place themselves at a distance from the everyday and from the real. That is to say, in the custody of the intellectual.

At a distance, too, and as far as it is possible, from oneself. This takes the form not only of "objectivity" but also of an ongoing effort to go beyond one's speciality, to remain concerned by all that matters to men and women.

Such attitudes would certainly tend to separate the subject from the great mass of his/her contemporaries. But there is separation and there is separation. We will not leave behind us the perversion of the intellectual's role that has characterized it since Plato's time, and again for the past seventy years, unless the intellectual genuinely becomes a *citizen* again. A citizen is not (not necessarily) a "party activist," but someone who actively claims participation in public life and in the common affairs of the city on the same footing as everyone else.

Here, quite evidently, appears an antinomy which has no theoretical solution; only *phronesis,* effective wisdom, can permit one to surmount it. The intellectual should want to be a citizen like the others; s/he also wants to be spokesperson, *de jure,* for universality and objectivity. S/he can abide in this space only by recognizing the *limits* of that which his/her supposed objectivity and universality permit of him/her; s/he should recognize, and not just through lip service, that what s/he is trying to get people to listen to is still a *doxa*, an opinion, not an *episteme*, a science. Above all, s/he must recognize that history is the domain in which there unfolds the creativity of all people, both men and women, the learned and the illiterate, a humanity in which s/he is only one atom.

Nor should this become a pretext for swallowing uncritically the decisions of the majority, for bowing down before force because it is the force of numbers. To be a democrat and to be able, if this be one's judgment, to say to the people, "You are mistaken," this too is what should be required of him or her. Socrates was able to do it during the Arginusae trial. After the fact the case seems clear-cut, and Socrates was able to rely upon a rule in formal law. Things are often much hazier. Here again, only wisdom, *phronesis*, and *taste*, can permit one to separate the recognition of people's creativity from blind adoration of "the power of facts." And be not surprised to find the word *taste* at the end of these remarks. One only had to read five lines of Stalin to understand that the revolution could not be *that*.

—2—

The "End of Philosophy"?

We are living through a protracted crisis of Western society and culture. The diagnosis is not invalidated by its innumerable repetitions—from Rousseau and the romantics through Nietzsche, Spengler, Trotsky to Heidegger and beyond. In fact the very ways along which many among these authors and others have tried to establish it are in themselves symptoms of the crisis and belong to it.[1]

To the crisis belongs also the proclamation—especially, but not only, by Heidegger—of "the end of philosophy" and the whole array of deconstructionist and postmodernist rhetoric. Philosophy is a central element of the Greco-Western project of individual and social auton-

---

1. For my part I have dealt with the subject in "Modern Capitalism and Revolution" (1960–61), available now in English in my *Political and Social Writings* (Minneapolis: University of Minnesota Press, 1988), tr. David Ames Curtis, 2 vols., vol. 2, especially pp. 271–96, and in various other texts, among which "The Crisis of Western Societies" is available in a (poor) English version in *Telos*, 53 (Fall 1982), pp. 17–28.

The ideas in this text were first presented during a lecture at the Goethe University in Frankfurt, in November 1986. The version published here is that of a lecture at Skidmore College (October 1988) published in *Salmagundi*, 82–83 (Spring–Summer 1988), pp. 3–23. My own French translation now appears in *Le Monde morcelé. Les Carrefours du labyrinthe III* (Paris: Seuil, 1990), pp. 227–46. [Translator's Note: I have translated and included a last paragraph which has been added to the French version. It appears here in brackets at the end of the present text.]

omy; the end of philosophy would mean no more and no less than the end of freedom. Freedom is threatened not only by totalitarian or authoritarian regimes, but also, in a more hidden but no less deep fashion, by the waning of conflict and critique, the spreading of amnesia and irrelevance, the growing inability to put into question the present and the existing institutions, be they strictly "political" or *weltanschaulich*. Philosophy has had a central, if mostly indirect, role in this critique. This role is being dissolved first and foremost by contemporary social-historical trends, which I will not discuss here.[2] But an effect of these trends, which in turn reinforces them, is the influence of the Heideggerian and post-Heideggerian adoration of brute "reality"—and the Heideggerian proclamation "we have nothing to do," "nothing is to be done."[3] The combination of both can be found in the glorification of a "*debile* thought," of a soft, weak, flexible thought expressly adapted to the society of the media.[4] Deconstructionist "criticism," carefully limiting itself to the deconstruction of old books, is one of the symptoms of the crisis.

The proclamation of the "end of philosophy" is, of course, not new. It is most clearly decreed by Hegel. It rests, both in Hegel and in Heidegger, on a philosophy which is, indissociably, an ontology (or a "thinking of Being"), a philosophy of history and a philosophy of the history of philosophy. It is not my purpose to discuss Hegel, nor Heidegger's ontology; however, some remarks do seem to me relevant here.

Heidegger's implicit philosophy of history—history as *Geschick*, destiny, destination, and donation of/by Being—and the entirety of his writing have as necessary condition Heidegger's congenital blindness before the political/critical activity of humans (at the root of his adher-

2. Cf. the texts in Note 1 and my "The Crisis of Culture and the State," Ch. 9 of this book.

3. Cf. for instance and among many other formulations, the "Conversation on a Country Path" concerning *Gelassenheit:* "We are to do nothing, but wait." (In *Discourse on Thinking*, tr. John M. Anderson and E. Hans Freund [New York: Harper and Row, 1966], p. 62.) The posthumous *Spiegel* interview is also very outspoken on this point.

4. Thus, *Il pensiere debole*, ed. Gianni Vatimo and P. A. Rovati (Milano, 1983), and Gianni Vatimo, *La fine della modernità* (Garzanti Editore, 1985).

ence to Nazism and the *Führerprinzip*). This blindness is fittingly complemented by a seemingly equally congenital blindness concerning sexuality and, more generally, the psyche. Here we have the bizarre spectacle of a philosopher talking interminably about the Greeks, and whose thought draws a blank in the place of *polis, eros,* and *psyche.* But an "interpretation" of Greek philosophy ignoring systematically the fact that philosophy was born in and through the *polis* and is a part of the same movement which brought about the first democracies, is bound to be irredeemably lame. If, as Heidegger once wrote, Greek is not "a" language, but *the* language, and therefore predestined for philosophy, what are we to make of the fact that Spartans spoke Greek—indeed, they spoke better than the other Greeks, *lakonizein*—but no Spartan philosopher is known?[5] The same blindness leads him to see in the present period only the domination of technique and "science"—in both cases, with an unbelievably naive stance before the supposed omnipotence of both—and makes him incapable of seeing the internal crisis of the technoscientific universe and, even more important, the activities of humans directed against the present system and the possibilities these activities contain.

This philosophy of history leads Heidegger to a method of interpretation of the history of philosophy which is, at its core, Hegelian, for the same deep reasons and, in fact, with the same results. In short: a true critical discussion of the philosophers of the past is forbidden or becomes impossible. Thereby philosophical democracy, the intertemporal *agora* of living and dead philosophers where they gather over the centuries and truly discuss, is abolished. With Hegel, critique of the past philosophers is only a sign that the critic does not understand what philosophy is. Past philosophers cannot be criticized, but only surmounted, *aufgehoben,* shown to lead "from inside" to the next philosopher, and so on till we arrive at Absolute Knowledge, that is the Hegelian system. (Of course, Hegel himself could not possibly remain

5. Except for the Lacedaemonian Hilon, one of the Seven Sages. Heidegger's monstrous (and, in the most important place, clearly political-reactionary) "interpretation" of the celebrated *stasimon* of Antigone ("many things are terrible . . .") at the end of his *Introduction to Metaphysics* shows how deeply alien he was to the Greek world and spirit.

faithful to this program.) The deep links of this attitude to Hegel's overall philosophy are as obvious as the intractable impossibilities it leads to. The end of philosophy is not a whim or an opinion of Hegel—it is the necessary implication of his whole system, which stands and falls with it. Things are not truly different with Heidegger. No critical discussion of the past philosophers can take place; the "thinkers," in fact, express moments in the "History of Being," Being talks through their mouths. (Of course, Heidegger also cannot remain faithful to his program.) Past philosophers can only be interpreted and "deconstructed" (the program of *Sein und Zeit* is *die Destruktion der Ontologie,* "deconstruction" is a more recent fruit). This means that it has to be shown, in each case, that they all partake of "metaphysics" understood as the covering up of the "ontological difference," the Forgetting of Being, the preoccupation with the being of beings, and the neglect of the question of the Meaning of Being, and that nevertheless and curiously, this forgetting somehow "progresses" (that is, regresses) in a quite Hegeloid fashion through history, toward more and more complete forms, so that the accomplishment/achievement of metaphysics and the forgetting of Being are there at once with Plato (and perhaps even the pre-Socratics), but are more completely completed with Hegel and, then, Nietzsche. Along this way, conflicts, contradictions, struggle among philosophers are ignored or covered up, and the whole history of philosophy is linearized so as to reach its destined result—the closure of metaphysics and its thinker, Heidegger. With Hegel, all philosophies are reduced to the same in the sense that all of them represent merely "moments" in the process of self-consciousness and self-cognizance of the Spirit—and in the sense that all these "moments" stand convicted as "moments" of the (Hegelian) System. With Heidegger, all philosophers are reduced to the same:[6] they represent various but, when we come to the heart of the matter, indifferent ways of forgetting Being, of thinking Being as presence, and of mixing up presence and that which is, in each case, present. With post-Heideggerians, this will become the unbreakable circle of Greco-Western onto-logo-theo-phallocentrism. But fortunately, we are not

6. Cf. the last pages of *Der Spruch des Anaximander* (1946), where Aristotle, Plato, Heraclitus, Parmenides, and Anaximander are presented as thinking "the same."

yet completely lost. With the help of the *Zeitgeist,* some noises about the possibility of evading this circle through recourse to the Old Testament (not of course the New, hopelessly contaminated by those damned Greeks), are increasingly perceptible. After we had been almost convinced of the nothingness of any "transcendental signified," we are now informed that Jehovah, his laws, and the ethic of the Hebrews can and must be restored in the place of a (meta- ? or post- ?) transcendental signified. Dare we hope that we only need to replace philosophy by revelation in order to be saved?

No wonder that, a few exceptions apart, philosophy is practiced less and less, and that most of what bears that name today is just commentary and interpretation, or rather, commentary squared and interpretation squared. This means also that the history of philosophy itself is becoming distorted, torn between spiritless and scholastic academicism and deconstructionist irrelevance.

How to approach the history of philosophy, that is, the work of important philosophers of the past, is of course a huge question in itself. Some cardinal points seem to me worth noting.

A philosopher writes and publishes because he believes that he has important and true things to say—but also, because he wants to be discussed. Being discussed entails also, possibly, being criticized and refuted. And all great philosophers of the past—up to and including Kant, Fichte, and Schelling—have explicitly discussed, criticized, and frequently refuted—or thought that they refuted—their predecessors. They thought, rightly, that they belonged to a transtemporal, social-historical public space, to the transhistorical *agora* of reflection, and that their public criticism of other philosophers was an essential factor in maintaining and enlarging this space as a space of freedom where there are no authorities, no revelation, no general secretary, no führer, and no *Geschick des Seins;* where different *doxae* are confronted and where everybody is entitled, at his own risks and perils, to express disagreement.

This is why for a philosopher there *can* only be a critical history of philosophy. Critique of course presupposes the most painful and disinterested attempt to understand the work criticized. But it requires also constant vigilance as regards its possible limitations—which result from the almost inevitable *closure* of any work of thought that accompanies its breaking of the previous closure.

But this is also why for a philosopher there *must* be a critical history of philosophy. If this history is not critical, he is not a philosopher, just a historian, an interpreter, a hermeneutician. And if there is no history in the full meaning of the word, the philosopher works under the fateful delusion that he is starting everything all over again—the delusion of the *tabula rasa.* Philosophy is a reflective activity that deploys itself both freely and under the constraint of its own past. Philosophy is not cumulative—but it is deeply historical.

In this sense, a circular situation obviously obtains, one which does not manifest any "logical defect," but expresses the very essence of self-reflection within the necessarily total horizon of philosophical thought—or the fact that its center *is* its periphery, and vice versa. A critical history of the past is not possible without a proper standpoint. But it is not possible, either, without some conception of what history is—human history in the widest and deepest meaning of the term—and what the place of philosophy in this history is. (In this respect, Hegel and Heidegger are, of course, formally correct.) This does not in the least mean "explaining" (and "refuting") Plato and Aristotle by the existence of slavery, Descartes and Locke by the rise of the bourgeoisie and all the well-known similar nonsense. But it does most emphatically mean that past (and present) philosophy has to take its place in the history of the human imaginary and of the painful, millenary struggle against the heteronomous institution of society. It would be just as silly to deny the essential *political* motives and determinations of Plato's philosophy, the fight against democracy, and their deep links to the whole of Plato's thought up to and including his ontology—as it would be silly to deny that Plato created and instituted again, for a second time, philosophy and that he remains to this day the greatest philosopher of all. Equally, and on a much more modest level, it would be silly to deny the deeply reactionary, antidemocratic motives and traits of Heidegger's thought, manifest already in *Sein und Zeit* (six years before the *Rektoratrede*) and persisting to the end (the posthumous *Spiegel* interview), and their intimate relation to the whole of his conceptions—as it would be silly to deny that Heidegger was one of the important philosophers of the twentieth century and to assert that a philosopher today could simply ignore him. The paradox apparently involved here certainly requires further examination, but this is not our present theme.

Philosophy is not cumulative—as science could be taken to be, though even here things are not so clear as they usually appear. For practical purposes, anyhow, one can learn physics or mathematics today by studying contemporary textbooks, and with no need to read Newton, Einstein, Archimedes, Gauss, or Cantor. Art is not cumulative either, though it is a different case. Immersion in the culture where a given work of art has been created is almost always a condition for "understanding" (not only externally) works of art. But this does not mean that one cannot be taken by Wagner, say, unless one has gone through all the steps from Gregorian chant to Beethoven, etc.

With philosophy it is a different matter again. As self-reflective activity of thought, philosophy entails that, ideally, *any* form of thought is obligatorily relevant for it; therefore also, for a philosopher, is obligatorily relevant what other philosophers have already thought. But self-reflectiveness means of course critique: a philosopher critical of past philosophers is exerting, so to speak, self-criticism (rightly or wrongly is another matter). I cannot wake up one morning with an idea contradicting what I thought up to then, and rush to develop it forgetting what I was thinking in all my previous life. Birds sing innocently anew every morning—but they are birds, and they sing the same song. In the same way, I cannot ignore the fact that my own thought, however original I may deem it to be, is but a ripple, at best a wave, in the huge social-historical stream which welled up in Ionia twenty-five centuries ago. I am under the double imperative: to think freely, and to think under the constraint of history. Far from forming a double bind, this apparent and real antinomy is a spring and a source of strength for philosophical thought. Putting it in the simplest, plainest way: the spring and the strength of a potentially immensely rich monological dialogue.

This means also, finally, that I must have—or gradually form—a conception of what philosophy is, of what self-reflective activity is about. Now, what philosophy is has been each time defined again, explicitly or implicitly, by every important philosopher—and each time in the most intimate relation with the content of his philosophy.

(No need to quote examples of this.) In other words, it is impossible to define what philosophy is without some understanding of what philosophers have said—this is almost a tautology—but also, without a critical stand (which may lead to just a reconfirmation) in regard to it. Thus the conception of philosophy I form is strongly linked with the conception of the history of philosophy I form, and vice versa. But it is also impossible to think what philosophy is without some conception of history, since philosophy is a social-historical datum. (Whatever the "transcendental" claims, I would stop discussion with somebody who asserted that Aristotle could have been Chinese or Hegel Italian.) And, to close the circle, this shows that a philosophy is impossible without a philosophy of the social-historical.

In this respect, I can only summarize here, dogmatically, my own positions. I believe it impossible to understand what philosophy is truly, without taking into account its central place in the birth and deployment of the social-historical project of (individual and social) autonomy. Philosophy and democracy were born at the same time and in the same place. Their solidarity comes from the fact that both express the refusal of heteronomy—the rejection of the claims to validity and legitimacy of rules and representations just because they happen to be there, the refusal of any external authority (even, and especially, "divine"), of any extrasocial source of truth and justice, in brief, the putting into question of existing institutions and the assertion of the capacity of the collectivity and of thought to institute themselves explicitly and reflectively.[7] To put it in another way: the struggle for democracy is the struggle for true self-government. As the aim of self-government is not to accept any *external* limits, true self-government entails explicit self-institution, which presupposes, of course, the putting into question of the existing institution—and this, in principle, at any time. The project of collective autonomy means that the collectivity, which can only exist as instituted, recognizes and recovers its instituting character explicitly, and questions itself and its own activities. In other words, democracy is the regime of (political) self-

7. Cf. my text "The Greek *Polis* and the Creation of Democracy," ch. 5 of this book.

reflectiveness. What laws ought we to have, and for what reasons? But the same is true about philosophy. Philosophy is not about the question: What is Being, or what is the meaning of Being, or why is there something rather than nothing, etc. All these questions are secondary, in the sense that they are all conditioned upon the emergence of a more radical question (radically impossible in a heteronomous society): What is it that I ought to think (about being, about *physis,* about the *polis,* about justice, etc.—and about my own thinking)?

This questioning goes on, and has to go on, incessantly, for a simple reason. Any being-for-itself exists and can only exist in a *closure*—thus also society and the social individual. Democracy is the project of breaking the closure at the collective level. Philosophy, creating self-reflective subjectivity, is the project of breaking the closure at the level of thought. But of course, any breaking of the closure, unless it remains a gaping "?" which does not break anything at all, posits something, reaches some results, and, thereby, risks erecting again a closure. The continuation and renewal of reflective activity—not for the sake of "renewal," but because this *is* self-reflective activity—entails therefore the putting into question of previous results (not necessarily their rejection—no more so than the revisability of laws in a democracy entails that they have to be changed wholesale every morning).

Thus, the birth of philosophy is not just coincident, but equisignificant with the birth of democracy. Both are expressions, and central embodiments, of the project of autonomy. Here one has to take up another aspect of the deformation Greece underwent and is constantly undergoing at the hands of the never fully de-Christianized Westerners. Greek political creation—the *polis* and democracy—has always been seen as a static "result," with the "merits" and "demerits" of the Athenian democracy discussed as if this regime were to be a model or an antimodel for ever and anywhere[8]—instead of being seen to show that what is really democratic in Athens over and above all the rest, and what is of paramount importance for us, is not any

8. What is worse: most of the time, Western political philosophers—e.g., Leo Strauss—usually talk about the "political thought of the Greeks," hereby meaning mostly Plato (and much less Aristotle). This is tantamount to speaking about the "political thinking of the French Revolution" quoting Joseph de Maistre or Charles Maurras.

particular institution established at a certain point in time (though many of them are full of lessons for us), but the continuous process of democratic self-institution, going on for almost three centuries: there is the creativity, there is the self-reflectiveness, there is democracy, and there is the lesson. In the same way, the important thing about Greek philosophy—over and above any "results" reached (we all know how weighty these remain)—is the continuing process of its self-institution. As soon as Thales appears, he conditions the appearance of another philosopher, and so on; a self-reflective movement of thought starts in a truly historical dimension, embodied also in continuous open and public discussion and criticism, and this is not a vain assertion of "individuality," since these thinkers continuously take cognizance of each other's positions and produce arguments (almost all of them still to be taken into account today), materializing thereby not a "dialectical progression" but a genuine historical self-deployment of thought. Not two or three "schools," frozen for ever and commenting interminably on the teachings of Confucius or Lao-Tzu, but many dozens of truly independent thinkers. The Pythagorians excepted, "schools" come into existence only when decadence sets in: with Plato and afterwards. With the fall of democracy and the Stoics, philosophy becomes rigidified in schools and given more and more to commentary and interpretation.

We can date the end of this period as synchronous with the end of the period of democratic political creation. The defeat of the Athenians in the Peloponnesian War in 404 and the death sentence against Socrates in 399 are symbolically of equal importance. Socrates is the last philosopher-citizen—and the *demos* of the Athenians is no more the *demos* of the sixth and fifth centuries. It may seem as a paradox that the decadent period then starting produced two of the greatest philosophers ever, Plato and Aristotle—though the matricide Plato was brought up and formed under democracy. With Plato starts the Platonic torsion which has dominated, ever since, the history of philosophy—or at least, its mainstream.

The philosopher ceases to be a citizen. He gets out of—or above—the *polis,* and tells people what to do, deriving it from his own *episteme.* He searches, and thinks he reaches, a unitary ontology—that is, a theological ontology. At the center of this ontology, as of all the rest, he places the meta-idea of determinacy (*peras, Bestimmtheit*). He tries to derive from ontology the ideal polity. And later (with the Stoics and much more so, with Christianity), he sanctifies reality, that is, he starts rationalizing that which exists in all fields.

We do not need to dwell upon the long intermediary period. A new birth takes place in Western Europe around the late twelfth and early thirteenth century, with the emergence of the protobourgeoisie and the constitution of political collectivities—the new or renewed cities—attempting self-government. From then on, philosophy, though under heavy Christian-theological constraints, again becomes involved with the Western emancipatory movement, but it never frees itself fully, in its dominant stream, from the main traits of the Platonic torsion. From the sixteenth century onward, the struggle becomes manifest within philosophy itself. Thus, the evolving galaxy of European philosophy, from Occam and Duns Scotus to Husserl and Heidegger, always presents antinomic characteristics. It is sometimes a participant in the emancipatory struggles, more frequently indifferent toward them or their scornful enemy. The system-building, reality-sacralizing, looking-down-upon-the-collectivity attitude remains, in various guises, the predominant one, with, sometimes, the most paradoxical outcomes: for instance, the "critical" thinkers Marx and Nietzsche clearly belong in the *sancta realitas* mentality (laws of history, "innocence of becoming," etc.). The main contribution of philosophy to the emancipatory movement during this whole period is to be found not so much in its "contents," but in its maintaining an open debate and a critical spirit. Though denying it in principle most of the time, it reinstaurates *de facto* the philosophical *agora*.

The traits I outlined earlier as characteristic of the Platonic (plus Stoic-Christian) torsion are evident (except for the idea of determinacy) in Heidegger and underlie his proclamation of the "end of philosophy." The *sancta realitas* principle is central with him. Planetary domination by technoscience is taken as insurmountable *not* by virtue of a reflection on the social-historical possibilities and forces (such a reflection could not, anyhow, reach a categorical result nor decide the case) but on the basis of strictly "metaphysical" (in the derogatory sense) and fully arbitrary pronouncements about the "destiny of Being." This is consonant, and combined, with the most uncritical and, in fact, uninformed view about contemporary technique and science.[9]

The "theoretical" ground for the proclamation of the "end of philosophy," briefly speaking, that philosophy is "metaphysics" and that metaphysics has been *restlos* ("absorbed") by contemporary science, only makes sense on the basis of Heidegger's thesis that there can be a *Denken des Seins* or a *Denken des Sinnes von Sein* as such, separated from any reflection concerning *Seiendes* or *das Sein des Seienden*. The thesis is both sterile and meaningless. Its sterility is immediately apparent in the fact that, with Heidegger himself, it has only led to pseudopoetic and pseudoprophetic high-sounding words (like *das Gevier,* etc.), and that nowhere can one see, even approximately, what the *Denken des Seins* consists in. No wonder that Heidegger's epigones proved unable to produce anything along this direction, and had to confine themselves to the endless "interpretation" and "deconstruction" of past philosophers.

But the thesis could make sense only on the faulty presupposition that

9. Heidegger writes (on the first page of *On Time and Being* [New York: Harper & Row, 1972]) that Werner Heisenberg was "searching" for "the full ultimate equation of the universe." [Translator's Note: the English translation simply says: "cosmic formula"; I have retained Castoriadis's translation of Heidegger.] An ultimate in absurd equations of which I have been able to find no trace in the writings of Heisenberg. There is at most one phrase (a banal one, for those familiar with the work of modern physics) in his Gifford Lectures of 1955–56 (*Physics and Philosophy* [London: Penguin, 1989], p. 154), expressing the "hope" that one day a "complete understanding of the unity of matter" will be achieved; this quite obviously is a reference to "unification" theories, which indeed have made some headway since then—and in no way to "the full ultimate equation of the universe." Heisenberg expresses, in completely express fashion, his doubts concerning the possibility of reducing the phenomena of living beings to simple physicochemical laws (*ibid.*, pp. 143, 187). It is highly improbable that Heisenberg could have uttered such an ultimate absurdity as "the full ultimate equation of the universe" (he was one of the last great physicists with a knowledge of and feeling for philosophy). But even if he had done so, a philosopher ought to have reacted with a sorrowful smile, both on grounds of principle and because he ought to know that, from Newton through Lord Kelvin through George Gamow and up to today's proponents of TOE (theory of everything), physicists have periodically proclaimed the advent of the theory to end all theories—and each time, journalists have been, of course, quick to spread the good tidings. Heidegger in fact believes naively in modern science and technique the way a bank teller amateur reader of vulgarized "scientific" magazines believes in it. He never saw the deep internal antinomies and aporias contemporary science is full of.

the object of philosophy would be, for instance, the question of Being, or why is there something rather than nothing, etc. In fact, as I said before, the object of philosophy is the question: What ought I, what ought we, to think—about being, about knowledge of Being, about "I," about "we," about our polity, about justice, etc. And one obvious result of the Heideggerian restriction is that any reflection on politics or ethics, for instance, becomes impossible, both on grounds of "substance," because "we are to do nothing but wait" (*Gelassenheit*)—this being, of course, the immediate consequence of the conception of history as "destination of Being"—and on the grounds of "method," since, for example, the *polis* and all that must be taken as belonging to the "ontic," therefore do not form a worthy object of the thought of Being.

How wonderfully all this fits *die geistige und politische Situation der Zeit,* the spiritual and political situation of the times, hardly needs saying. This of course does not forbid anybody from discussing its substance. But neither can one fail to see that these proclamations appear at a time when the questions: What are we to think? What are we to do? are taking on a tragic immediacy and urgency. In this sense, the Heideggerian philosophy and its offshoots are but one of the expressions of (and a minor factor in) the more general trend toward the decomposition of Western society and culture—that is, toward the vanishing of the project of autonomy. But this trend, undoubtedly real and more and more threatening (we have not waited for Heidegger to see and say that), nobody can today consider as definitively and irreversibly victorious. We do not yet live in fifth-century Rome or Constantinople.[10]

---

10. Sometimes, nice, sincere, and honest people say: but you cannot deny that Heidegger *is* the critique of modern technique. This is of course "epochal" parochialism and ignorance. The critique of modern technique starts at least with Rousseau and the Romantics, is there through the whole of the nineteenth century (e.g., William Morris, Ruskin, etc.) and becomes the *lieu commun* in Germany around the turn of the century with Max Weber, Tönnies, A. Weber, Simmel, etc. The chapter "Reification and the Consciousness of the Proletariat" in *History and Class-Consciousness* of G. Lukács (1923), developing ideas of Marx and Weber, contains, of course in a Marxist garb, most of what is of some substance, in this respect, in *Sein und Zeit* (1927) and the *Einführung in die Metaphysik* (1935). The Frankfurt School should also be mentioned in this respect. (Nobody seems to have noted that most of Foucault's writing is but an application of the central ideas of Lukács and the Frankfurt School in some particular

There is, in fact, no real possibility for philosophy to become absorbed by technoscience. What is possible, and indeed taking place, is that genuine philosophical questions get buried deeper and deeper under a thick layer of a quiet and soft dogmatism of positivistic metaphysics (in secret complicity with an "anarchism/scepticism" *à la* Feyerabend: "anything goes" is a thoroughly positivistic position. Anything goes and nothing goes really, but some things work provisionally; the question of truth is a "metaphysical" question, etc.), while, in other buildings of Academia, historians of philosophy go on chewing the dried fruits of their specialty, and, in the glorious free market of ideas, "philosophical" punk sects supply ideoclips for the consumption of the various media.

I must leave aside here the question whether, in the present social-historical situation, a single person recognizing what I take to be the genuine tasks of philosophy and working on them can do more than bring forward a personal *oeuvre*. What the resonance of such an *oeuvre* may be, what stimulus it could provide for a renewal of philosophical activity, these are of course questions which can never be answered in advance. In this respect as in other domains, the only valid maxim is: *fais ce que dois, advienne que pourra.*

But one example will help, I hope, to understand why I consider impossible—*de jure*—the "disappearance of philosophy within the world of technicized science."

Virtually the whole of inherited philosophy, when talking about the world or physical (and psychical) being, has in view either the

---

fields.) In brief: the critique of modern technique and its world, of reified society, the *Entzauberung der Welt*, etc. were flowing in the gutters of Weimar Germany (and in other European countries: cf., e.g., D. H. Lawrence) and belonged to both the "right wing" and the "left wing" of opponents of capitalist society. What Heidegger "added" to it was to make technique the *result* of "Western metaphysics," instead of seeing that (1) the birth of capitalism and the work of Descartes/Leibniz, say, were parallel manifestations of a *new* social-historical imaginary (neither Plotinus's nor Thomas Aquinas's metaphysics "produced" technique or capitalism); and (2) parallely, and antinomically, the project of autonomy (the emancipatory or democratic movement) never ceased to manifest itself and to interfere—in an extremely complex relation of antagonism and mutual contamination—with the capitalistic project of unlimited expansion of pseudorational pseudomastery. But, of course, for Heidegger the democratic movement could be nothing more than another expression of the modern Forgetting of Being.

Lebenswelt (most ancient philosophers, partly Kant, fully of course the later Husserl and Heidegger), or the "classical" world of mathematical physics (from Descartes onward). In both cases these *images* have played a decisive role both as paradigms of "being" (*Seiendes*) and as the basis for a method. Now, the *Lebenswelt* (that is, the return of old Husserl to Aristotle's starting point) is an indispensable common initial ground—but slippery and full of holes and quicksands. And the "classical" edifice lies in ruins.

Things, time, space, matter have become riddles more than they ever have been. Modern physics, generally without knowing it, is uneasily sitting simultaneously on all four pairs of the Kantian antinomies—and adds to them plenty of new ones. Its wonderful "instrument," mathematics, displays more and more its terrifying efficiency—for no apparent reason (the Kantian reasons are of no avail for a quasi-Riemannian four- or perhaps ten-dimensional manifold). The dazzlingly rapid progression of mathematics, while unveiling the gap in its own foundations (undecidability theorems—Gödel, Turing, Church) and based on paradoxical assumptions (axiom of choice) has led to a situation (Gödel and Paul Cohen on the continuum hypothesis) where an indefinite number of "non-Euclidian" ("non-Cantorian") set theories appear possible. Mathematics appears more and more as a free creation of human imagination working under certain constraints (consistency, economy). But it also appears as (1) strangely related to the physical world (any physical theory is mathematized, though sometimes in a very weird way, e.g., quantum theory, and purely mathematical considerations play a tremendous heuristic role in today's physics), and (2) bumping against no man-made constraints, necessities, and intrinsic kinships. We seem to be creating a multilayered "ideal" world which, in the most strange and uninspectable way, *encounters* both a multilayered physical world *and* an "ideal" world *in itself.*

Everybody knows, or ought to know, the chaotic theoretical situation in fundamental physics—a situation that is all the more puzzling as it does not in the least interfere with the experimental, observational, and practical accuracy and efficiency of physics, nor with its predictive capacity. The two main theories—general relativity and quanta—are, both, continuously corroborated by observation and experiment, while each of them contains as yet unsolved deep problems and while they contradict each other. The classical edifice of categories—by no means causality alone—is a broken machine that still turns out wonderful products. And I could go on for pages.

It would be silly to speak of all this as just "epistemological" or even "metaphysical" (in the Heideggerian sense) problems. They go directly at the heart of the ontological question. What is the being of this being (humans), that can freely create forms, which then turn out to have something to do with, and *encounter,* something externally given? What is the being of these forms? And what is the being of the externally given? But then: What ought we to think of being as such, if being belongs also to a being capable of a free creation which both meets and fails to meet whatever there is? It would be ridiculous to think that these questions are eliminated by the "ontological difference"—or by the supremacy of the question about "the meaning of Being." The question of the "meaning of Being" in the resolutely un- and anti-Aristotelian turn Heidegger wants to imprint on it is meaningless, except as an anthropomorphic/anthropological and/or theological question. Who told you that there is a meaning of Being? And the "ontological difference" is just a terminological nicety, without substantive import. Being is inseparable from the modes of being, themselves in turn inseparable from beings. To put it in the fashionable jargon: presence as such is obviously different from that which is present—but presence itself is each time different, is in a different mode in relation to that which presents itself. The presence of a lover is not the presence of a crocodile (not necessarily, at any rate). The phenomenality of the phenomena is not itself a phenomenal datum, to be sure. But the phenomenality of, for example, thought, is not the phenomenality of a star. To talk just about phenomenality (or presence, or presence/absence, etc.) becomes of necessity empty talk (*logikon kai kenon,* Aristotle would say), meaning simply: something is given—*es gibt*—something has to be given. Far from absorbing philosophy, in the sense of integrating the philosophical questions within its methods and its procedures, contemporary science both returns to these and puts them in a new light.

Something is given—something has to be given—but *to whom,* and *how*? Is mathematics "given" to us—or are we creating mathematics? In what place are infinite-dimensional Hilbertian spaces "given"? And *who* is thinking of Being? Is it the *Dasein*—this bastard and composite construct (bastard and composite as the philosophical "subject" almost always is), ignorant of its constituent elements, an artificial juxtaposition of psychical, social-historical, and reflective components peppered with a powder strongly smelling both of the social-historical situation of the time and of its creator's idiosyncrasies and value choices?

If we are doing philosophy (or even, "thinking the meaning of Being"), we have to ask: Who is that "we," and what is he or she? Who and what am I, when I stop being simply a *Dasein* and start reflecting on the question: Who and what am I *qua Dasein*? Now the latest era has witnessed the flourishing of an eclectic, incongruous, and unthoughtful hodgepodge, proclaiming "the death of the subject" (and of man, of meaning, of history, etc.), under the sign of Marx, Nietzsche, and Freud, but—strangely—with Heidegger as the philosophical guarantor. Yet one could not note, in all this, the slightest awareness of the true questions raised, on the philosophical level, by psychoanalysis or by whatever is of value in Marx or Nietzsche. I leave aside the obvious objection of the clever high-school adolescent: if everything you say is determined by your unconscious (or your social position), or is just an interpretation, then so too is this very conception of yours (this was already well known in Athens around 450 B.C.). But the substantive problem is: given that *it is true* that at the core of the "subject" (whatever that may mean) an unconscious psyche most of the time motivates its acts (therefore, also, its pronouncements); given that *it is true* that nobody can ever jump over his times or extract himself from the society to which he belongs; given that *it is true* that any statement contains an irredeemable element of interpretation corresponding to the interpreter's position, outlook, and interests—how can it be that we are capable of any self-reflective activity, including the one leading us to the above statements and all the others?

In the face of this situation—which, by the way, is *not* fundamentally new in its form (but I will not dwell upon that now)—and barring a self-silencing radical skepticism, only two positions seem possible.

Either we accept that this or that individual or philosopher—for instance, Heidegger, or *stultiores minoresque alii*—has been endowed, *for no reason,* with the capacity to utter the truth—or the meta-, or the post-truth—anyhow: to make pronouncements valid for everybody, but about which no further enquiry is possible. Then we revert simply to the consecration of a particular philosopher as a prophet—that is, we revert to the religious position.

Or we stand in the Greco-Western tradition, and recognize no prophets—whether it be God or Being talking through their respective mouths. Then we remain under the obligation of *logon didonai*—of giving account and reason for whatever we say and do publicly. *Logon didonai* does not mean, of course, mathematical demonstration or experimental corroboration, neither does it mean the search for and the exhibition of a "foundation." But it means that we accept critique and discussion; and discussion is not possible without the requirement of a minimal *consistency* (which is *not* ensemblistic-identitary consistency).

Then we have to face this challenge: How is it that a psychical being, which is at the same time social-historical, can become a reflective subjectivity? For various reasons, the Kantian position will not do. We cannot be satisfied with the "transcendental" point of view—or, in other terms, with the simple distinction between the *quaestio juris* and the *quaestio facti*—because the "subject" we are interested in—and which is of critical importance for whatever we think and do—is not a "Transcendental" subject but an *effective* subject.[11] We find ourselves facing two, *prima facie* antinomical considerations: we know, and cannot pretend to forget, that for whatever we do and think, there are psychical and social-historical conditions (not "causes"!); and we cannot pretend to ignore that we attempt to think, to discuss and to judge irrespective of these conditions, that we intend validity for what we say irrespective of place, moment, motives, and conditions. We therefore have to recognize both the effective and the reflective point of

11. As is, or ought to be, known, Kant wavers on this point. He continually speaks of "us humans," and of the interest of *our* reason—and constructs a "transcendental subject" of which we never know if it represents the way we actually function or the way we ought to function. In brief: the "transcendental" answer leaves us in the dark as to the ontological status of the knowing subject. See also my text "Portée ontologique de l'histoire de la science," in *Domaines de l'homme. Les Carrefours du labyrinthe II* (Paris: Seuil, 1986), pp. 419–55, and, concerning the relation between psyche and reflective thought, the first part, "Psyche," of *Crossroads in the Labyrinth* (Brighton: Harvester, and Cambridge, Mass.: M.I.T., 1984), and chapter VI of *The Imaginary Institution of Society*, tr. Kathleen Blamey (Oxford: Polity Press, and Cambridge, Mass.: M.I.T., 1987).

view. And we have to face the fact that it is only in and through the social-historical (and leaning on certain capacities of the psyche) that the reflective (of which the "transcendental" is a dimension) becomes effective. If we cannot think the possibility and the effectivity of a marriage between *jus* and *factum,* we simply cannot think anymore.

But we know that reflective thinking, no more than democracy, was not there all the time. It emerges, it is created through human activity at a certain time in a certain place (after which, of course, it becomes virtually accessible to all humans). We therefore have to recognize in them human creations; we are thus led to recognize also, beyond that, the otherwise obvious fact that human history is creation—of significations and institutions embodying them, of the social individual out of the "raw material" of the psyche, and of self-reflective subjectivity. We then can see—from the vantage point of a tradition to which philosophy and democracy belong—that almost all societies have instituted themselves as heteronomous, in and through the closure of their institutions and significations. Then we see that democracy and philosophy are the twin expressions of a social-historical rupture, creating the project of (social and individual) autonomy. The meaning of this project is the refusal of closure, and the establishment of another relationship between the instituting and the instituted at the collective level, between radical imagination and the socialized individual at the level of the singular human being, between the incessant reflective activity of thought and its results and accomplishments at any given moment.

These are creations. There is no way of showing that the condensation of galaxies, the Big Bang, or the combinatory properties of carbon were necessary and sufficient conditions for the emergence of democracy and philosophy. On the one hand, this leads us again into the ontological issue: there is at least a type of being capable of altering its mode of being—and since this is a mode of being therefore it pertains to what we think of Being. On the other hand, this creation contains the creation of a social-historical space where, and of a type of individual—self-reflective subjectivity—for whom, the question of truth can arise and be elucidated in a nonvacuous fashion. That means that the reflective belongs to the effective—and that the effective can bear the reflective. This has nothing to do with a *Geschick des Seins,* a destination/donation of Being. The creation of the project of autonomy, the reflective activity of thought and the struggle for the creation of self-reflective, that is, democratic institutions, are the results and the manifestations of the making/doing of humans. It is human activity that gave birth to the claim for a truth each time breaking the walls of the instituted representations of the tribe. It is human activity that has created the claim for freedom, equality, justice, in its struggle against established institutions. And it is our free and historical recognition of the validity of this project, and the effectivity of its partial realization up to now, that binds us to these claims—the claim for truth, the claim for freedom, equality, and justice—and that motivates us to move forward in this direction.

To work under these claims is therefore both a political and a philosophical task, in all senses of these terms. From the more specifically philosophical point of view, the closure we are up against is the ensemblistic-identitary character which has more and more, since the Stoics, dominated philosophy. At this level, the idea of an "end of philosophy" expresses essentially impotence in overcoming the ensemblistic-identitary closure and the vain attempt to escape from it by taking refuge in pseudopoetical and pseudoprophetical utterances masquerading as thought.

[Night has fallen only for those who have let themselves fall into the night. For those who are living,

helios neos eph'hemerei estin

the sun is new each day (Heraclitus, Diels 22, B 6).]

Frankfurt, November 1986–Paris, October 1988

3

The Social-Historical: Mode of Being, Problems of Knowledge

The best a "positive" conception of history can offer is this: history is the sum total of actions of human beings through space and time. We may as well start with it. Immediately, though, questions arise. What are those human beings and where do they come from? Can there be human beings without history, outside history? Are they not shaped into very different forms *within* history, possibly *through the action of* history? Do these actions of human beings take place in a vacuum? Is there any possible meaningful human action outside an instituted society, the relations, the meanings, the purposes, the values posited by this instituted society? Unless by "history" we mean the mere unfolding of a sequence of any sort of events over time (as, e.g., in the phrase: "the history of the Solar System"), have we ever encounted history without society? Should we then say that history, in the proper sense, is the product of societies? But can we forget that social forms, particular societies as defined by their specific institutions, are themselves "products" of history? Is society generating history, or the reverse? Or is this opposition meaningless?

Meaningless it is, indeed. And it would even be inadequate to say that society is the "product" of history, or that history is the "work" of

Originally written in English for *Thought* (forthcoming).

society. History is the self-alteration of society—an alteration whose very forms are each time the creation of the society considered. Repetition itself—as, for instance, in primitive or traditional societies—is never, of course, strict repetition; in its actual occurrence and in order to occur, repetition is heavily slanted by the basic orientation of the whole set of institutions of these societies. At a deeper level, it would still be inadequate to say that history is a *dimension* of society, the dimension by virtue of which the past of a society is always immanent in its present, this present always being inhabited by a future of some unspecified content and form. History is the self-deployment of society in time; but this time is, in its essential characteristics, a creation of society, both once for all as *historical* time and in each particular case as *the* time of this particular society with its particular tempo, significant articulations, anchorages, prospects, and promises. In the same way, there is a self-deployment of society in space, a topic which I will not dwell upon here. By space I do not mean "geographical expansion" (or location), but the creation of a simultaneously ordered "natural" and "social" multidimensionality proper to each and every society. As society cannot be without this self-deployment in time, as society *is,* indeed, this self-deployment in time, we would better speak, in philosophical terms, of *the social-historical.*[1]

History does not happen to society: history is the self-deployment of society. By this affirmation, we contradict the entire spectrum of existing tenets: history as the product of the will of God; history as the result of the action of ("natural" or "historical") "laws"; history as a "subjectless process"; history as a purely random process. It is not my purpose, however, to discuss or to refute these tenets here.[2]

We posit history *in itself* as creation and destruction. We are speaking at an ontological level here, for we are concerned with the creation and destruction of *forms,* of *eide.* Creation is not "production," the bringing forth of an exemplar of a preexisting *eidos;* it is the *ab ovo* positing of such an *eidos.* Even less would it be the random emergence of a numerically singular combinatorial configuration. De-

1. *The Imaginary Institution of Society,* tr. Kathleen Blamey (Oxford: Polity Press, and Cambridge, Mass.: M.I.T., 1987), pp. 167–220.

2. Cf. *Institution,* pp. 9–70, 115–64.

struction is, here, ontological destruction. When a star or a galaxy runs its course and eventually disappears as this star or this galaxy, there is no destruction properly speaking. The form star or galaxy is unaffected, and stars and galaxies of the same type could be (and certainly are) produced again. And even if such were not the case, the *eidos* would not be destroyed: an ideal scientist-observer could, in principle, reconstitute this form. In a certain sense, nothing is really "lost" with the explosion of a supernova or the disappearance of the dinosaurs (whatever the empirical gaps and problems thereby created for biologists); however, the destruction of the Athenian *polis,* of the Roman religion, of Florence as it was from the twelfth to the sixteenth century, is the destruction of the singular, unique, *eidos* embodied in each of these historical entities. It would be meaningless to say that this *eidos* is ideally preserved in the sense one may say the Pythagorean theorem would be ideally "preserved" even after the disappearance of the Earth and the end of the human race. Because the being of a social-historical entity is not purely (not even essentially) "intelligible" or reducible to "intelligible" elements, it is in principle impossible to recover, after it is destroyed, the *eidos* it embodies and realizes. It is not only the glory that was Athens or Rome that has vanished. It is the whole world of meanings, of affects, and of intentions—of social imaginary significations—created by these societies and holding them together that cannot be recovered, but only approximated with the greatest difficulty, on which more later.

Even more than the creation of *eidos,* the *destruction* of *eidos* must remain wholly unthinkable for the inherited ontology. Just as the creation of social-historical *eidos* is not a combinatorial pasting together of "immutable elements" (e.g., the "pairs of opposites" of structuralist theories), destruction of *eidos* in history is not the decomposition of components, of "elements" which have been combined in this form and could be recombined in another. There are no such "elements" in the human domain. The "elements" of social-historical life are, each time, created *as* elements, in their relevancy, meaning, connections, etc., in and through the particular institution of society to which they "belong." Thus, each social-historical form is truly and genuinely *singular;* it possesses an essential, not numerical or combinatorial, singularity (strict speaking, structuralism and poststructuralism assert that the singularity of a society—or indeed, for that matter, of an *oeuvre* ("a work")—is, and must be of exactly the same character as the singularity of the number, say, 556,632,413). Indeed, the "proof" that social-historical *eidos* is created is that it can be destroyed in a way that no other *eidos* can. For instance, any physical form (whether it be taken concretely or abstractly, as type) can have its elements "taken apart" and can subsequently, at least in principle, be recomposed. (That this may well *not* be the case even in physics, as might be inferred from some aspects of contemporary cosmology and quantum theory, is an indication that perhaps even sheer physical being cannot be fully captured in the ensemblistic-identitary categories of inherited ontology.)

The specificity of the social-historical is not just being-for-itself, "meaning for . . . ," "representation," "affect," "intention" (or "desire"): these are already creations of the living being as such—though, of course, they acquire completely different contents in the social-historical field.[3] The social-historical is, first of all, the phenomenological specificity of the forms it creates and through which it exists: institutions embodying social imaginary significations, and their concrete product, bearer and reproducer, the living individual as social-historical form. More importantly, however, the social-historical is the ontological form that *can put itself into question* and, through self-reflective activity, *explicitly alter itself.* To be sure, this is not a fated or necessary result, nor does it happen *os epi to polu,* but rather as an exception. Nonetheless, it is only in the social-historical domain that we encounter an *eidos* that puts into question its own laws of existence (politics in the proper sense) and that, more particularly, puts into question the transmitted representations it has for itself of a world and of itself (philosophy). We not talking about an "immanent" or "essential possibility" of the social-historical. Democracy and philosophy are not the outcome of natural or spontaneous tendencies of society and history. They are themselves creations, and they entail a radical break with the previously instituted state of affairs. Both are aspects of the project of autonomy. But the emergence of this project (of which ontology and the self-

3. "The State of the Subject Today" (1986), tr. David Ames Curtis, in *Thesis Eleven,* 24 (1989), pp. 5–43.

ontology of the social-historical as embodied in this very self-reflection are an aspect) has taken place at this level of being only.

This essential feature of the social-historical lays bare to our scrutiny the abyssal question of social-historical knowledge. Of course it is not our conception that produces the question. The question is there, manifest in the innumerable substantive difficulties of social-historical knowledge and hardly veiled by the various "theories" about society and history formulated by historical materialism, functionalism, structuralism, etc., as it cries loudly for recognition over the Procrustean beds on which all these theories lay their social-historical "material." Our conception simply allows us to gain, from the start, a clear vision of the infinitely enigmatic character of the question.

Each and every society creates, within what must be called its cognitive closure—or, even better, its *closure of meaning*—its own world, which is both "natural" (and "supranatural") as well as "human." Our fountains are inhabited by Nymphs, our stars are palaces for our gods, only a young virgin woman may marry honorably, and so on. In this world, other societies (other human groupings) have a (generally very poor) limited and defined place, meaning, and role. Knowledge referring to them is scant, mostly pragmatic (they trade salt, they use poisoned arrows) and religio-mythical in character (they are heathen, under the curse of God, etc.). As far as we know, only two societies, the Ancient Greek and the Western European, have developed a genuine interest in the others *as* others and attempted to attain a knowledge and an understanding of their ways of being. And this is the tradition in which we find ourselves.

The attempt to "know," as far as possible, other societies than our own, be they "present" or "past," immediately raises two questions: Why, and how? Let us eliminate facile answers to the first question. Of course, we may want to accumulate a knowledge of sorts about the others (in a sense, all societies do) in order, e.g., to exploit, conquer, dominate, or proselytize them. (*The Use of Geography Is to Make War* is the title of a recent French book.) I am asking, however, for a reasonable, defensible, arguable answer. This can only be found in the implications of our project of autonomy. In attempting to know, to understand the others irrespective of any "practical use" of this understanding, we go over and beyond the *closure of meaning* of our own institution. We stop dividing the human world between "us" and "them"—us: the only true human beings; the others: savages, barbarians, heathens, and so on. We stop considering our own institution of society as the only good, reasonable, truly human one and the institutions of the others as curiosities, aberrations, "primitive nonsense" (Engels), or divine punishment for their devilish nature. We also stop considering our representation of the world as the only *meaningful* one. Without necessarily abandoning our institutions—since, after all, *these* are the institutions that made this questioning possible—we can take a critical stand against them: we can discover, as did the Greeks in the sixth and fifth centuries, that institutions and representations belong to *nomos* and not to *physis,* that they are human creations and not "God-given" or "nature-given." This opens up immediately the possibility of questioning *our own* institution and of *acting* in regard to it. If its origin is *nomos* and not *physis,* then it could be changed through human action and human reflection, and this leads immediately to new questions: Ought we to change it? For what reasons? Up to what limits? How? This is why a genuine interest in the institutions of other peoples as such appears in fact only in the two social-historical formations, Ancient Greece and Western Europe (which includes, of course, the United States), where true *politics*—in the sense of calling into question the existing institutions and of changing them through deliberate collective action—and true *philosophy*—in the sense of calling into question the instituted representations and meanings and of changing them through the self-reflective activity of thought—were created. What I have in mind here is not a "causal" or "chronological" sequence. Geography, historiography, and ethnology (as distinct from chronicles of priests and kings and accounts of marvelous/mythical voyages) were in fact born as part of philosophy in the largest (and truest) sense, which is itself a dimension of the democratic and emancipatory movement born in the Greek *poleis* and reborn—much later, following a long period of regression—in the cities of Western Europe after the height of the "Middle Ages."

Of course, once born, this interest starts feeding on what becomes our unquenchable thirst for knowledge per se. This thirst is one of the manifestations of our freedom, or autonomy: we constantly put into question the inherited (be it "scientific" or "philosophical") representation of what there is, we constantly shake the walls of our own closure. Indeed, this is the very meaning of truth, as created in the Greco-Western world. Of course, in every society there must be some sort of "truth"—but we should rather call that *correctness:* the canonical correspondence of statements and representations with what the instituted and closed world of meanings of the society considered has once and for all established as the "real" state of affairs as well as the instituted criteria whereby this correspondence is, each time, judged. In the Greco-Western world, truth is created as the perpetual movement of doing away with the closure of meaning (the movement is perpetual because this closure can never be eliminated). In the particular case of social-historical knowledge, however, our interest has as well another, equally strong motivation: to grasp human beings' essential possibilities. We consider their social-historical creations, and their, or our own, sublime or monstrous deeds, and we thereby enlarge the view of our own possibilities. If Socrates existed, this is something a human being can be. If Hitler existed, this too is something a human being can be. And so too can the social-historical formations which made these human exemplars possible.

But *how* can we know other societies and historical epochs? What we do know is heavily, perhaps exhaustively, conditioned by what we are as social individuals brought up in and fabricated by this particular society, our own. This goes far beyond "prejudices," and far beyond epistemology and theory of knowledge. The question has an ontological grounding. We are, and are what we are, because we share in a world which, far from being free-floating or neutral (assuming "humanization" or "socialization" in general) is created and instituted by our own society. Neither Kant nor Husserl writes in a transcendental language. They both write in German. And the German language—as any other—conveys an entire world.

Therefore, the first presupposition is the calling into question of the institution which made us what we are and of the ways of thinking it has furnished us. This is of negative value only. We thereby avoid uncritically imputing to others motives, feelings, and value orientations that have currency and meaning among us, and even "rationality" in general. (And, by the way, who said that our "rationality" is rationality *tout court*?) The first task in this respect is indeed to start probing our so-called rationality—and this would be the first *rational* task. As we know, this task remains in fact incomplete and is, in principle, incompletable (except in trivial domains which exclude the infinite and exclude self-reference, that is, exclude by definition the self-reflective activity of thought). And we recognize, to begin with, that another society lives literally in another world—its own world (this was already known to Herodotus, as shown by his remarks about Cambyses and the Egyptians, or Darius and Greek and Hindu burial customs). How can we enter this other world, or, in fact, even approach it?

As I have done in the preceding pages, I offer these conclusions without benefit of "proofs" (i.e., without the necessary argumentation and empirical corroboration).[4] There are some scant and (unless they be trivial) always problematic social-historical universals. They fall into two broad classes. The first belongs to what I call the ensemblistic-identitary (for short: *ensidic*) dimension of the institution of any society. Given what we are and what we know, we can deduce them almost a priori. For instance, if a society is to have language, it must be familiar with predication, and it must divide statements into correct and incorrect. It also must have some arithmetic and geometry as well as functionally adequate descriptions and classifications of the part of the physical world in which it is living (the "first natural stratum"), including human beings as "biological" entities. Now, it happens (*sumbainei*) that we share with all humans the same biological constitution and the same "physical world" and know something about its properties. If a society is to last, it has to "function adequately"—maintain and reproduce itself—and therefore it must, up to a point, construct its world in some correspondence with the given first natural stratum and in accordance with some requirements of ensidic logic—to which, we find, the first natural stratum also "corresponds." It would be easy, and tiresome, to multiply *ad infinitum* examples of the constraints thereby imposed upon the creation of social institutions.

---

4. See *Institution*, passim, and *Crossroads In the Labyrinth*, tr. Martin H. Ryle and Kate Soper (Brighton: Harvester, and Cambridge, Mass.: M.I.T., 1984), pp. 119–44.

But this does not take us very far. It boils down to this: given the physical environment of the Earth and the biological properties of human beings, each and every society, if it is to maintain and reproduce itself (i.e., if it is to remain *observable*), will have to provide for its material and sexual reproduction. To this purpose, it will have to create some coherent fragments of ensidic logic and of "applied" knowledge of this world. Yet this would also be true of an "ape group"; and it would not in the least make intelligible the almost unlimited variety of societies and their corresponding institutions and social imaginary significations. Our knowledge of these constraints, and their particular character (geographical environment, inherited or borrowed techniques, and ensidic "knowledge") only points, in each particular case, to some of the beams used and to some of their particularities that have helped and/or hindered a society in the building of its institutions. The plan, the form, the articulations, the purpose of the building, these are another matter—and that is what we are chiefly interested in. It is not the properties of stone that tell us the difference between the Pyramid of Cheops, the Parthenon, and the cathedral of Amiens. Neither is it the (problematic) sameness of their syntactic structures that will teach us anything about the difference between "the apple is a fruit borne by a tree" and "life is a tale told by an idiot."

The construction of its own world by each and every society is, in essence, the creation of a world of meanings, its social imaginary significations, which organize the (presocial, "biologically given") natural world, instaurate a social world proper to each society (with its articulations, rules, purposes, etc.), establish the ways in which socialized and humanized individuals are to be fabricated, and institute the motives, values, and hierarchies of social (human) life. Society *leans upon* the first natural stratum, but only to erect a fantastically complex (and amazingly coherent) edifice of significations which vest any and every thing with *meaning* (think again of language). This is also a transhistorical universal, and, up to a point, we can elucidate it and some of its implications. Society socializes (humanizes) the wild, raw, antifunctionally mad psyche of the newborn and imposes upon it a formidable complex of constraints and limitations (the psyche must renounce absolute egocentrism and omnipotence of imagination, recognize "reality" and the existence of others, subordinate desires to rules of behavior, and accept sublimated satisfactions and even death for the sake of "social" ends). Society thereby succeeds to an unbelievable degree (though never exhaustively) in diverting, orienting, and channeling the psyche's egotistic, asocial (and, of course, fully "arational") drives and impulses into coherent social activities, more or less "logical" diurnal thinking, etc. But "in exchange," as it were, the psyche imposes upon the social institution an essential requirement: the social institution has to provide the psyche with *meaning*. Viewed from the standpoint of the psyche, the process whereby the psyche abandons (though never fully) its initial ways and objects and invests (cathects) socially meaningful ways of behaving, motives, and objects is *sublimation;* viewed from the standpoint of society, it is the social fabrication (nurturing, rearing) of the individual. Thereby a new *eidos* (different in each particular society) is created: the social individual (you, me, and the others). The individual is, in fact, the effective concrete bearer of the institutions of its society, and it is, in principle, bound by construction, as it were, to maintain and reproduce them. That this binding is more or less broken with the appearance of societies containing the germ of autonomy and the corresponding type of individual raises a further question.

The substantive task of "knowing" another society is thereby brought back to the attempt to penetrate, make accessible, and reconstitute the world of its social imaginary significations. (And, insofar as the concrete bearer of the emerged parts of these significations is the individual, some degree of "methodological individualism" is legitimate, though by no means sufficient.) The term "social imaginary significations" should not, however, be given an "intellectualistic" or even simply "noematic" content. The imaginary significations construct (organize, articulate, vest with meaning) the world of the society considered (and lean each time upon the "intrinsic" ensidic organization of the first natural stratum). Yet, in the same stroke and indissociably, they also do much more than that. To borrow, metaphorically, the distinctions correctly made by ancient psychology, they determine at the same time the representations, the affects, and the intentions dominant in a society. In fact, one can show almost a priori that these distinctions necessarily correspond to the fundamental ways of being of any entity which is "for itself"—and, in their own way, both society and the social individual are "for themselves."[5] Not only is the "noematic" ("representational") construction of the natural and social world a creation, each time different, of each and every society, but also each society posits its own important and dominant *intentions* (to live calmly with music and dance, to worship God and be saintly, to be *kalos kagathos,* to conquer the world, to expand the "forces of production," to "build socialism," etc.); moreover, and this point is usually ignored, it creates its dominant and characteristic *affects.* Even the sheer characterization of these affects is extremely difficult and can drag us onto very slippery ground or into the swamps of pseudoliterary *à peu près.* One example may help to understand what I mean. After describing Thomas Aquinas' philosophy and his tremendous effort to import Aristotle into Christian philosophy, Etienne Gilson comments, "But for Thomas, faith remains primordial." Now, this sentence would be Chinese for Aristotle—or, indeed, any classical Greek. *Pistis* in classical Greek, *fides* in classical Latin, have only a homonymic relation to what *pistis* and *fides,* faith, became with Christianity. (The possible antecedents in Judaism need not detain us here.) Faith, as this complex of *Erlebnisse* which is centrally and decisively organized around an *affect,* is a historical creation of the Christian institution of religion (and, for fifteen centuries, of society itself). We can follow its instauration from Paul and the Greek Fathers to Augustine; we can point to specific aspects of theological and mystical texts, of hymns, of church architecture, of paintings; we can force people to listen for hours to the *Matthaüs Passion;* we can describe crusading, pious, or caritative behavior. But we can neither show nor demonstrate faith (neither exhibit nor define it); and without this, any description, let alone understanding, of a Christian society would be hopelessly mutilated.

Thus, after the "external description" of a society (of its ensidic and functional organization), we have to attempt to grasp its particular *eidos.* This leads us to the need to penetrate and understand the magma of its singular social imaginary significations. *Some* "constitu-

5. Cf. "Subject," passim.

ent parts" of this magma, and some institutional forms, may be universal—and this may help (but also create illusions about) our work. What matters, however, is the singularity of this magma.[6] Of the three "vectors," so to speak, that characterize this magma, the least difficult to describe is that of the "intentions" of the society considered—since they can be read immediately in its effective actions. Even in this case, though, things are far from simple. It is relatively easy to "understand" the "intentions" (the "drive," the "push") of capitalist society (or of the capitalist component of today's Western societies). Let it be granted that they can be adequately described by the expression: "unlimited expansion of 'rational' mastery." (The innumerable problems conveyed by this expression and the actual facts to which it refers need not detain us here.) The relative facility of access, in this case, is not only due to our proximity to, or participation in, this society. The very nature of the "goals" of the capitalistic system and of the means it uses (as, more generally, of the world it constructs) make it to a large extent amenable to considerations of ensidic logic (*Zweckrationalität*). How individuals in this society live the universal expansion of pseudorationality, and why on earth a society would aim at it, is another part of the story.

The situation is very different, however, in most other cases. Consider, for instance, Aztec society or even, much nearer to us, the "true" Christian societies (from the fifth to the twelfth centuries). Here the "intentions" are so intimately entangled with "meanings" (in the narrow sense) or "representations," on the one hand, with "affects," on the other (cf. what has been said earlier about faith) that, very often, one's understanding risks remaining external or simply verbal. Some aspects of Max Weber's considerations about "World-religions" seem to me to exemplify this risk. To use an image: in music we always have rhythm, melody, and harmony. Of course there are monophonic melodies, but even in this case harmony is embedded in the melody since melody cannot exist if it does not belong to a mode, which confers upon each note its potential har-

6. Concerning this, see *Institution*, pp. 340–44 and "La Logique des magmas et la question de l'autonomie," in *Domaines de l'homme. Les Carrefours du labyrinthe II* (Paris: Seuil, 1986), pp. 385–418.

monic value. Even bare rhythm, e.g., the monotonic banging of a tam-tam, contains a "melody" as a borderline case (here the "melody feature" is simply *a, a, a . . .*).

The situation is akin to that implied by having *full* possession of a "foreign" language (and the simile is not gratuitous, since language bears and conveys virtually the whole of the life of a society and a substantial part of its "history"). Such possession is possible, though very difficult, and perhaps not easily accessible to all people. (We are not committed to the thesis that everybody must be able to understand each and every foreign language, even less than we are committed to the thesis that everybody must be able to master, with equal facility, all branches of contemporary mathematics, say.) But the knowledge thereby acquired is not readily "translatable" in the native language of the student. As in the case of language, the "translation" (the transposition of meaning) would entail the restitution of all the relevant connotations of the second culture in the first—which is strictly speaking impossible and can only be posited as a limit or an ideal. This by no means implies that all statements about a foreign society (or, for that matter, about our own), are equivalent, that "anything goes." The validity of the attempts to understand and reconstitute a foreign culture can be judged on the basis of the following criterion: To what extent are they capable of making sense of this other society, of encompassing as many as possible of its aspects and dimensions, and of plausibly (reasonably) showing that there is a magma of social imaginary significations, distinct from our own, that accounts for the specific organization of the society considered, holds it together and stands behind the "observable" activities and works (*oeuvres*) of the individuals belonging to it?

One should not confuse this last criterion with Max Weber's conception of *Idealtypen* and their "comparison" to "actual" behavior. Not only is the *zweckrational* component of behavior (its "instrumental" or "functional" dimension) for us the least important one and itself, as such, only instrumental in character; it is, each and every time, a *creation* of the society considered and deeply permeated with the imaginary significations of that society. The universality of even purely instrumental "rational" determinations throughout different social-historical forms is both a datum (mostly in its trivial aspects) and a question (for the more important ones). But there is much more than that. Any reconstruction of "understandable" individual behavior starting from observable social realities has to recognize the fundamental constraints of coherence, complementarity, and (ideally speaking) completeness. Ideal types are not pieces of garment hanging on a coat rack. They have to be *internally* connected, and, by necessity, they refer to each other and all together to the institution of society and its social imaginary significations. The Roman *pater familias* refers from within—and not because the theoretician "constructs" it so—to the Roman spouse, the plebeian to the patrician, and all of them to the laws of the *urbs,* the Roman religion, etc. They must fit together in order to produce not only a society as a functionally going concern, but a *coherent world of* (what is to us) *alien meaning*—and there is the rub. To be able to proceed to such a reconstruction, we would therefore have to be able to penetrate, to a nontrivial degree, the Roman imaginary of, say, the first three centuries of the Republic, and to reconstitute it, more or less satisfactorily (via various types of circumlocutions), in our own idiom. The fundamental precondition for this endeavor is, of course, the philosophical one: to understand that nothing of this idiom of ours can be taken for universally granted (even, for instance, or perhaps particularly, "rational economic behavior"). As was hinted at earlier, the easiest part of this reconstitution concerns the "intentional" "vector"—the drive or push of a society—for it can be deciphered from its activities and its hierarchy of values. The difficulties of reconstructing the "representational" vector are larger, but once we have shaken open *our* world and partially broken its closure, our imagination allows us to invent different, even violently "exotic," world schemes and to compare them with the observable social-historical phenomena. The most difficult—and, in principle, inaccessible—task is the reconstruction of the "affective" vector. Nobody will ever be able to say how the Greeks lived their religion, nor what initiation into the *mysteria* of Eleusis meant for a newcomer.

And here the circle closes upon itself. Because of the essential unity of the social space defined by these three "vectors," our inability to relive the *Stimmung* of an alien society does not make social-historical knowledge vain, but instead stamps it with an essential lacunarity.

Tinos, August 1987–Paris, December 1987

— 4 —

Individual, Society, Rationality, History

As an old admirer of Max Weber,[1] I want to take this opportunity to reexamine a series of questions which, as far as I am concerned, have been settled for a long time but which the "spirit of the times" has raised again in a fashion I find to be regressive, and whose decisive elucidation a critical confrontation with Weber, it seems to me, would allow.[2]

1. My first published writings in Greece (1944), which Ypsilon has just republished in Athens (1988), included among other things a translation with extensive commentary of Weber's "Methodological Foundations" in *Economy and Society* and an "Introduction to Theory in the Social Sciences," the composition of which was heavily influenced by Weber.

2. I will cite Philippe Raynaud's book by the abbreviation PhR; *Economy and Society,* ed. Guenther Roth and Claus Wittich (Berkeley: University of California Press, 1978) will be indicated by *E&S* followed by a page number, and by a section number in those cases where the "Methodological Foundations" section is cited. [Translator's Note: I have in many instances altered this translation of Weber's posthumous work in

Originally published as "Individu, société, rationalité, histoire," in *Esprit,* February 1988, pp. 89–113. Translation by David Ames Curtis appeared in *Thesis Eleven,* 25 (1990), pp. 59–90. For reasons of space and interest to English-speaking readers, several references to Philippe Raynaud and his *Max Weber et les dilemmes de la raison moderne* (Paris: PUF, 1987)—hereafter PhR—which occasioned this essay, have been eliminated.

The Question of Individualism

We all know that Max Weber taught what he called an individualist method. The ultimate goal of sociological and historical inquiry—for Weber, and rightly so, there is at bottom no distinction between these two objects of inquiry—would be to refer all phenomena investigated back to the effects of the acts and behavior (*Verhalten*) of "one, few or many" determinate—that is to say, separate and definite—individuals. As he himself says in *Economy & Society* (p. 15, sect. 9), it is only in this way that "something more" becomes accessible, something "never attained in the natural sciences": "the understanding of the behavior of the singular individuals that participate in these social structures." This is certainly a very important point: all physical processes are describable, and they are often explainable, that is to say, they lead us back to "laws" which govern them. But they are not understandable, and in truth there is nothing there to be understood. On the other hand, various instances of human behavior are—at least partially, at least virtually—understandable. Squabbles between children, a fit of jealousy, most often these sorts of behavior can be understood as such and as they unfold, even in extraordinary and improbable ways (whereas it would be, strictly speaking, impossible to provide an "explanation" in the sense of the exact sciences). This task of the understanding is conditioned by the possibility that we can have what Weber calls *sympathisches Nacherleben*, a sympathetic (or empathic) reliving or recapturing of the behaviors and motivations of another.[3] This

order to make the English conform more closely to Castoriadis's original French translation from the German.] As I have treated this question at length elsewhere, the reader may, if interested, consult my 1964–65 essay, "Marxism and Revolutionary Theory," which now appears as the first part of my 1975 book, *The Imaginary Institution of Society*, tr. Kathleen Blamey (Oxford: Polity Press, and Cambridge, Mass.: M.I.T., 1987), and is cited as *MRT;* the second half of *The Imaginary Institution* cited as *Institution;* also, *Domaines de l'homme. Les Carrefours du labyrinthe II* (Paris: Seuil, 1986), cited as *Domaines;* and finally my 1986 essay, "The State of the Subject Today," tr. David Ames Curtis, in *Thesis Eleven*, 24 (1989), pp. 5–43, cited as "Subject." All italicized words and passages are in the original, unless stated to the contrary.

3. Let us note in passing that not so long ago this possibility of a sympathetic or empathic reliving of experience provoked bursts of laughter from vanguard Parisian psychoanalysts. Quite clearly, without this possibility, social life itself would quite simply be impossible.

"empathic reliving," however, is not, as we shall see, the basic characteristic of "the understanding."

What Max Weber calls the individualist method seems to be opposed to a substantialist or ontological individualism. The sociology Weber wants to promote proceeds by constructing (or restituting) a subjectively understandable *meaning* of the behavior (*Verhalten*) of single (*einzelnen,* "one or more"; *E&S,* p. 13, sect. 9) individuals. It accedes to this meaning all the better, or rather it only can attain it to the extent that this meaning is "rational." This attainment of meaning is accomplished via the construction of ideal types (of individuals, or of instances of behavior). I will return to these as well as to the enormous question of whether "the *signification* of social phenomena is *constructed* by the social scientist starting from a particular standpoint" (PhR, p. 51) and of whether no presuppositions are made during this construction relative to its object.

Fully anticipating the possible perversions of this view, Weber characterized in advance as a "monstrous misunderstanding" (*ungeheuer Missverständnis*) the attempt to draw from this "individualist *method*" an "individualist system of values" in any sense as well as every attempt to draw from "the unavoidable tendency of sociological *concepts* to assume a rationalist character" any conclusions concerning the "*predominance* of rational motives" in human action or even a "positive *valuation* of rationalism" (*E&S,* p. 18, sect. 9, emphasis added; cf. also *E&S,* pp. 6–7, sect. 3). Those who are familiar with his violent and obsessively repeated criticisms of Rudolph Stammler can easily imagine the harsh sarcasm he would have heaped upon the "individualism" and "rationalism" found in the social sciences today—not to speak of the pseudopolitical conclusions that have been drawn therefrom, using arguments that resemble nothing so much as the syllogism that "unicorns exist, therefore the universe is made of quince preserves." Upon such arguments Freidrich von Hayek has made his reputation.

From this perspective, what can be said of "social collectivities" or "social formations"? Weber's expressions are, in these cases, so categorical that it can immediately be seen that if the individualist method does not involve taking an "evaluative," and still less a political, position, it is nevertheless tantamount to an ontological decision concerning the Being of the social-historical: "For the interpretive understanding of behavior . . . these social collectivities must be treated as solely (*lediglich*) the resultants and modes of organization of the particular acts of *individual* persons since, for us, these alone can be treated as comprehensible agents of meaning-oriented action" (or "bearers of meaningful behavior": *sinnhaft orientiertem Handeln; E&S*, p. 13, sect. 9).

This powerfully worded statement is accompanied by three remarks concerning the relation between "the subjective interpretation of action" and "these collective concepts":

1. It is often necessary to use expressions such as "State," "family," etc.—but one must avoid confusing them with the corresponding juridical concepts by imputing to them a "collective personality."
2. The process of understanding must take into account that these "collective formations" are also "*representations* in the minds of real men," and that they thus can "have a powerful, often a decisive (dominant, *beherrschende*) causal influence on the course of action of real individuals." But clearly, in this context such "representations" can be thought of only as the *result* of the action of other "real individuals."
3. There is an "organic" school of sociology that tries to explain social behavior on the basis of "functional" considerations, the "parts" accomplishing the functions necessary for the existence of the "whole." These kinds of considerations may have value, says Weber, as a "practical illustration," for they may establish a "provisional orientation" for one's investigations (but beware of the risk of "reifying concepts"!) or they can be heuristically useful (allowing one, for example, to detect the most important actions within a given context). But all this is just a prelude to the work of sociology proper, which alone accomplishes the true task: the understanding of the behavior of individual participants (*E&S*, pp. 13–14, sect. 9; cf. also the remarks on Othmar Spann's "universalistic method" or "holism," *ibid.*, pp. 17–18).

These remarks clearly have no import on the level of basic principles. Weber's individualist method does not prevent him from ultimately deciding the ontological question in the most categorical of terms: "The real empirical sociological investigation begins with the question: What motives *have determined* and *do determine* the singular (*einzelnen*) members and participants in this 'collectivity' to behave in such a way that this community came into being (was formed, created: *entstand*) in the first place and that it *continues to exist*?" (*E&S*, p. 18, sect. 9, emphases added).

Only individual acts, therefore, would be "understandable" or "interpretable." But in what does this comprehensibility of theirs consist? Weber's "initial" formulations are broad and exhibit his prudence in this matter: "The basis for certainty in understanding can be either rational . . . or it can consist of an emotionally or artistically appreciative empathic reliving (*einfühlend Nacherleben*)"; at the same time, he speaks of how difficult it is for us to understand "many ultimate 'ends' or 'values' toward which experience shows that human action may be oriented" if, when we "relive them in the empathic imagination" (*einfühlende Phantasie*), they depart too radically "from our own ultimate values" (*E&S*, p. 5, sect. 3). He thus seems to maintain a balance between the two opposing poles, and their difference arises only from the relative difficulties involved in understanding each one. Let us note in passing, however, the underlying imprecision of this opposition: we understand more easily an action oriented toward ends or values that are near to our own and/or that unfold according to a rationality of means relating to ends; we have more trouble understanding, and sometimes we do not understand at all, actions that occur in conformity with ends that are not our own and/or whose application appreciably departs from the rationality of means relating to ends. (In line with what is becoming more and more the current usage, I will call the later "instrumental rationality." Weber's term, *Zweckrationalität*, which in this one case is rather unfortunate, really means *Mittelnrationalität*, "rationality of means used," which obviously can be adjudged only in relation to an end that an actor has set forth and intended, whereas the literal translations, "end-related rationality" or "rationality according to ends," create an intolerable ambiguity.)

In reality, however, if one attentively rereads the section of *Economy and Society* entitled "Methodological Foundations" while keeping this problem in mind, there is little possible doubt about the double movement being made there. On the one hand, the "understanding" is reduced more and more to the understanding of instrumentally rational action. On this point, let me quote at length from this section, for the passage (*E&S,* pp. 18–19, sect. 10, emphases added) sheds light on almost all aspects of the entire matter at hand:

> These laws [which interpretive sociology tries to establish] are both comprehensible and univocal to the highest degree insofar as at the foundation of the typically observed course of action lie pure instrumentally-rational motivations, . . . and insofar as the relations of means and end are, according to the rules laid down by experience, also univocal. . . . In such cases one may assert that *insofar as* the action was rigorously rational in an instrumental way, it *would have had to* (*müsste,* in the sense of necessity and not obligation) occur *in this way and no other* . . .

The examples cited (arithmetical calculation, insertion of such and such a proposition in such and such a place in a proof, rational decision of a person acting according to the determinate interests involved in undertaking an action corresponding to the results s/he would expect) are clear-cut. On the other hand, Weber amasses a series of examples of behavior that are not instrumentally rational: *all* traditional activity, many aspects of charismatic actions (*E&S,* p. 17, sect. 9)—and of course, reactions—then (*E&S,* pp. 21–22, sect. 11) the quasitotality of "real action" which "goes on in the great majority of cases in a state of apathetic (vague, numb: *dumpf*) semiconsciousness or unconsciousness of the 'meaning one intends.' " "In most cases the individual's action is governed by impulse or habit. . . . Really effective meaningful behavior (*sinnhaftes Handeln*), where the meaning is fully conscious and explicit [whether it be "rational or irrational"] is a marginal case." Whence the conclusion, already formulated: "All these facts do not discharge interpretive sociology from the obligation, in full awareness of the narrow limits to which it is confined, to accomplish what it alone *can* do" (*E&S,* p. 17, sect. 9, emphasis added).

So that no one hastens to object that within traditional, habitual, semiconscious or unconscious behavior can be found a sort of "rationality," let us note that there are two unsatisfactory options: either we know nothing about it or, in order to establish its existence, we would have to have recourse to ideas of "objective rationality" which Weber had dismissed in advance—and rightly so, given the horizon of his philosophical views—for, as he says, "we shall speak of 'action' insofar as the acting individual attaches a subjective meaning to his behavior." Such meaning "may refer first to the actual or effective (*tatsächlich*) existing meaning in the given concrete case of a particular actor, or to the average or approximate meaning attributable to a given plurality of actors; or second, to the meaning subjectively *intended* by the actor or actors *thought of* as types within a conceptually constructed *pure* type" (*E&S,* p. 4, sect. 1, emphases added). And in any case, a mystery would remain: Why and how do the great majority of individuals in the great majority of their acts act simply because they have become habituated to act in that way, what does it signify in relation to the *very being* of human individuals, and what can we say of the *instauration* (each time pristine) of these "habits" or of "tradition"? What can we say, too, of the prospects and chances for interpretive sociology if the latter, when faced with 95 percent of human history, must confine itself to saying: that is not understandable, but it is traditional?

We will have to criticize the philosophical foundations of Weber's position. Before doing that, however, we must understand the logic (and, arising from its foundations, the necessity) of his attitude.

Sociology must understand, and not (or not simply) explain. (I will return later to the mistaken idea that one can *separate absolutely* these two moments.) What can one understand? Meaning. And, according to Weber, there is no meaning except "in," "through," and "for" actual individuals (even if it is simply for the social scientist who "constructs" this meaning), in any case, as an *intended* meaning (*gemeinter;* the German word strongly suggests the "subjective" side, and it is quite close to the Greek *doxazo*). But what sociology is to understand is not simply an "isolated" meaning, supposing that such a thing could exist. It has to understand the concatenation of people's acts—the socially oriented behavior of individuals—and not "explain" them, as physics does, by mere acknowledgment of incomprehensible irregularities. And as far as possible, sociology has to understand these concatenations as *necessary*. It is thus, and thus alone, according to Weber, that it can be a science. Its task is to furnish "a *correct* causal *interpretation,*" and this requires that "the process which is claimed to be typical must appear adequately grasped on the level of meaning and at the same time that its interpretation must to some degree be shown to be causally adequate" (*E&S,* p. 12, sect. 7, emphases added). For Weber, causality is essential. Now, what must really be called, in the last analysis, Weber's rationalistic (methodological, but also ontological) individualism depends entirely upon this connection between causality (necessity) and understanding, which is inevitably represented (we shall soon see why) by rational intelligibility. Indeed, in opposition to the "stupid regularities" of physical nature, a rationally connected concatenation of acts is bound to appear to us as both intelligible and necessary—intelligible in each of its moments and in their connection, and likewise necessary. (To Weber's chosen examples, cited earlier, one can add that of the general who, under given circumstances and with given means at his disposal, would have made those decisions that were instrumentally rational in view of the end he had set for himself; here we would be able to "*explain* in causal terms" the distance, the margin of deviation of his actual acts, by the intervention of "misinformation, strategical errors, logical fallacies, personal temperament or considerations outside the realm of strategy"; *E&S,* p. 21, sect. 11.)

Now, causality signifies neither "irreversibility" nor any kind of temporal ordering and still less, quite clearly, a mere, empirically established, regular succession from one phenomenon to another. Causality signifies the regularity of a succession whose *necessity is expressed by a universal law.* In the case of the physical sciences, the universality of the law, *formaliter spectata,* is a prerequisite for scientific thought and, *materialiter spectata,* it is represented by the, in principle indefinite, reproducibility of the particular succession under investigation. (I am leaving aside here such distinctions as experimentation, observation, indirect inference, and so on, which are of only secondary importance in relation to my theme.) But in the case of social-historical phenomena (I repeat that for Weber there is in this regard, and rightly so, no essential distinction between society and history) both reproducibility and even nontrivial repetition properly speaking are beyond our grasp, for a thousand reasons that have been stated many times and which still could be enlarged upon. Now, it is precisely this absence of reproducibility which, from his causalist perspective, gives substance to Weber's remarks on "rationality" and intelligibility. The intrinsic intelligibility of a concatenation of motivations and acts is precisely what effectively substitutes for the kind of reproducibility found in the experimental sciences (as it increases, moreover, our "understanding"). Experimental reproducibility is replaced, in effect, by a *statement of potentially indefinite reproducibility* of the sort: "Every other rational individual in X's place would have decided, when faced with the same circumstances, to employ the same means, Y." Or, if you prefer: *qua* rational individuals, we are all substitutable for one another and each of us "would have to reproduce" the same sorts of behavior when confronted with the same conditions. (Let us note that under these conditions the very singularity of historical events is dissolved, except in the form of a numerical singularity, or of irrational deviation: "What would you have done under these conditions?" "Exactly what he did." "And why didn't you do it?" "I drank too much champagne.")

If such potential reproducibility, itself issuing from considerations of "rationality," is, however, lacking, what Weber calls the *Fehlen an Sinnadäquanz*—a lack or shortage of adequation of meaning—comes into play, thus reducing the observed regularity to an "incomprehensible" or "statistical" regularity (*E&S,* p. 12, sect. 7)—that is to say, it makes us retreat to the side of the observational physical sciences. And this is true even for "psychic elements": "the more precisely they are formulated from the point of view of natural science, the less does one understand them. This is never the road to interpretation in terms of an intended *meaning*" (*E&S,* p. 13, sect. 9, emphasis added). Certainly, as Weber adds, incomprehensible processes and regularities are not for all that any less "valuable"; but for sociology their role is the same as that of all factual situations established by other scientific disciplines (from physics to physiology). They belong to the conditions, obstacles, requirements, incitements, and so on that the nonsocial world presents to people in their capacity as social actors.

Is there not then beneath all of this any philosophy (other than a "theory of knowledge of the social sciences")? Oh, indeed there is! It is not even worthwhile entering into discussion over the untenable idea of the existence of some "method" (or "theory of knowledge") that would involve *no* ontology. Without the two interconnected assertions, that is, that *there is* something comprehensible in society and history and that what is understandable *is* (*par excellence,* if one wants to insist on the point) the "rational" dimension of *individual* action, Weber's method would no longer possess an object of investigation (and one would no longer understand why he has chosen to apply this method to society and history rather than to the expansion of galaxies). There is no point in adding such phrases as "we do as if . . ." (Why not use this same "as if" in molecular biology?) or "we are speaking of the parts covered by our method without making any judgments about the totality" (therefore *there very well are* parts which your method takes in, and this fact cannot depend upon your method *alone* since the other parts resist its application). The origin of the idea that the comprehensible is the product of individual action can be traced back to Vico and his celebrated statement, *verum et factum convertuntur*—truth and (human) deeds/facts are interchangeable, or, more freely but still faithfully: only that which we have done is intelligible and everything that we have done is intelligible—and upstream from Vico, all the way back to Hobbes. Of course, the origin of this idea is to be found in theological philosophy: when, in the *Timaeus,* Plato wants to "explain" the world, he makes its constitution *understandable* "as much as possible" by putting himself in the place, so to speak, of a "rational" demiurge (indeed, one placed at the summit of "rationality": a mathematician and geometer) who works on the basis of a model that is itself "rational." (If the world is not completely "rational," it is that Plato, who in spite of everything remains Greek, has contrived for his demiurge to work upon matter that is itself irrational and independent. This option is not open for the Christian theology of an omnipotent God.) Clearly, the same scheme predominates in German idealism (the intelligible is correlative to the action of a subject—finite in Kant, infinite according to Hegel). In all events, Weber's Kantian and neo-Kantian roots are well known and quite evident, especially in this regard.

To air out the discussion a bit and to expose more clearly the stakes involved, let us take our distance in the most brutal terms possible. Without prejudicing the moment of partial truth it contains, Vico's statement as well as the whole constellation of ideas denoted by it are false. We would not live in the world we live in, but in another, if everything we did was intelligible and if what we did was alone intelligible to us (as individuals or as a collection of individuals designatable by name). It hardly is worth recalling that not all of what we do or of what others do or have done is intelligible (or, oftentimes, even understandable, however broadly we expand the meaning of this term). And many things—the most decisive—are intelligible to us without us having done them or without us being able to "redo" them, to reproduce them. I have not made up the idea of a norm or law (in the effective, sociological sense, not in the "transcendental" one); I might invent a particular law but not the *idea* of a social law (the idea of institution). In vain will it be said that concretely designatable persons have taught me language; to teach me language, they already had to have possessed it. Will one go so far as to maintain that "rational individuals," driven by their "interests" or their "ideas," have *consciously* made up language (language in general, or some particular language)? Will one go even further and maintain that it is only to the extent that language has been made *consciously* that it is intelligible? Let us stop laughing, and simply ask: *Without language,* is a "rational" and "conscious" individual conceivable as an effective individual (*and even* as a "transcendental subject")?

We know how Dilthey, starting from a perspective of "individualistic" (and, at the beginning, "psychological") understanding and borrowing from Hegel while rejecting Hegelian metaphysics, was led to take into account the manifestations of what he calls, following Hegel, but with a meaning much larger than what is found in the latter's philosophy, the "objective spirit" (which practically overlaps completely with what I call the institution): language, custom, forms of life, family, society, State, law, etc. Though as early as 1883 he had characterized the individual as an abstraction, one may also rightly note the persistance in Dilthey of the principle of *verum factum:* "The field [of the sciences of the mind] is identical to that of the understanding and consequently the object of understanding is the objectivization of life. Thus the field of the sciences of the mind is determined by the objectivization of life in the outer world. *The mind can understand only what it has created*" (from Dilthey's *Der Aufbau der Geschichtlichen Welt in den Geisteswissenschaften* in *Gesammelte Schriften* [1915], vol. 7, emphasis added; cited by PhR, p. 86). Dilthey's philosophical position here is clearly confused. *Something* is objectivized that is not Hegelian Reason or the World Spirit; it is called, incidentally, "life" or "mind"—and that in which it objectivizes "itself" is *de jure* understandable to us (across differences in times and places). In addition, the conditions for this understanding remain obscure: it could be said that we participate in this "life" and in this "mind"—but is that a sufficient condition, especially once it is no longer a matter of understanding "rational" activities alone but also the totality of human experience *and above all* its "objectivized" forms?

This was not a problem for Max Weber—since, as we have seen, collective entities "appear anew as simple givens which the understanding must seek to reduce to the activity of individuals" (PhR, p. 121). But at what a cost! One must endorse an ontology (that of critical philosophy) which affirms: *If there is* meaning, it is because *there is* a subject (an ego) that posits it (intends it, constitutes it, constructs it, etc.). And *if there is* a subject, it is because it *is* either the source and unique origin of meaning or meaning's necessary correlate. That this subject is named, in philosophy, "ego" or "consciousness" in general and, in sociology, the "individual" undoubtedly creates serious questions (notably the problem of how to pass from the transcendental subject of critical philosophy to the individual effectively acting in society, who, according to the principles of Kantian and neo-Kantian philosophy, can only be the "psychological," "empirical," "phenomenal" subject), but it basically changes nothing. In both cases, the postulates and intentions of thought are clearly *egological*. Whatever one then does, there is one thing one cannot avoid doing: namely, presenting the social-historical as the "product" of the cooperation (or of the conflict) between "individuals" (or claiming, in an attenuation of this individualist methodology, that we can think about it only to the extent that it is individual).

What are these "individuals"? Two paths open up, and both lead to untenable conclusions:

1. Either it will be said that the essential aspect of individual behavior is "rational" (or progress toward "rationality")—and if I can understand the individual, it is because I participate in the same "rational-

ity." We immediately proceed, full steam ahead, toward a (Hegelian) absolute idealism as concerns history, even if this is labeled "reconstruction of historical materialism," as it is in Habermas. That one might happen, within this "rationality," to distinguish between a "logic of interests" and a "logic of ideas" (or "representations") changes nothing: it is still a matter of logic; and if there be conflict, it would be a conflict between two logics. Everything that does not come under this heading, everything that cannot be rationally reconstructed in a philosophy seminar—not much, really, just the totality of human history—is scoria, a gap to be filled in progressively, a learning stage, a passing failure in the "problem solving" exercises assigned to humanity (by whom and for what purpose?) or—why not?—"primitive nonsense," as old Engels said.

2. Or, following Terence (*humani nihil alienum puto*) and the great classical philosophers, I take the "individual" in its fullness, with its capacity for "rationality" but also with its passions, affects, desires, etc. I then find myself faced with a "human nature" that is more or less determined but assuredly identical across space and time—and whose latest avatar is a pseudopsychoanalytical marionette which, it must be said, Freud himself had a substantial hand in fabricating. Even supposing that, following the path that leads from *The Republic, The Leviathan, Totem and Taboo,* etc., I might be able to understand why and, above all, how this being could produce a society, I remain with the following enigma: Why and how has it produced so many different societies, and why has it produced a history (and indeed many of them)?

Two things fill me with an ever-renewed sense of wonderment: the starry sky above me and the ineradicable hold these schemata have on my contemporary fellow authors. Learning, we are told once again today, is the basic motor of human history. Considering the ease with which people "forget" psychoanalysis, ethnology, prehistory, history—or, more concretely, two world wars, gas chambers, the Gulag, Pol Pot, Khomeini, and so on and so forth—we must concede that learning is not a motive force, not even a secondary one, for contemporary reflection in this domain.

The Social-Historical and the Psychical

We do not "understand" all individual acts of behavior, not even our own—far from it—and we can understand "objects" that are irreducible to individual acts of behavior when they belong to the field of the social-historical. The social-historical world is the world of meaning—of significations—and of the effective or actual [*effectif*] meaning. This world cannot be thought of as a mere "intended ideality," it must be borne by *instituted forms,* and it penetrates into the very depths of the human psychism, decisively fashioning it in almost all of its discernible [*repérables*] manifestations. "Effective meaning" does not necessarily mean (and, moreover: *never* exhaustively means) meaning for an individual. The dividing line between "nature" as the object of the "experimental" sciences and the social-historical does not have to do with the existence or nonexistence of individual behavior. Whether it is a matter of acts of individuals, collective phenomena, artifacts, or institutions, I am always dealing with something that is constituted as such by the *immanent actuality of a meaning*—or of a *signification*—and this is sufficient for me to place the object within a horizon of social-historical apprehension. That there may be limit cases (Is this pebble "natural," or has it been worked upon?) does not weaken our assertion any more than does the fact that we might have trouble deciding whether someone is trembling with rage or shaking because s/he is suffering from a neurological condition. The understanding is our mode of access to this world—and it does not necessarily, nor by its essence, require recourse to the individual. If, in reading the *Parmenides* or the *Lex duodecim tabularum,* I understand these writings, it is not because I am sympathetically reliving someone's behavior. Faced with a social-historical phenomenon I have the (in the immense majority of cases, enigmatic) *possibility* of "sympathetically reliving" or "reconstituting" a meaning *for* an individual; but I am *always* gripped by the presence, the "incarnation" of meaning. That I might try to make understandable as well the "intentions" of an author, the possible "reactions" of his/her potential readership, changes nothing. The social-historical object is co-constituted by the activities of individuals, which incarnate or concretely realize the society in which they live. And in extreme cases I can take account of these activities only "nominally." A dead language studied as a no longer evolving corpus, Roman law as a system, these are *institutions* that are accessible as such; they do not refer back to individual actors except "at the margin" or in a wholly abstract manner. And, far from considering language as the "product" of cooperation between individual thoughts, it is language that tells me, first of all, what was thinkable for individuals and how it was so.

In opposition to a substantialist or ontological individualism, a methodological individualism would be an approach that refuses (as Weber does explicitly) to ask questions of the kind: "Is it the individual or society that comes 'first?' "; "Is it society that produces individuals or individuals that produce society?" while asserting that we are not obliged to answer such "ontological" questions, the only thing that we might (come to) understand being the behavior of the (actual or ideal-typical) individual—this behavior itself being all the more comprehensible when it is "rational" (or at least "instrumentally rational"). But what is the actual [*effectif*] individual—and what is *effective* rationality?

The individual is not, to begin with and in the main, anything other than society. The individual/society opposition, when its terms are taken rigorously, is a total fallacy. The opposition, the irreducible and unbreakable polarity, is that between *psyche* and society. Now, the psyche *is not* the individual; the psyche *becomes* individual solely to the extent that it undergoes a process of socialization (without which, moreover, neither it nor the body it animates would be able to survive an instant). We need not pretend we do not know when we do. Surely, Heraclitus has not been "surpassed": as he says, we will not reach the limits of the psyche, even after having traversed its entire path (or all its paths). We know, however, that human beings are born with a given biological constitution (which is extremely complex, rigid in certain respects, and endowed with an incredible plasticity in others) and that its make-up includes a psyche so long as it is functioning. Though we are far from knowing everything about the latter, we nevertheless know quite a lot. The more we explore it, the more we discover that it is essentially alogical, that in this regard the terms "ambivalent" and "contradictory" give us an idea of its mode of being only to an immensely slight degree. Yet we also know when exploring the psyche that we encounter on all its strata the effects of a process of socialization that it undergoes as soon as it comes into the world—and this is so not only because the patient of psychoanalysis must put his dreams into words or because the psychoanalyst must think on the basis of certain categories.

This process itself is certainly a social activity. And, as such, it is always necessarily mediated by identifiable individuals, the mother for example—but *not only* by them. Not only are these individuals always already themselves socialized, but what they "transmit" goes far beyond them: let us say, roughly speaking and so as to point out merely one feature, that they provide the means and the modes of access to virtually the whole of the social world as it is instituted in each instance, this whole being a totality which they in no way need to possess in actuality [*effectivement*] (and which, moreover, they *could not* in fact "possess" in actuality). Moreover, there are not only individuals: language *as such* is an "instrument" of socialization (though it certainly is not only that!) whose effects go immeasurably beyond everything the mother who teaches it to her child could "intend." And as Plato already knew, children (and youths and adults) are socialized by the very walls of their city well beyond any explicit "intention" of those who constructed them.

I will not repeat here what I have set forth at length elsewhere on many occasions.[4] I will simply summarize my views by saying that the socialization of individuals—itself a socially instituted process, and in each case a different one—opens up these individuals, giving them access to a *world* of social imaginary significations whose instauration as well as incredible *coherence* (the differentiated and articulated homology of its parts as well as their synergy) goes unimaginably beyond everything that "one or many individuals" could ever produce.[5] These significations owe their actual (social-historical) existence to the fact that they are *instituted*. They are not reducible to the transsubstantiation of psychical drives: sublimation is the psychical side of the process whose social side is the fabrication of the individ-

4. *Institution*, ch. 6; "Subject," passim.

5. *MRT*, pp. 135–56.

ual. And they are obviously not reducible to "rationality," whatever breadth one grants to the meaning of this term. To state that they are is to oblige oneself to produce, here and now, a "rational dialectic" of history and even of histories in the plural; one would have to explain, for instance, in what way and how during the fourteenth and fifteenth centuries, the civilizations of the Aztecs, Incas, Chinese, Japanese, Mongols, Hindus, Persians, Arabs, Byzantines, and Western Europeans, *plus* everything that could be enumerated from other cultures on the African, Australian, Asian, and American continents, represent simply different "figures of rationality" and, above all, how a "synthesis" of them could be made—here's the state of the World Spirit in 1453, for example, and here's why, in and through this diversity on the phenomenal level, the underlying unity of Reason, whether human or not, manifests itself—or, lacking this, here's how these civilizations could be *ordered* rationally (for, a Reason that could not, even "dialectically," give order to and establish a hierarchy for its manifestations should be put out to pasture). The thick-headedness displayed in the various versions of contemporary rationalism when confronted with these questions—which questions themselves could be muliplied indefinitely and which are as basic as they are incapable of being circumvented—clearly shows that it represents much less a stage in the history of thought than a regression of an *ideological* nature (the motivations behind this ideology cannot detain us here). The philosophy of history does not begin with a reading of Kant but with a study of human sacrifices among the Aztecs, the massive conversions of Christian peoples to Islam in half of the Eastern empire, or Nazism and Stalinism, to take a few examples.

On the other hand, if we grant the existence of a level of Being unknown to inherited ontology, which is the social-historical *qua* anonymous collective, and its mode of being *qua* radical imaginary in its capacity as *instituting* and *creative of significations,* we will be able to keep in mind the weighty evidences social-historical phenomena themselves present to us: that is, the irreducibility of the institution and of social significations to "individual activity"; society's coherence, beyond the functional level, in matters relating to *meaning;* the mutual irreducibility of different social-historical formations; and of all of them to some sort of "progress of Reason." The existence of this level is shocking only because people do not wish to depart from settled habits of thought; in itself, there is nothing more (or less) astonishing about it than that other level of being whose existence everyone stupidly accepts, if I dare say so, because they believe they have always seen it: namely, life itself. The existence of the social-historical is revealed (and even "proven") by its irreducible effects; if we do not grant its existence then we must, in no uncertain terms, make of language, and of languages in the plural (and this is only *one* example), a biological phenomenon (as Habermas practically does). These same effects reveal its creative character: Where else does one see a *form of Being* like the institution? It is a creation that manifests itself, *inter alia,* by the enormous diversity of social forms as well as in their historical succession. And this creation is *ex nihilo:* when humanity creates the institution and signification, it does not "combine" some "elements" that it would have found scattered about before it. It creates the *form* institution, and in and through this form it creates *itself* as *humanity* (which is something other than an assembly of bipeds). "Creation *ex nihilo,*" "creation of form," does not mean "creation *cum nihilo,*" that is to say, without "means," unconditionally, on a *tabula rasa.* Apart from one (or perhaps several) point(s) of origin which is (are) inaccessible and unfathomable and which itself (themselves) *lean(s) on* properties of the first natural stratum, of the human being as biological being, *and* of the psyche, all historical creation takes place upon, in, and through the already instituted (not to mention whatever surrounding "concrete" conditions there may be). This conditions it and limits it, but does not *determine* it; and quite clearly, still less does it do so in a "rational" manner since in major instances what occurs is a passage from one magma of social imaginary significations to another.[6] Thus it is a mere rhetorical objection to state that if there is creation in history then Homer could have been located somewhere between Shakespeare and Goethe. None of these "phenomena" (authors) can be detached from its own social-historical world—and it just so happens that, in *this* case, these worlds succeed one another by "being conscious," more or less, of those that preceded them in *this*

6. *Institution,* ch. 7; "La Logique des magmas et la question de l'autonomie," in *Domaines,* pp. 385–418.

segment of human history. The existence of conditions during a succession of such phases does not suffice to make such a succession "rationally causal." My reading of Hegel enters into the conditions for my thinking at this moment; if, against all odds, I succeeded in thinking something *new,* Hegel will not have been the "cause" of such an occurrence. The world built upon the ruins of the Roman Empire from the fifth century onward is inconceivable without Greece, Rome, the New Testament, and the Germanic barbarians. This in no way signifies that it springs from an "addition," "combination," or "synthesis" of elements from these four sources (and others one could think of). It is a creation of new social-historical forms (which are, moreover, radically other in the Eastern empire and in the Western barbarian kingdoms); they confer an essentially new meaning upon the very elements which preexisted them, and which they "utilize."[7] To speak of a "synthesis" in such instances is pure mental laziness and a dreary repetition of old clichés; they blind one, for example, to the fact that the "utilization" of Greek philosophy by Christian theology would have been impossible without a huge distortion of this philosophy (whose effects, moreover, are still making themselves felt) or that the institutionalization (and already the spread) of Christianity has required the abandonment of essential elements of the New Testament faith, such as its acosmic outlook and the purported imminence of Parousia (the Second Coming). Far from being able to "explain" or "understand" the Byzantine world on the basis of these elements, I must, quite to the contrary, understand the Byzantine world as a form for itself and a new magma of instituted significations in order to "explain" and "understand" what its preexisting elements have become through the new meaning they have acquired. In the actual practice of such an investigation, there is certainly always a give-and-take between the two approaches, but this in no way alters the main point on the level of principle.[8]

Of this, at least, Weber was thoroughly convinced *as well*—even if his terminology differs from ours. The true referent for the "incomparability" or "incommensurability" of "values" and ultimate "ends" of

---

7. *Domaines,* pp. 231–33.

8. For a sketch of the problems involved in, and the means available to, the understanding, see "The Greek *Polis* and the Creation of Democracy," ch. 5 of this book.

"people's social acts" and for the "war of the gods" is the otherness or *alterity* of different social-historical worlds and of the imaginary significations that animate these worlds. They express his acute perception of the problem created by the irreducible multiplicity of the forms through which the social-historical deploys itself as well as his profound awareness of the impossibility of giving these forms, when considered in themselves, any hierarchical ordering; however, this allows an ineradicable antinomy to remain in his thought. As clear as is his refusal to consider modern "rationality" and "rationalization" as *de jure* "superior" to other forms of social existence (and I will add, for my own part, that from *other* points of view, notably philosophical and political, this refusal is highly criticizable and ultimately unacceptable) his "violent rejection [*refus*] of historical irrationalism" (PhR) *compels him,* due to the irreducibility of "ultimate values" (i.e., of other imaginary significations), to set up a rationalist individualism (which, we have seen, cannot simply be "methodological" in character) and to establish instrumental rationality as the horizon of intelligibility for the social-historical. We should now be capable of seeing how the two terms of the antinomy feed upon each other: the more people's acts are motivated "in the last analysis" by adherence to mutually irreducible "ultimate values" (and, of course, to "Reason"), the more "scientific" analysis has to fall back on instrumental rationality as the only solid field of investigation; and the more "rationality" is postulated as the ultimate horizon of the understanding, the more the "ultimate values" of different cultures become *de facto* inaccessible and the understanding of the social-historical world finds itself reduced to the reconstitution of a few fragments, or instrumentally rational dimensions, of human action.

But what is this "instrumental rationality" itself?

The "instrumental rationality" of human individuals is, each time, socially instituted and imposed. (That this imposition encounters in the psyche what, through a difficult and painful process, makes it possible, is another question; cf. "Subject"). It is, for example, impossible without language. Now, every language conveys the totality of the social world to which it belongs. There are, of course, some "elements" of this rationality which, in the abstract, are transhistorical:

$2 + 2 = 4$ is undoubtedly valid in every society. These are the elements that belong at the intersection (the common part) of the ensidic (the ensemblistic-identitary) understanding which every society must, at minimum, institute and which also correspond, sufficiently as to need [as Aristotle would say], to the ensidic component of the first natural stratum upon which every society lives.[9] These elements, however, are *always* co-determined to a great extent by the magma of social imaginary significations in which they are immersed, and which each time they instrument. Without such instrumentation, these significations could not even be *voiced;* but without these significations, the "rational" (ensidic) elements would have *no meaning*. A book in mathematics written entirely in formalized terms and containing *no* explanation of its symbols, its axioms, and its rules of deduction, is totally incomprehensible. Thus, if one cannot avoid taking these transhistorical elements into consideration (a condition which does not take us very far, however), it is impossible to have a *correct* access to these same elements as they are actually given in a certain society unless one first has viewed the imaginary institution of this society. I must know something of the Christian religion to avoid seeing in the statement "$1 = 3$," as propounded by a believer in or a theologian of the Holy Trinity, a pure and simple instance of absurdity. It is therefore impossible for me, in trying to carry out the Weberian "methodological" program, to consider individual behavior as composed of a central "rational" (ensidic) component that is supposed to be (if [only] "methodologically") *everywhere and always the same* and of *individual* deviations from this "rationality." The understanding is instituted social-historically, and it is immersed in the overall imaginary institution of society. To speak in crude but clear terms: what is different in another society and another epoch is its very "rationality," for it is "caught" each time in another imaginary world. This does not mean that it is inaccessible to us; but this access must pass by way of an attempt (certainly always problematical; but how could it be otherwise?) to restitute the imaginary significations of the society in question.

In the second place—and this is another aspect of the same thing—

9. *Institution,* ch. 5.

the difference, the alterity, the deviation through which the object of social-historical inquiry is presented—and which constitutes the principal difficulty for this inquiry—is of an entirely other order than the deviation of an instrumentally rational form of behavior from the actual behavior observed. Marc Antony gave up the battle of Actium when he saw Cleopatra's vessel depart—though, "rationally speaking," he still had a chance of winning; this interference of passion in the application of instrumental rationality offers us no great enigma to resolve. What really astonishes us, and what constitutes the difficulty involved in the attainment of social-historical knowledge, is the enormous and massive alterity separating the representations, affects, motivations, and intentions of the subjects of another society from our own. How can we begin to understand the behavior of Arab warriors during Islam's great period of expansion, Christian soldiers during the Crusades, participants in the religious wars that tore apart Europe from 1530 until the Treaty of Westphalia, if the only instrument we have at our disposal is the ridiculous comparison between the instrumentally rational component involved in each of these cases and that which deviates from this component? I will have understood nothing if I have not tried to penetrate an entirely other *world* of significations, motivations, and affects; these certainly contain an ensidic component of *legein* and *teukhein,* but they are irreducible to it. Nearer to us, or rather closer to home: What good would it do me if I tried to understand the behavior of Hitler, the SS and members of the Nazi party or Stalin and members of Stalinist parties as instances of instrumentally rational behavior which, on certain precise points, have deviated from this rationality (the two parts of this statement being, moreover, quite true)? What would I have understood then of totalitarianism? And how can one avoid seeing that in this case the very implementation of such a demented "instrumental rationality," sometimes applied down to its tiniest details, has been dependent to a massive degree upon the imaginary of totalitarianism as well as decisively codetermined by it? Once again, one cannot avoid thinking that the return in force of such a "rationalist" individualism, and even of a certain rationalism, is actually motivated today as well by the desire to put an end (in words and philosophically) to the horrors of the twentieth century, even while these horrors continue to happen and diversify before our very eyes.

The situation is reversed, but the question is rendered no more solvable, in the opposite case: alterity tends toward a minimum—and ideally toward zero—when the object of investigation is the researcher's own society. In this case, the risk is that the researcher will consider the "rationality" of his/her society (and his/her very own rationality) as going without saying, as unquestionable, and that, for this very reason, s/he will fail to recognize the imaginary that lies at the basis of his/her society and founds it in its singularity. Need we recall to what extent this risk has trapped some of the greatest thinkers—from Hegel and Marx to Freud and Max Weber himself, not to mention those among our contemporaries who are legion? It is in this way that the Prussian monarchy, capitalist technique and the capitalist organization of production, the patriarchal family and the modern bureaucracy have, each in their turn, appeared as the incarnations of an unquestionable ("instrumental" or substantive) rationality.

Ideal Types

As conceived by Weber, the intended purpose of the ("scientific") construction of ideal types is to establish "typical" concatenations of individual motivations and acts (which ought, in the "perfect" case, to be both "adequate as to meaning" and "causally adequate") and thereby also to establish ideal types *of individuals,* at least with regard to an aspect of their activity ("king," "official," "entrepreneur," "magician," to take examples Weber cites in *E&S,* p. 18, sect. 9). Now, one of the paradoxes of his work is that several of the ideal types he has constructed (or elucidated)—and among these, some of the most important are terms that were formerly imprecise or vague and to which he has given a much more rigorous content—do not refer to individual behavior or to individuals but to great collective artifacts; that is to say, they refer in fact to institutions and types of institutions: the city, the market, varieties of authority, bureaucracy, the patrimonial or legal State, etc. Of course, Weber was seeking to find out to what extent in each case a specific instance of a class of phenomena, taken as belonging to the same term, approaches or diverges from its ideal type (cf. what he says about "the market," *E&S,* pp. 82–85), which is not of interest to us here, and on the other hand, to reduce these artifacts each time, ideally, to "individual behaviors"—an objective that is in truth rarely, not to say never, attained, given that it is intrinsically unattainable. To reduce, for example, the "market" to the maximizing behavior of "rational individuals" is both to make individuals of that type fall down into place from the sky and to neglect the social-historical conditions by which the "market" as institution has been genuinely *imposed* upon people (Polanyi has already said a good deal of what there is to say about this). What is constructed in each case is the ideal type of an *institution* which certainly has to accommodate "individuals"—no institution can survive if it does not—but which concerns another level of being than "purely individual" existence and which, much more important, is the general and specific *presupposition* for our being able to speak about the "rational behavior" of individuals. It is because *there is, already there,* a bureaucratic universe that my behavior *qua* bureaucrat would or would not be "rational"; even in modern bureaucracy, to be a bureaucrat with instrumentally rational behavior signifies behaving according to "rational" (and just as often, "absurd") rules instaurated by the bureaucracy in general and by the particular bureaucratic corps to which I belong.

Yet there is much more. The social-historical world is a world of effective and immanent meaning. And it is a world that has not waited around for the theoretician in order to come into existence as a world *of meaning,* nor in order to be, to a fantastic degree, *coherent,* for without coherence it would not exist. ("Coherent" means neither "systematic" nor "transparent.") This sets requirements on the construction of ideal types; to an extent, these requirements were tacitly admitted by Weber; to another extent, he ignored them.

Ideal types have a *referent* which is the effective social meaning of the "phenomena" (behaviors) observed. That this actual meaning is never "given immediately," that there is always necessarily an (in principle interminable) circulation back and forth between the theoretical construct and its confrontation with the (significant) "facts" changes nothing on the level of principle. Contrary to what Popper believes, one can say idiotic things about ancient Greece (I am not speaking here in terms of geography or demography) or about any other society—and one can show, with the aid, for example, of an ancient Greek text, that they are indeed idiotic. There are an infinity of absurd "interpretations" and few *prima facie* plausible ones relating to the historical "material" at hand. The validity of an ideal type can only be judged by its capacity to "make sense" [*sens*] of the historical phenomena, which are already *in themselves and for themselves* bearers of meaning [*sens*].

Now, such meaning is never "isolated." It always participates in the overall institution of society as institution of imaginary significations, and it is of a piece [*solidaire*] with it. This is also why—and independently of all "empirical" and "vulgar" refutations—I cannot insert the ideal type "shaman," for example, in a capitalist society or the ideal type "financial speculator" among the Aranta. *It just won't stick.* More generally speaking, the ideal types that I construct for a given society under study have to be *coherent, complementary,* and (ideally) *complete* or *exhaustive.* If I construct an ideal type of "Roman patrician," for example, it must be able to *hold together* with the ideal type "Roman plebeian," the two with that of "Roman slave," Roman "*pater familias*" and "*mater familias,*" etc.; but none of these ideal types can be constructed without reference to Roman law, Roman religion, the Roman army, the possibilities of the Latin tongue, etc. It is not that, *at the end* of this work, I will have reconstructed Roman society in its entirety; rather, it is that I cannot undertake *the first step* in this task unless I have this society *as such* in view. "Social facts" and "individual behaviors" are *effectively* possible (as "facts" *and* as meaning) only because there is, each time, a society which "functions," as is said in English, "as a going concern." (This has nothing to do with any sort of "functionalism." I simply mean that society exists, that it reproduces itself, changes, etc.) It is not because the ideal types constructed in order to grasp a given society have been constructed with a eye toward its coherence that they "produce" a coherent society—it is because society *is* coherent (even during civil war and in concentration camps) that the theoretician can try to construct ideal types that hold together somehow or other. I do not "freely" construct the Athenians' relation to their *polis;* it is because this relation has actually [*effectivement*] existed, in its historical singularity, in its coherence, and in its relative permanence, that I have before me the *polis* and the Athenian as objects of knowledge. As a coherent totality, society exists first of all in and for itself; it is not a "regulative Idea." "Total understanding" of it is, of course, an inaccessible ideal—but that is something else entirely.

Rationality and Politics

In order to appreciate the *constraint* that Weber's idea of "rationalization" as a *historically active factor* (and therefore one which is *immanent* to history and not "constructed" by the theoretician in order to better understand it) imposes, we should have discussed in precise detail Weber's immense work on the question of religion (the three volumes of the *Gesammelte Aufsätze zur Religionssoziologie* as well as Chapter 5 of *Economy and Society,* pp. 399–634, in particular the paragraph on "theodicy," *ibid.,* pp. 518–26). It is impossible to do so here: given the intrinsic importance of the subject and its revival in contemporary discourse, I hope to be able to return to this topic very shortly. Nevertheless, in the meantime I want to note that I consider completely false Weber's idea, which has been revived and expanded by Habermas, that "all religions have to resolve the problem of theodicy" and that there is an "*internal logic of religious representations*" which drives them toward a *movement* of "rationalization," whatever qualifications one will add to fix up this thesis.

I will conclude with a few remarks concerning Weber's political views and their relation to his philosophy and social theory, especially with regard to what must be called Weber's "decisionism" in matters political, or the idea of a "politics of the will" (PhR, p. 183).

Ultimately, Weber's "decisionism" boils down to saying that just as in the social-historical world the ultimate "values" orienting human activity are mutually irreducible and incommensurable, so the action of the politician (and of each of us, inasmuch as we are political subjects) rests on ultimate values which no amount of "rational" argumentation can impose upon those who do not share these same values. Let us note, first of all, that if Weber did not free himself, as we have seen, from Kantian rationalism in the domain of knowledge, he breaks with it in the domain of action; second, that this position (the "politics of the will") is in reality hardly weakened at all by Weber's marked preference for an "ethics of responsibility" (which takes the results of action into account) as against an "ethics of conviction" (which enjoins one to act according to certain principles or "for the greatness of the cause," whatever the real consequences of one's actions might be). The distinction is itself untenable, if not on the (descriptive) sociological plane, then in any case on the logical and normative, the only one of interest to us here. All "responsibility" is responsibility with regard to certain *ends*. If my "ethic of responsibility" prevents me from undertaking some political action—because, for example, it might entail the sacrifice of human lives—it is quite obviously because I posit human life as the supreme value, or at least superior to all others, this being a "conviction." And if I want to promote the "greatness of a cause" by any means possible, come what may, I greatly run the risk of destroying this cause. (One can think in terms of an absolute "ethic of conviction" without contradicting oneself only if this ethic is oriented in a completely acosmic fashion.) Third, quite obviously the choice to take on "responsibility" itself follows from a "conviction." Finally, as Philippe Raynaud notes, "the ethic of responsibility itself presupposes the limits of its own validity *and can thus grant the irreducibility of conviction*" (PhR, p. 184, emphasis added).

The irreducibility of conviction to anything else is another way of saying that nothing allows one to provide a "foundation" for ultimate choices and to escape the "combat of the gods." Nothing can save us from our *ultimate responsibility:* to choose and to will in view of the consequences. Not even Reason, that latest historical figure of a Grace that would shower upon those who entreat her with sufficient ardor.

There are two ways to attempt to go beyond—I would rather say, avoid—this situation, and both appear to me untenable.

Raymond Aron thought he could "escape from the circle in which he [Weber] enclosed himself" by invoking "universal rationality" as exemplified by "scientific truth." But "scientific truth" (and even the fact that "it addresses itself to all men") is a value and criterion only for those who have *already accepted* the value of "universal rationality" *and* who (this additional condition is absolutely essential) have passed from the latter to a practical and political/ethical universality. The first condition makes this statement into a tautology, the second reveals the fallacy that lies within. I see no incompatibility between the acceptance of "$2 \times 2 = 4$" (Aron's example) or quantum theory, and a call to kill the infidels, to convert them by force, or to exterminate the Jews. Quite the contrary, the *compatibility* of these two classes of assertions is the massive fact of human history. And it is particularly striking to witness the fact that it is in the twentieth century—the century that, more than any other, has monstrously demonstrated, and continues to demonstrate, that it is possible to dissociate the techno-scientifically "rational" from the politically reasonable—and *after* the experience of Stalinism and Nazism, that people have begun again to whistle in the dark the tune of universal rationality as a way of building up their courage.

We must again, we must always make distinctions. An ensidic "rationality" exists, it is universal up to a certain point, and it can take us very far (up to the point of manufacturing H-bombs). It was there before Greco-Western science and philosophy, it does not commit anybody to anything, and it could continue, for an indefinite period of time, upon an inertial course even if philosophy and science in the strong sense were to suffer a temporary or definitive eclipse. And Khomeini can, without any contradiction, consider Western science null and void—since all truth is in the Book—and buy from Satan such effective products as Stinger missiles so as to put them in the service of the One True God. And even if this were a contradiction it would change nothing. Contradicting oneself never prevented anyone from existing. But scientific *truth*—which is of the same nature as philosophical *truth:* namely, it perpetually puts to the test the closure in which thought is, every time, caught—contains the possibility of a *historically effective* universality only by effecting a *rupture* with the world of traditional or authoritarian instituted representations. (It is actual historical universality with which we are concerned when we confront the political question, not "transcendental universality.") Now, to "give oneself" this rupture as something already effectuated—which is what Aron does when he speaks of a "community of minds across boundaries and centuries"—is to assume that the problem is already resolved. In this effective sense, scientific or philosophical universality presupposes subjects who have *actually* put into question their belonging to some particular social-historical world. In a sense, it is, even, just that. It is therefore tied to the exigency of a universal ethics and politics only *at its root:* both of them express and try to realize the project of autonomy. This project, therefore, has to be posited *before* one can draw out any argument whatsoever in favor of scientific universality—and the latter will be valid only for those for whom this project is valid. *Downstream* from this project, everything becomes effectively an object of reasonable debate from which gains can be expected in all domains. But these gains, this debate, this project itself, what value have they then for a genius like Pascal, who renounces, so to speak, the invention of infinitesimal calculus because everything that *distracts* the soul from its relation to God is pure diversion or *distraction?* ("Martha, Martha, thou art careful and troubled about many things; But one thing is needful," *Luke* 10:41–42.) And upon what basis other than personal faith ("conviction"!) or a parochial cosmo-historical prejudice will one judge Pascal's and Kierkegaard's God worthy of respect while saying that of Khomeini is not?

Certainly, the term (or idea) of "authenticity" is not useful for this debate, and the idea that an "autonomous" individual is one that, in its actions, "obeys values" is untenable. In what way is a religious fanatic who drives an explosives-filled truck against an embassy's gates "inauthentic," and how could it be said that s/he does not obey "values"? Either "values" are arbitrary and mutually equivalent or else not all values are the same, and to say this already means that one has already accepted the reasonable discussability of values as one's supreme value and criterion. It is impossible to circumvent the necessity of affirming the project of autonomy as the primary position, one which can be elucidated but which cannot be "founded," since the very intention of founding it presupposes it.

I cannot take up here again the discussion of the idea of autonomy.[10] But we must reiterate that the question will remain intractable so long as autonomy is understood in the Kantian sense, that is, as a fictively autarchic subject's conformity to a "Law of Reason," in complete misrecognition of the social-historical conditions for, and the social-historical dimension of, the project of autonomy.

Let us now take up the normative standpoint (the political/ethical

10. Cf. *MRT*, pp. 101–14; "Une Interrogation sans fin" (interview), in *Domaines*, pp. 241–60; "The Greek *Polis*," ch. 5 and "The Nature and Value of Equality," ch. 6 of this book; and "Subject."

one, the two being at bottom indissociable). There is a goal which a few of us have set for ourselves: the autonomy of human beings, which is inconceivable except as the autonomy of *society* as well as the autonomy of *individuals*—the two being inseparably linked, and this link being in fact an analytic judgment (a tautology) when we understand what the individual is. We set autonomy in this sense as the goal for each among us, both with respect to each one of us and with respect to all the others (without the autonomy of others there is no collective autonomy—and outside such a collectivity I cannot be *effectively* autonomous). Since 1964[11] I have called the activity that aims at autonomy *praxis:* this activity aims at others as (potentially) autonomous subjects and tries to contribute to their efforts to attain full autonomy. (The term "*praxis*" therefore has here only a homonymic relation to the meaning Aristotle assigns to it.) This activity may take on an intersubjective form in the precise sense of unfolding in a concrete relation to determinate beings *intended as such*. Its most obvious cases are then pedagogy (also and especially "informal" pedagogy, which occurs everywhere and always) and psychoanalysis. But it also has to, under penalty of lapsing into total incoherence, take a form that goes far beyond all "intersubjectivity": *politics* [*la politique*], namely, the activity that aims at the transformation of society's institutions in order to make them conform to the norm of the autonomy of the collectivity (that is to say, in such a way as to permit the *explicit*, reflective, and deliberate self-institution and self-governance of this collectivity).

It is by starting with this position that we can understand why, contrary to what some may think, Habermas' efforts to found a theory of action on the ideas of "communicative action," "interpretive understanding," and "ideal speech situations" do not really go beyond "the mere critique of Max Weber's subjective convictions" and cannot "culminate in a fruitful attempt to redefine the tasks of social theory" (contrary to PhR, p. 190). There certainly is a "communicative" dimension (more simply put: there is communication) almost everywhere in social action (just as there is, everywhere, "instrumental," that is, ensidic, activity, a *legein* and a *teukhein*). Communication, however, is

11. *MRT*, pp. 71–79.

hardly ever an "end in itself," and it is totally inadequate as a way of bringing out criteria for action.

Let us consider the simplest cases, those apparently most favorable to Habermas' thesis. Both in pedagogy and in psychoanalysis, "communicative action" and "interpretive understanding" are certainly important *moments* of these activities. But in no way do they define either their *meaning* or their *end*. The *end* of psychoanalysis is not "interpretive understanding" between the analyst and the patient (which in no way is intended as such, and which is highly asymmetrical, as also is the case in pedagogy), but rather a contribution to the patient's access to his/her *own* autonomy (his/her capacity to challenge him/herself and lucidly to transform him/herself).

And again, these are (the most important) instances of "intersubjective" action. Now, activities that aim at autonomy have to (under penalty of succumbing to an annihilating incoherence) take on a *social*—that is to say, a *political*—form. And here we must dispel a radical misunderstanding and expose an ideologically based terminology that has reigned in philosophy at least since Husserl. The philosophers do not know (or rather, what is worse, do not *want* to know) what *the social* [*le social*] is. The term "intersubjective" systematically serves to evacuate the genuine (theoretical as well as practical) question of society and to mask their inability to think it. The term "intersubjectivity" expresses their continued enslavement to a metaphysics of the "substantive individual" (of the "subject") and the desperate attempt (already found in Husserl) to escape from the solipsistic cage to which egological philosophy leads—an attempt which, moreover, fails, the "other" always remaining in this perspective an incomprehensible prodigy.

But the social is something entirely other than "many, many, many" "subjects"—and also something entirely other than "many, many, many" "intersubjectivities." It is only in and through the social that a "subject" and an "intersubjectivity" become possible (even "transcendentally"!). The social is the always already instituted anonymous collective in and through which "subjects" can appear, it goes indefinitely beyond them (they are always replaceable and being replaced), and it contains in itself a creative potential that is irreducible to "cooperation" among subjects or to the effects of "intersubjectivity."

It is the *institution* of this social sphere [*le social*] that is the aim of politics, which therefore has nothing to do with "intersubjectivity" or even with "interpretive understanding." Politics intends the institution as such, or the grand options affecting society as a whole. It "addresses itself" to the anonymous collective, both present and to come. Certainly, it always acts through a determinate public, but it does not *aim for* interpretive understanding between the political actor and this public; rather, it aims at the fate of the collectivity for a period of time that is, in principle, indeterminate. The fact that the orator has to express him/herself in a comprehensible way, or even that we want, and consider of capital importance, that the decision result from the most reasonable discussion possible, is not even worth mentioning here. The intended end, and the actual result, are something else entirely, these being the adoption of a new law, or engagement in some important common endeavor. In important cases, all these decisions *modify* not only the individuals presently involved but also those to come. All this goes far beyond "communicative action" and "interpretive understanding." These latter are, so to speak, only the atmosphere indispensable to *political* life and creativity—and their very existence depends upon instituting acts. The *end* or *goal* of these acts goes far beyond the establishment of an ideal communication situation, which is only part of that end, and really just a mere *means*.

Now, if one now adopts not a *normative* standpoint (we want autonomy, what it presupposes and what it entails), but rather a descriptive-analytic one concerning society and history in their actuality—as is, in reality, the case with Habermas—Habermas's attempt to elicit from the *very fact* that "communicative action" occurs everywhere and always some sort of *exigency* can be seen only as an enormous logical blunder. As "reproducing product" of society, "interpretive understanding" is everywhere: among fifth-century B.C. Athenians, New Yorkers, and French people today, the Communards of 1871—as well as among the oligarchic Spartans, the Waffen-SS, or Khomeini's pajdarans. What distinguishes for us the second group from the first does not relate in any way to some kind of deficiency in the capacity for intersubjective communication (which is, perhaps, at a maximum within a homogeneous group of fanatics of any sort), but to the fact that such communication is *always already structured* exhaustively by the given institution of society in such a way that it is *effectively impossible,* from the social-historical point of view, for the participants to put into question this institution (which they are doomed to reproduce indefinitely) and, *by this very fact,* to open themselves to the reason of others. It is the institution as it is given each time that always assures communication and traces the limits of the humanity with which one can, in principle, "communicate." It is therefore this *institution* as such that has to be aimed at if the field of such communication is to be enlarged. And if we will to enlarge it, it is not because we will communication for itself, rather we will it in order that all humanity be put in a position where it would be able to work in common toward the creation of institutions that will advance its freedom of thought and creative making/doing [*faire*].

Habermas's attempt "rationally" to educe, once again, right from fact—the idea of a "good" society from the *reality* of the conditions of social life—appears to me just as untenable as the other attempts of the same kind that have been made in the past, and which he repeats. It leads him, in a totally characteristic way, to seek a mythical *biological* foundation for the questions of social theory and political action. The following passage, one among many others, bears witness to this: "The utopian perspective of reconciliation and liberty is ingrained in the conditions for the communicative sociation of individuals; it is built into the linguistic mechanism of the reproduction of the species."[12] Since when has biology (the "linguistic mechanism of the reproduction of the species") ever "built into" it a "utopian perspective"? Why would such a "mechanism" not be compatible with the preservation of closed societies—which it has, on the contrary, safeguarded almost everywhere, almost always, throughout history? And why would freedom be "utopian"? Freedom is neither a "utopia" nor a fatality. It is a social-historical project without whose already occurring, yet still partial, realization neither would Habermas be in a position to write what he writes nor would I to object to it. (Here, as in all contemporary parlance, "utopia" clearly is a replacement for the Kantian "regulative Idea"; it removes the disagreeable "idealist" con-

---

12. *Theorie des kommunikativen Handelns,* vol. 1, pp. 532–33; *The Theory of Communicative Action,* tr. Thomas McCarthy (Boston: Beacon Press, 1984), p. 398.

notations as it confers upon it, now that Marxism has gone bankrupt, an agreeable "pre-Marxist revolutionary" scent.) To found the project of freedom philosophically in reason is already a bad usage of reason, for the very decision to philosophize is but a manifestation of freedom; to philosophize is to try to be free in the domain of thought. To want to "found" it on "the linguistic conditions for the reproduction of the species" is to revert to a biological positivism that leads to an incoherent paradox: it makes of freedom both a fatality inscribed in our genes and a "utopia."

From the moment we have left the closure of the sacred institution; from the time when the Greeks posed the questions: "What ought we to think?" "What ought we to do?" in a world they had built in such a way that the gods had nothing to say about those questions, there is no longer any possible evasion of responsibility, choice, and decision. We have decided that we want to be free—and this decision *is already* the first realization of this freedom.

Tinos, August 1987–Paris, January 1988

5

The Greek *Polis* and the Creation of Democracy

How can we orient ourselves in history and politics? How can we judge and choose? It is from this political interest that I start—and in this spirit that I ask: In ancient Greek democracy is there anything of political relevance for us?

In a sense, Greece is obviously a presupposition of this discussion. The reasoned investigation of what is right and wrong, of the very principles that are the basis of our ever being able to say, beyond trivialities and traditional preconceptions, that something is right or wrong, arises for the first time in Greece. Our political questioning is,

---

The principal ideas found in this article were presented for the first time during a lecture given on October 29, 1979, to a seminar at the Max Planck Institute in Starnberg led by Jürgen Habermas; Johann Arnason, Ernst Tugendhat, and Albrecht Wellmer were among the main participants. Since then, these ideas have been at the center of my work in my seminar at the Ecole des Hautes Etudes en Sciences Sociales in Paris, beginning in 1980, and they have provided the substance for a course in August 1982 at the University of Sao-Paulo, a seminar in April 1985 at the University of Rio Grande do Sul (Porto Alegre), and several other presentations. The text published here is that of a lecture read on April 15, 1982, in New York, during one of the Hannah Arendt Memorial Symposia in Political Philosophy organized by the New School for Social Research which dealt with "The Origins of Our Institutions." The original English version was published in the *Graduate Faculty Philosophy Journal* of the New School, 9:2 (Fall 1983), pp. 79–115. A French translation appeared in my *Domaines de l'homme. Les Carrefours du labyrinthe II* (Paris: Seuil, 1986), pp. 261–306.

ipso facto, a continuation of the Greek position, although of course we have transcended it in many important respects and are still trying to transcend it.

Modern discussions of Greece have been plagued by two opposite and symmetrical—thus, in a sense, equivalent—preconceptions. The first, and most frequently encountered over the last four or five centuries, is Greece as eternal model, prototype, or paradigm.[1] (One contemporary outlook merely inverts this preconception: Greece as antimodel, as negative model.) The second and more recent preconception involves the complete "sociologization" or "ethnologization" of the examination of Greece. Thus, the differences between the Greeks, the Nambikwara, and the Bamileke are only descriptive. No doubt, this second attitude is formally correct. Not only, needless to say, is there not nor could there be any difference in "human value," "worthiness," or "dignity" between different peoples and cultures, but neither could there be any objection to applying to the Greek world the methods—if there be any—applied to the Arunta or to the Babylonians.

The second approach, however, misses a minute and decisive point. The reasoned investigation of other cultures and the reflection upon them does not begin within the Arunta or the Babylonian cultures. Indeed, one could show that it could not have begun with them. Before Greece and outside the Greco-Western tradition, societies are instituted on a principle of strict closure: our view of the world is the only meaningful one, the "others" are bizarre, inferior, perverse, evil, or unfaithful. As Hannah Arendt has said, impartiality enters this world with Homer.[2] This is not just "affective" impartiality. It is the impartiality of knowledge and understanding. The keen interest in the other starts with the Greeks. This interest is but another side of the critical examination and interrogation of their own institutions. That is to say,

1. Marx himself wrote in the *Introduction to a Critique of Political Economy* that Greek art presented an *inaccessible* model, not insuperable or insurmountable—but *inaccessible*.

2. "The Concept of History," in *Between Past and Future* (New York: Viking Press, 1968), p. 51.

it is a component of the democratic and philosophical movement created by the Greeks.

That the ethnologist, the historian, or the philosopher is in a position to reflect upon societies other than his own and, indeed, even upon his own society becomes a possibility and a reality only within this particular historical tradition—the Greco-Western tradition. Now, on one hand, this activity may have no theoretical privilege over any other—say, poison divination by the Azanda. Then, for example, the psychoanalyst is but a Western variety of shaman, as Lévi-Strauss has written, and Lévi-Strauss himself, along with the entire society of ethnologists, is but the local variety of sorcerer within this particular group of tribes exorcising, if you will, the alien tribes. The only difference is that rather than fumigating them out of existence, they structuralize them out of existence. Or on the other hand, we may postulate or posit a qualitative difference between our theorizing about other societies and about "savages" and attach to this difference a specific, limited but firm, positive valuation.[3] Then, a philosophical discussion starts. *Then,* and not before. To start a philosophical discussion is to imply that one has already affirmed that for oneself unrestricted thinking is the way of entering upon problems and tasks. Thus, since we know that this attitude is by no means universal but extremely exceptional in the history of human societies,[4] we have to ask how, under what conditions, in which ways, human society was capable, in one particular case, of breaking the closure in virtue of which it generally exists?

In this sense, though describing and analyzing Greece is equivalent to describing and analyzing any other randomly chosen culture, thinking and reflecting about Greece is not and cannot be. For in this latter case, we are reflecting and thinking about the social and historical conditions of thought itself—at least, thought as we know and prac-

---

3. Needless to add, this in itself does not allow any "practical" or "political" conclusions.

4. Linguists seem to recognize and register some 4,000 languages extant *today*. Though there is of course no one-to-one correspondence between language and total institution of society, this gives a very rough indication of the order of magnitude of different types of society that have existed in the very recent past.

tice it. One has to eliminate these twin attitudes: there was, once upon a time, a society which remains for us the inaccessible model; *or,* history is essentially flat, there are no significant differences between cultures other than descriptive ones. Greece is the social-historical *locus* where democracy and philosophy are created, thus, of course, it is our own origin. Insofar as the meaning and the potency of this creation are not exhausted—and I firmly believe that they are not—Greece is for us a *germ,* neither a "model," nor one specimen among others, but a germ.

History is creation: the creation of total forms of human life. Social-historical forms are not "determined" by natural or historical "laws." Society is self-creation. "That which" creates society and history is the instituting society, as opposed to the instituted society. The instituting society is the social imaginary in the radical sense.

The self-institution of society is the creation of a human world: of "things," "reality," language, norms, values, ways of life and death, objects for which we live and objects for which we die—and of course, first and foremost, the creation of the human individual in which the institution of society is massively embedded.

Within this wholesale creation of society, each particular, historically given institution represents a particular creation. Creation, as I use the term, means the positing of a new *eidos,* a new essence, a new form in the full and strong sense: new determinations, new norms, new laws. The Chinese, the classical Hebrew, the ancient Greek, or the modern capitalist institution of society each means the positing of different determinations and laws, not just "juridical" laws, but obligatory ways of perceiving and conceiving the social and "physical" world and acting within it. Within, and by virtue of, this overall institution of society emerge specific creations: science, for example, as we know and conceive it, is a particular creation of the Greco-Western world.

There follows a series of crucial questions, about which I can only sketch some reflections here.

First, how can we understand previous or "foreign" institutions of society? (For that matter how and in what sense can we say that we understand our own society?) We do not have, in the social-historical domain, "explanation" in the same sense the physical sciences do. Any "explanation" of this sort is either trivial or fragmentary and conditional. The innumerable regularities of social life—without which, of course, this life would not exist—are what they are because the institution of this particular society has posited this particular complex of rules, laws, meanings, values, tools, motivations, etc. And this institution is nothing but the socially sanctioned (sanctioned formally or informally) magma of social imaginary significations created by this particular society. Thus, to understand a society means, first and foremost, to penetrate or reappropriate the social imaginary significations which hold this society together. Is this at all possible? We have to take into account two facts here.

The first, indisputable fact is that *almost all* of the people in a given society do not and cannot understand a "foreign" society. (I am not speaking, of course, about trivial obstacles.) This points to what I have called the cognitive closure of the institution. The second (which can be and is disputed, but to which I nevertheless hold) is that under some very specific social, historical, and personal preconditions, some people can understand something about a foreign society. This points to some sort of "potential universality" in whatever is human for humans. Contrary to inherited commonplaces, the root of this universality is not human "rationality" (if "rationality" were at stake here, nobody would ever have had understood anything about the Hebrew God, or, for that matter, about any religion whatsoever), but creative imagination as the core component of nontrivial thinking.[5] Whatever has been imagined strongly enough to shape behavior, speech or objects can, in principle, be reimagined (rerepresented, *wiedervorgestellt*) by somebody else.

Two significant polarities have to be stressed here.

In this social-historical understanding, there is a distinction between "true" and "false"—and not just in the trivial sense. One can talk sense about "foreign" societies, and one can talk nonsense—of which there is no dearth of examples. The "true" cannot be subjected in this case (as,

5. Relying on "rationality" alone has led, e.g., to the nineteenth-century characterizations of primitive religion and myth as sheer nonsense (or "junk," as Marx and Engels wrote)—or to contemporary structuralism and other Procrustean beds.

more generally, it never can in matters of thought) to the banal "verification" or "falsification" procedures which are currently (platitudinously and wrongly) considered to demarcate "science" from "non-science." For instance, Burckhardt's realization of the importance of the agonistic element in the Greek world (which looms so large in Hannah Arendt's thinking about Greece), is *true*—but not in the same sense as $E = mc^2$ is true. What does "true" mean in this former case? That the idea of the agonistic brings together an indefinite class of social and historical phenomena in Greece that would otherwise remain unconnected—not necessarily unconnected in their "causal" or "structural" relation but unconnected in their *meaning;* and that its claim to possess a "real" or "actual" referent (i.e., that is not just a delusion, or convenient fiction, or even an *Idealtypus,* an observer's limiting rational construction[6]) can be discussed in a fecund way, though this discussion may be and, in the decisive cases, *has* to be interminable. In brief, it *elucidates* and initiates a process of elucidation.

The situation is different, at first glance, when we are speaking about our own history or tradition, about societies which though "other" are not "foreign" since there is strong genealogical connection between their imaginary significations and ours, since we still somehow "share" the same world, since there is still some active, intrinsic relationship between their institutions and our own. It would seem that since we succeed this creation but fall within the same concatenation, since we find ourselves, so to speak, downstream, since we live, at least partly, within the mental framework and the universe of beings which is posited, our understanding of our "ancestral" societies would present no mystery. But of course, other problems arise. This "common belonging" is by necessity partly illusory, but often tends to be taken as fully real. Projective "value judgments" become important and interfere with understanding. The proper distance between ourselves and "our own past" is very difficult to establish; the attitudes toward Greece cited earlier are examples. The illusion of the *Selbstverständlichkeit* can be catastrophic: thus, people today consider democracy or rational inquiry to go without saying, naively projecting onto

6. A "central limit" one would say in mathematics. [Note added in 1986.]

the whole of history the exceptional situation of their own society, and are unable to understand what democracy or rational inquiry could mean for the society where they were created for the first time.

The second question is: If history is creation, how can we judge and choose? It is to be stressed that this question would not arise if history were simply and strictly a causal concatenation, or if it did contain its *physis* and *telos*. It is precisely because history is creation that the question of judging and choosing emerges as a radical, nontrivial question.

The radicality of the question stems from the fact that, despite a widespread naive illusion, there is not and cannot be a rigorous and ultimate foundation of anything—not of knowledge itself, not even of mathematics. One should remember that this foundational illusion has never been shared by the great philosophers: not by Plato, not by Aristotle, not by Kant, not by Hegel. The first outstanding philosopher who was under the delusion of "foundation" was Descartes, and this is one of the respects in which his influence has been catastrophic. Since Plato, it has been known that every demonstration presupposes something which is not demonstrable. Here I want to stress one other aspect of the question: the judgments and choices we make belong to the history of the society in which we live and depend upon it. I do not mean that they depend upon particular social-historical "contents" (though this is also true). I mean that the sheer fact of judging and choosing in a nontrivial sense presupposes not only that we belong to that particular history, to that particular tradition where judging and choosing first become effectively possible, but that we have already, before any judgment and choice of "contents," judged affirmatively and chosen this history and this tradition in this respect. For this activity of judging and choosing, and the very idea of it, is a Greco-Western activity and idea—it has been created within this world and nowhere else. The idea would not and could not occur to a Hindu, to a classical Hebrew, to a true Christian, or to a Moslem. Classical Hebrews have nothing to choose. They have been given the truth and the Law once and for all by God, and if they started judging and choosing about that, they would no longer be Hebrew. Likewise, true Christians have nothing to judge or choose: they have to believe and to love. For it is written: *Judge not, that ye be not judged* (*Matt.* 7:1). Conversely, Greco-Westerners ("Europeans") who produce rational arguments for rejecting the European tradition confirm *eo ipso* this tradition and that they belong to it.

But neither does this tradition offer us repose. For while it has produced democracy and philosophy, both the American and the French Revolutions, the Paris Commune and the Hungarian Workers' Councils, the Parthenon and *Macbeth,* it has produced as well the massacre of the Melians by the Athenians, the Inquisition, Auschwitz, the Gulag, and the H-bomb. It created reason, freedom, and beauty—and it also created massive monstrosity. No animal species could ever create Auschwitz or the Gulag; to create that you must be a human being. These extreme possibilities of humanity in the field of the monstrous have been realized *par excellence* in our own tradition. The problem of judging and choosing thus also arises within this tradition, which we cannot validate for a moment *en bloc.* And of course, it does not arise as a simple intellectual possibility. The very history of the Greco-Western world can be viewed as the history of the struggle between autonomy and heteronomy.

It is well-known that the problem of judging and choosing is the object of Kant's third *Critique,* and that Hannah Arendt in her later years turned toward the third *Critique* in her search for some grounding for these activities of the mind. I feel a form of illusion is spreading among some of Hannah Arendt's followers or commentators (1) that somehow or other Kant "solved" this problem in the third *Critique,* and (2) that his "solution" could be transposed to the political problem or at least facilitate the latter's elaboration. Facilitate, indeed, it does—but in a negative way, as I will try to show briefly.

I submit that the whole affair is a strange (but philosophically commonplace) *chassé-croisé* of correct insights arrived at for the wrong reasons. It begins with Kant himself. Why is Kant, nine years after the first edition of the *Critique of Pure Reason,* driven to the question of *Urteil* and *Urteilskraft*?[7] The apparently watertight answers given to

7. It is true that in his initial plans dating back to 1771, when he projected writing a work entitled "Limits of Sensibility and Reason," Kant proposed to treat in the same framework theoretical reason, ethics, and taste; but the way in which the last of these objectives was realized in his 1790 book and especially its connection with the "teleology of nature" seems to me to justify the remarks in the text. [Note added in 1986.]

this question in the Preface and Introduction to the third *Critique* I consider to be rational reconstructions or rationalizations, Kant's dressing up in systematic and systematizing garb deeper and not fully conscious philosophical motivations.

First among these, no doubt, is the realization that the whole edifice of the *Critique of Pure Reason* stands on air, that any "given" just is not sufficient to produce *Erfahrung* (experience), that the organization of a "world" out of the *Mannigfaltigkeit* (diversity) of the given entails that this *Mannigfaltigkeit* already be intrinsically organized to a minimal degree, since it must be at least *organizable*. No catagory of causality could ever legislate a *Mannigfaltigkeit* which would follow this law: if y once succeeded an x, never again will a y succeed an x.[8] (Of course, in such a "fully chaotic" world the existence of an actual, effective "knowing subject" would be impossible—but this is a second and equally strong argument against the monocracy of subjective transcendentalism. The object of the legislation has to be forthcoming as "legislatable," and the legislator actually has to "exist" as well. Both entail a world that is not completely chaotic.

A worthy philosophical answer is not supplied to this question by the "happy accident" (*glücklicher Zufall*), the "contingent" character of the "systematic unity" of the laws of nature and of their capacity to fulfill the requirements of *Verstand*—which is indeed, in a sense, the truth of the matter. Hence, the turn to a reflective and not constitutive teleology of nature: though we cannot "prove" it, nature works as if it were organized according to ends. For these workings of nature, the human work of art provides an analogy, since in it we can see "imagination in its freedom as determinable by the understanding according to ends" (§59).

The second motivation is precisely the recognition of the specificity of the work of art.[9] Kant has to bring together his desire (or need) to

8. The problem is already stated in the *Critique of Pure Reason*, A 653–4. See *Critique of Judgment*, Introduction, V and VI—where the expression "happy accident" (*glücklicher Zufall*) occurs.

9. A useful and informative recent survey of the widespread preoccupation of that period with the work of art and imagination is given by James Engell, *The Creative Imagination* (Cambridge, Mass.: Harvard University Press, 1981).

provide an "aesthetics" in the usual sense, a philosophy of the beautiful and philosophical *locus* for it, and his dim realization of the ontological specificity of art as *creation*. This is, of course, where Kant transcends the classical tradition and its ontology. The great work of art does not follow rules but posits new rules—it is *Muster* and *exemplarisch*. The artist, the genius, is not able to "describe" or "scientifically explain" his product, but posits the norm "as nature" (*als Natur,* § 46). Nature of course is here *natura naturans,* not *natura naturata,* not the nature of the *Critique of Pure Reason,* but a "living" power of emergence, bringing together matter under form. The genius is *Natur*—and *Natur* is genius!—*qua* free imagination determinable according to finality.

The third motivation is Kant's increasing preoccupation with the questions of society and history. This is manifest in his numerous writings of the period related to these subjects and expressed in the third *Critique* through the ideas of a *sensus communis* and of the distinction between objective and subjective universal validity (*Allgemeingültigkeit*).

Before addressing the questions arising from the frequent contemporary recourse to the third *Critique* in connection with the activities of judging and choosing, it is necessary to point to a paradox of the first magnitude: Why should one have recourse to the *Critique of Judgment* when the whole of Kant's *practical* philosophy is explicitly directed toward supplying rules and maxims of judgment and choice in "practical" matters?[10] Why is the apparently firm ground offered by Kant's practical philosophy in matters of ultimate political judgment neglected in recent discussions while it abundantly inspired, eighty years ago, neo-Kantian socialists and Austro-Marxists, for example? If the categorical imperative as such is an empty, simple form of abstract universality, as Schiller and Hegel rightly saw, if Kant's attempts to derive substantive injunctions and interdictions from the principle of contradiction are flawed, certainly the same cannot be said about Kant's maxims. "Be a person and respect others as persons"; "respect humanity in every human being"; "treat others as ends and never

10. Richard Bernstein has rightly and clearly stressed this point in "Judging—the Actor and the Spectator," a paper delivered in the Conference on the Work of Hannah Arendt held in New York in October 1981.

simply as means"—if these principles hold, one may certainly still be shocked by Eichmann and what he represents, but one will not wonder about the possibility of judging him. Then Hans Jonas would not have to worry about being able to say to a Hitler "I will kill you," but not "you are wrong."[11]

But of course the matter does not end here. First, Hitler would be right in answering: You cannot *demonstrate* to me the validity of your maxims. Second, he would answer nothing of the sort. Nazis and Stalinists do not discuss, they just draw their guns. Third, the maxims escape the flaw of indeterminacy only because we are used to giving a more or less determinate content to the terms "person," "humanity," etc. This is not philosophical hairsplitting. Not so long ago, the Church was burning people at the stake in order to save their "humanity"—their souls. Maxims (or any similar rules) are of value only within and for a community where (1) reasonable (not "rational") discussion is accepted as a means of overcoming differences, (2) it is recognized that everything cannot be "demonstrated," and (3) there is a sufficient (even if tacit) degree of consensus beyond logical definition about the meaning of terms like "person," "humanity"—or for that matter, "liberty," "equality," and "justice." It will be noted that these terms refer to social imaginary significations *par excellence.*

The similarities between these prerequisites and those of any discussion about art are obvious. This of course does not mean that political and aesthetic judgments are species of the same genus—but that it is not, *prima facie,* unreasonable to explore the conditions under which a community can discuss and agree upon matters beyond those accessible through procedures of strict demonstration.

It is equally obvious, however, that these conditions are so restrictive as to be of no use when we come to ultimate questions. Kant's third *Critique* in fact presents a description of rather than a "solution" to the problem of judging. Significant as this description is, it offers no help in the search for "foundations." As a "solution," from a logi-

---

11. See Michael Denneny, "The Privilege of Ourselves: Hannah Arendt on Judgment," in *Hannah Arendt: The Recovery of the Public World,* ed. M. A. Hill (New York: St. Martin's Press, 1979), pp. 259 and 273. See also, *ibid.,* the exchange between Hans Jonas and Hannah Arendt, pp. 311–15.

cian's point of view, it only begs the question; in the terms of my framework, it describes the primitive circle of social-historical creation without actually understanding it. To this I now turn briefly.

Let us note from the outset that, as far as I know, the invocation of the *Critique of Judgment* in regard to the issue of social-historical creation refers only to the idea of "taste" and "reflective judgment," and not at all to the idea that the great work of art is a creation. In this way, a central and fatal *aporia* in Kant's work is ignored or concealed.

For Kant, the aesthetic "reflective judgment" possesses a *subjektive Allgemeingültigkeit* (a subjective universal validity)—as opposed to the objective universal validity of, e.g., determinative judgments in the theoretical field. It appeals to *taste* and is founded upon the possibility of the subject's placing itself "in the other's place." No such condition is required for judgments of objective universal validity. Where "the other" is, from the point of view of *quid juris,* is irrelevant.

Where does this subjective universal validity of the judgment of taste derive from? From the fact that in aesthetic judgment I do not say "It pleases me," or, "I find this beautiful," but "This *is* beautiful." I claim universality for my judgment. But this of course will not do. It is perfectly possible that I give (or that I am bound to give) the form of universality to a class of my judgments without any content corresponding to this form in a valid way. It is perfectly possible that I formulate a claim to universality, and that this claim remain frustrated and vacuous. The logical-transcendental trap does not work here. When I say not "I believe P to be true," but "P is true," the question of the objective universal validity of my judgment can be settled in principle by rules and procedures. And if someone tells me, "nothing is ever true," or "truth is a matter of whim," he walks, *de jure,* out of the room of rational discussion. I need not worry about him, and more generally (in Kant's eyes), in theoretical matters I do not even need the approval of "the other," nor need I look at things "from his point of view."[12] Not so for the reflective judgment, where I *do* need to intro-

12. In fact even in the theoretical field this is not so; but I cannot enter here into the question of the social-historical conditions of thought. Suffice it to say that "objective universal validity," as Kant conceives of it, is virtually equivalent to the perfect isolation

duce the other's point of view. Now, if the other were "pure taste"—if such a thing as "pure taste" exists, *even* "transcendentally," that is, in the same way *reiner Verstand* must "exist"—the judgment would be mere wordplay. The other would be just another concrete instance of the same "universal" (though of course not a logical or "discursive" universal) of which I would also be an instance. For if "pure taste" exists, this would entail that it owe nothing to the "empirical particularities" of the subjects concerned nor be affected by them (just as in the cases of knowledge and ethics). But in the domain of the aesthetic judgment, the other has to be taken into consideration precisely *qua other.* He does not differ from me "numerically," as the scholastics would say, but substantively. Despite the connotations of the term "reflective," in reflective judgment the other is not a mirror. It is *because* he is other (nontrivially different) that he can function where Kant locates him. It is because *different* people *can* agree on matters of beauty that the aesthetic judgment exists and is of a nature other than theoretical or pure practical (ethical) judgments. In the latter cases, the agreement is both necessary and superfluous. Universality, there, is identity through or across indefinite and indifferent numerical "instantiations." But the "subjective universal validity" of the aesthetic judgment is commonality through or across nonidentity. The other has to find—or does find—the *Nightwatch* beautiful even though he is nontrivially different from me.

But different how, to what extent, up to what point? Different just enough, not too much, and not too little. Would my judgment of *Oedipus Rex* become shaky if a throng of very refined Tang, Song, or Ming mandarins found the play repugnant? Should I think of Hokusai's point of view when looking at *Les demoiselles d'Avignon?* Kant speaks repeatedly, of course, about the "education of taste." But education of taste gives rise to two intractable philosophical problems (intractable at least from *this* perspective). First, education of taste is

---

or disembodiment of "theoretical consciousness," and thus to some sort of solipsism. For instance, Kant completely ignores the inseparability of thought and language, as a *theoretical* (not "psychological") problem. At the same time, he asserts (in the third *Critique*), strangely enough from the "transcendental" point of view, that without communication there is no knowledge.

impossible unless (1) beauty is already there, and (2) it is rightly recognized as such. Whence, by whom, and on what basis? Who shall educate the educators? Either education of taste is a meaningless expression, or beauty is a historical *Faktum* (as, indeed, *Erfahrung* also is) and its "recognition" or "reception" cannot be "explained" or "understood" (let alone *be* founded) any more than its creation (Kant says "production," *Erzeugung*) can. What we discover here again is the primitive, originary circle of creation: *creation presupposes itself.* Second, if we think of historically effective education, then we would have (as indeed we do) the *imposition* of a given "taste" in a particular culture. Uniformity of taste will then be more or less "obligatory," and reflective judgment will provide no more input than that already injected into the historical subjects.

Now if beauty is a historical *Faktum,* there is not only one history of this *Faktum,* but a vast plurality of such histories—and thus also of tastes. We have been educated and continue educating our offspring in and through the creations of our own particular history. It is also our own history—*and this history alone*—that has educated us so that we find beauty in the sculpture of the Mayas, the painting of the Chinese, or the music and dance of the Balinese, while the reverse is not true. To be sure, some of the best interpreters of Mozart today are Japanese. But they attain to this insofar as they have been "Westernized"—not so much in that they have learned the piano, Mozart, and so forth, but in that they have accepted this very opening, this movement of acculturation, with its corollary: that the music of some barbarians is not to be rejected beforehand but may be worth the effort of appropriation.[13]

If the other is not a shadow or a mannequin, he belongs to a definite and concrete social-historical commonality. Concrete means particular: a particular community, and its particular "education"—that is, tradition. But then, the appeal to the other's point of view floats uneasily between vacuousness and tautology. It is vacuous if the addressee is supposedly to be found in each and every particular commu-

13. A well-known story reports that two centuries ago the Chinese emperor turned down the proposal of an English embassy for a trade treaty with the remark: I can well see why the barbarians would wish to have our products, but I do not see how they could offer a worthwhile equivalent.

nity. It is tautologous if it is an appeal to our own community: for then it is an appeal to go on judging as beautiful what has already been so judged.

That this should be so is, of course, the consequence of what I called the cognitive closure between the different social-historical worlds. This applies to art as well as to "science," to sufficient reasons for dying as well as to table manners. To be sure, there is a distinction to be drawn between "science" and the rest, or at any rate between science and art. Even if we disdain pragmatic arguments of the sort "the universal validity of our science over against savage magic is 'proven' by the fact that we kill savages much more effectively than their magic can kill us," it remains that the chances for effective "universal validity" in science are much greater than those in art. For in the case of science, the component that supplies the identity among its variations (*legein* and *teukhein*) is paramount, and this component is less variable among different cultures.[14] For instance, insofar as causality is recognized everywhere (magic itself operates on some sort of causality postulate), you can convince any savage with a few operations that X causes Y. The chances that you could bring him to love *Tristan und Isolde* are immeasurably less: for this you would have to educate him in and through several centuries of European culture. This is of course no accident: "art"—which has never been just "art," except for a short and recent historical period—is much more strongly and deeply linked to the kernal of a society's imaginary significations than is "knowledge of things."

Of course, to all this there is a Kantian answer, and at least a threefold one. First, the work of art addresses itself "to the subjective element, which one can presuppose in all men (insofar as it is required for possible knowledge in general)" (§38). This is to be found in the combination of the free play of imagination with the legality (*Gesetzmässigkeit*) of understanding (§35), in a proper proportion (§21). Second, the foundation of the "necessity" of the judgment of taste must lie in an "indeterminate concept," the concept "of a supersensible

14. On these terms and the problem itself see my *Imaginary Institution of Society*, tr. Kathleen Blamey (Oxford: Polity Press, and Cambridge, Mass.: M.I.T., 1987), ch. 5.

substratum of phenomena" (§57). Third, there exists a historical process, equivalent to a progress in education of taste—and certainly to an actualization of effective universality through convergence—and this is manifest in the development of civilization in general and in *Aufklärung* in particular (§41).

It is neither possible nor necessary to discuss these points here. I will only note regarding the first one that it implies much more than it initially appears to do. One can easily grant that imagination, understanding, and a "productive" interplay of the two are present in all humans: but the question of taste entails much more than such abstract universal "faculties," it pertains to their concrete historical specification (and Kant is well aware of this, as the third point shows; cf. also the Remark to §38). Of much greater importance, however, these ideas imply the whole of Kant's philosophy—both "pure philosophy," and "philosophy of history." Without it, the third *Critique* hangs in the air. I find it puzzling that those who today advocate recourse to the third *Critique* do not seem to realize that they have to take into the bargain as well the idea of a "supersensible substratum of phenomena," and of "humanity" (in the *Kantian* sense of "supersensible"). Nor do they seem to realize that beauty is "the symbol of the moral good" (§59). I find it even more puzzling that they are able to disregard the essential link between Kant's theory of taste and judgment and the historical world, which is Kant's unequivocal and firm position on the *Aufklärung*. If all the human tribes, after long wanderings in the wild forests of precivilization, were to gather now in the glades of the *Aufklärung* where, we, the first comers, were to greet them as they arrive, the problems would surely be quite different. But have we not been told that it was precisely because of the shattering crisis within the *Aufklärung*'s ideas and standards that the whole discussion began?

Consider now the other kernel of the third *Critique*. The fine arts are arts of genius; and the work of genius is a *creation*—though Kant does not use the term.[15] It is new, not "numerically," but essentially, in that

15. Only once (§49) does he speak of *schöpferische Einbildungskraft*, "creative imagination." As this last expression was current in the eighteenth century, Kant's insistence on always calling the imagination *productive* cannot be fortuitous.

it posits new norms: it is a new *eidos*. Thus it is a "model" or "prototype" (*Muster*).

But a model of what, and for what? The term is strange, since one would naturally expect it to be a model for imitation—and Kant rejects and severely and rightly condemns imitation and insists strongly on essential originality as the distinctive character of the work of art, that is, of genius.

The work of genius is a prototype of nothing and for nothing—if we take "prototype" in the formal sense.[16] Yet it is indeed a prototype in two other ways. It is a prototype of the "fact" of creation: it proposes itself as an "example" not for imitation (*Nachahmung* or *Nachmachung*), but for "succession" or "continuation" (*Nachfolge*), for the fact and feat of creation to be reenacted. And it is a model for the education of taste. In both respects, however, the circle of historical creation is present, and no "logical," "analytical" construction allows us to escape this paradoxical situation. The *chef d'oeuvre* can only be a model for taste if there is already taste enough to recognize it as a *chef*

16. Of course, the work of art is also a "presentation" of the Ideal of morality. But in the present context, this notion is irrelevant. Moreover, it can only be taken into consideration if one accepts Kant's metaphysics. This follows from the supersensible character of that which is to be presented (*dargestellt*). Finally, we have an apparent *aporia:*

- any *Darstellung* (by artistic genius) is adequate;
- any *series of Darstellungen* is insufficient, since it never "exhausts," so to speak, that which is to be presented.

One can see here another important ground of the dependence of Kant's aesthetics (and theory of judgment) on his metaphysics—comparable to the one in the *Critique of Practical Reason:* the infinite or insuperable distance between humanity and the Idea—and the (vain) attempt at once to maintain *and* cover it through some sort of infinite walk. In the *Critique of Practical Reason* this leads, *inter alia,* to the nonsensical argumentation on the immortality of the soul. In the *Critique of Judgment* (where an "immanent" historical progression is clearly envisaged) it leads to the idea of an unending series of *Darstellungen*. The difference is that in the first case (moral action) we are permanently deficient (nobody is ever a saint, says the *Critique of Practical Reason*); in the second case (art) the work of genius is certainly not deficient.

The point bears further elaboration, which should take into account Kant's *Anthropologie,* and which cannot be given here. Let me only add that, in truth, the absolute adequacy of the *chef d'oeuvre* is nothing but its presentation of the Abyss (the Chaos, the Groundless), and that the inexhaustibility of art is rooted in the ontological character of the Abyss as well as the fact that each culture (and each individual genius) creates its own way into the Abyss—the second being again a manifestation of the first.

d'oeuvre. And it is a model for the reenactment of the creative act if it is already recognized as the embodiment of such an act.

Behind Kant's apparently watertight construction and beyond the realization of its precariousness, we find a deep intuition of the truth of the matter. Art as creation cannot be "explained." Nor can the reception of the great work of art be "explained." The "educative" function of the new, of the original, is both a fact and a paradox.[17] It is an instance of the fact and the paradox of each and every historical creation.

Kant's theory of aesthetics is the only part of his fundamental writing in which he is forced to go beyond his strictly dualistic approach and to consider what later neo-Kantians (e.g., Rickert) would call *das Zwischenreich des immanenten Sinnes* (the in-between realm of immanent meaning). It is also the part in which he comes closest to recognizing creation in history—at least in substance, though he does not and could not name it. Beauty is created. But it is characteristic, first, that Kant have an "exceptionalist" view of creation: only genius creates, and it does so "as nature." (This "nature" of course has nothing to do with the "nature" of his theoretical philosophy. It is easy to see that it is an uneasy pseudonym for God; "genius" is a fragmented offshoot of the creative intelligent power that reflection on the teleology of "nature" must posit.) Second, that creation has to be restricted to the ontologically weightless domain of art. What Kant has to say about scientific work in the third *Critique* shows that it is intrinsically necessary for him to trivialize and reduce it to a cumulative process. In the domain of art, the effective validity, recognition, and reception of the norms (meanings, or "values" in neo-Kantian parlance) must take on decisive importance. Hence the move from "objective" to "subjective universal validity," and from "determinative" to "reflective": determination does not depend upon the opinion of the other, while reflection does indeed involve it. Thus, the irreducible character of creation and the commonality/community of

17. See also my text "The Sayable and the Unsayable," in *Crossroads in the Labyrinth*, tr. Martin H. Ryle and Kate Soper (Brighton: Harvester, and Cambridge, Mass.: M.I.T., 1984), in particular pp. 137–38.

humans acquire, however half-heartedly, some philosophical status, even if only as problems.

Kant believes that he answers the question of the essence of beauty (of what beauty *is*) and of the "necessity" of its common recognition. Of course he does no such thing. We have to recognize the decisive importance of the third *Critique, not* for the question of judging but for its insights into creation and human commonality. We also have to recognize the limitations of these insights—and the necessary origin of these limitations in the "main body" of Kant's philosophy (the two other *Critiques*). To remove these limitations, this main body must be exploded, but then, the insights of the third *Critique* gain a completely different meaning, and lead in unexpected directions. Because of these limitations—which are, in fact, common to the mainstream of the inherited philosophical tradition—it is not possible for Kant to think the radical social imaginary or instituting society; he cannot really think the sociality of history, even the historicity of society.[18] Hence the restriction to "genius" and to "art": the creation of institutions is ignored, or, at best, has to be presented as a purely "rational" affair (cf. the "nation of devils" in *Zum ewigen Frieden*). This is why the primitive circle of creation (that creation presupposes itself) can only loom confusedly and indistinctly between the lines and behind the aporias of Kant's treatment: beauty is recognized because there is taste, and taste is there because men have been educated, and men have been educated because they have already been in touch with beauty—in other words, because they recognize beauty before being, in principle, capable of doing so.

In the field of art, the social-historical consists in self-institution. "Genius" is here both a particular case of, and a pseudonym for, historical creation in general. The reception of the work of art is a particular case of the active and self-creative participation and cooperation of human communities in the institution of the new—in the insti-

18. This is also why he has to confine his insights on imagination to its strictly "individual-subjective" dimension. See my text, "La découverte de l'imagination," in *Libre*, 3 (Paris: Payot, 1978, [and now in *Domaines de l'homme. Les Carrefours du labyrinthe II* (Paris: Seuil, 1986), pp. 327–63].

tution *tout court*. "Reception" is no less paradoxical—and no less creative—than creation. And of course, nothing in all of this brings us any closer to deciding how to judge and choose. The generalization and radicalization of Kant's insights can only bring about a generalization and radicalization of the aporias involved. For, everybody always judges and chooses not only within but by means of the particular social-historical institution—the culture, the tradition—which formed him. Indeed, without this he would not be *able* to judge and choose anything. That Kant is both capable of knowing this and ignoring it is typical of his essential stand as an *Aufklärer:* in truth, there is but *one* history—and for all that really matters, this one history coincides with our own (or, our own history is the "transcendentally obligatory" meeting point of all particular histories). One might be tempted to treat this stand as "empirical" and dispensable, but that would be a mistake. For, this postulate—the "transcendentalization" of the historical fact of the *Aufklärung*—is necessary, if the semblance of an answer is to be given in "universal" terms to the original question. If all of us belonged substantially to the same tradition—or if one tradition was, *de jure,* the "true" one—we could appeal to the "same" taste (but even then, only on the counterfactual supposition that creative breaks within that tradition remain within some sort of undefinable bounds).

We can now conclude on the *chassé-croisé* of correct insights and wrong reasons which occur within the contemporary invocation of the third *Critique.* Kant's theory of judgment is appealed to because of the delusion that it could contribute an answer to the question of judging and choosing—which it does not. And the third *Critique* is *not* appreciated for what is, in truth, its most precious germ: the insight into the fact of creation. But this is no accident. For, contemporaries repudiate (at least tacitly) the main body of Kant's philosophy; if they did not, there would be no need to resort to the third *Critique* in matters of practical-political judgment. Now, when liberated from the transcendental scaffolding, and from the postulates referring to the supersensible, the idea of creation becomes uncontrollable. If norms themselves are created, how is one to escape the abhorrent thought that Right and Wrong themselves are social-historical creations? Consequently, refuge is taken instead in some vaguely perceived *sensus communis* regarding matters of Right and Wrong—forgetting again that it was the actual breakdown of this *sensus communis* that initiated the very discussion in the first place.

Can we go farther than stating the obvious facts—that judging and choosing always take place within and by means of an already existing social-historical institution or else spring out of a new creation in the face of which no criteria are available except the ones this new creation establishes for the first time? And how can we confront reasonably, if not "rationally," the question of judging and choosing between different institutions of society—the political question *par excellence?*

I will not discuss this problem here. I will only repeat: the absolute singularity of our Greco-Western or European tradition lies in its being the only tradition wherein this problem arises and becomes thinkable. (This does *not* mean that it becomes "soluble"—*pace* Descartes and Marx.) Politics and philosophy *and* the link between them have been created here and only here. Of course, this *does not* mean that this tradition can be "rationally" imposed upon—or defended against—another tradition that ignores or rejects this setting. Any rational argumentation presupposes the common acceptance of rationality as a criterion. It is not so much pragmatically ineffectual as it is logically absurd to argue "rationally" with Hitler, Andropov, Khomeini, or Idi Amin Dada. Indeed, "pragmatically," such argumentation can be defended as a political ("pedagogical") activity: there is always a chance that some followers of these men may be or become inconsistent and thus permeable to "rational" arguments. But to take a more dignified example, can argumentation invoking rationality, the equal value of all humans *qua* humans, for example, carry any weight against a deeply held belief that God has revealed himself and his will—the latter entailing, for instance, the forced conversion and/or extermination of the infidels, sorcerers, heretics, etc.? Silly, modern parochialism is capable of laughing at this idea as "exotic"—even though it was central to all "civilized" societies as recently as two centuries ago.

Judging and choosing, in a radical sense, were created in Greece, and this is one of the meanings of the Greek creation of politics and philosophy. By politics I do not mean court intrigues or fighting among social groups over interest or position (both of which existed elsewhere), but a collective activity whose object is the institution of society as such. In Greece we have the first instance of a community explicitly deliberating about its laws and changing those laws.[19] Elsewhere laws are inherited from the ancestors or given by gods or by the One True God; but they are not posited as created by men after a collective confrontation and discussion about right and wrong law. This position leads to other questions, which also originated in Greece: not only, "Is *this* law right or wrong," but "What is it for a law to be right or wrong, that is, what is justice?" Just as in Greek political activity the existing institution of society is called into question and altered for the first time, similarly Greece is the first society where we find the explicit questioning of the instituted collective representation of the world—that is, where we find philosophy. Further, just as political activity in Greece leads to the question not merely of whether this particular law is right or wrong, just or unjust, but of what justice is in general, so philosophical interrogation leads rapidly to the question not only of whether this or that representation of the world is true, but of what truth is. Both questions are genuine questions—that is, they must remain open forever.

The creation of democracy and philosophy and the link between them has its essential precondition in the Greek vision of the world and human life, the nucleus of the Greek imaginary. This can perhaps best be clarified by the three questions in which Kant summarizes the interests of man. About the first two: What can I know? What ought I to do? an endless discussion begins in Greece, and there is no "Greek answer" to them. But to the third question: What am I allowed to hope? there is a definite and clear Greek answer, and this is a massive and resounding *nothing*. And evidently it is the true answer. "Hope" is not to be taken here in the everyday trivial sense—that the sun will again shine tomorrow, or that a child will be born alive. The hope to which Kant refers is the hope of the Christian or religious tradition,

19. I cannot agree with Hannah Arendt's idea that in Greece legislative activity was a secondary aspect of politics. This would hold only in a limited sense of the term "legislative." Aristotle counts thirteen "revolutions" in Athens, that is, changes in the fundamental ("constitutional") legislation.

the hope corresponding to that central human wish and delusion that there be some essential correspondence, some consonance, some *adequatio,* between our desires and decisions, on the one hand, and the world, the nature of being, on the other. Hope is the ontological, cosmological, and ethical assumption that the world is not just something out there, but *cosmos* in the archaic and proper sense, a total order which includes us, our wishes, and our strivings as its organic and central components. The philosophical translation of this assumption is that being is ultimately good. As is well-known, the first one who dared to proclaim this philosophical monstrosity clearly was Plato—after the classical period had ended. This remained the fundamental tenent of theological philosophy in Kant, of course, but in Marx as well. The Greek view is expressed as early as the myth of Pandora. For Hesiod hope is forever imprisoned in Pandora's box. In preclassical and classical Greek religion, there is no hope for an afterlife: either there is no afterlife, or if there is one, it is worse than the worst life on earth—as Achilles reveals to Odysseus in the Land of the Dead. Having nothing to hope from an afterlife or from a caring and benevolent God, man is liberated for action and thought in *this* world.

This is intimately linked with the fundamental Greek idea of *chaos.* For Hesiod, in the beginning there is chaos. In the proper, initial sense "chaos" in Greek means void, nothingness. It is out of the total void that the world emerges.[20] But already in Hesiod, the world is also chaos in the sense that there is no complete order in it, that it is not subject to meaningful laws. First there is total disorder, and then order, *cosmos,* is created. But at the "roots" of the world, beyond the familiar landscape, chaos always reigns supreme. The order of the world has no "meaning" for man: it posits the blind necessity of genesis and birth, on one hand, of corruption and catastrophe—death of the forms—on the other. In Anaximander, the first philosopher for whom we possess reliable testimony, the "element" of being is the *apeiron,* the indeterminate, indefinite—another way of thinking chaos. Form,

20. As Olof Gigon has clearly established in *Der Ursprung der greichischen Philosophie von Hesiod bis Parmenides* (Basel, 1945). [Note added in 1986.]

the particularized and determinate existence of the various beings, is *adikia,* injustice—one may well call it *hubris.* That is why the particular beings have to render justice to one another and pay compensation for their injustice through their decay and disappearance.[21] There is a strong though implicit connection between the two pairs of opposite terms, *chaos/cosmos* and *hubris/dike.* In a sense, the latter is the transposition of the former into the human domain.

This vision conditions, so to speak, the creation of philosophy. Philosophy, as the Greeks created and practiced it, is possible because the world is not fully ordered. If it were, there would not be any philosophy, but only one, final system of knowledge. And if the world were sheer chaos, there would be no possibility of thinking at all. But this vision of the world also conditions the creation of politics. If the human world were fully ordered, either externally or through its own "spontaneous operation," if human laws were given by God or by nature or by the "nature of society" or by the "laws of history," then there would be no room for political thinking and no field for political action and no sense in asking what the proper law is or what justice is (cf. Hayek). But furthermore, if human beings could not create some order for themselves by positing laws, then again there would be no possibility of political, instituting action. If a full and certain knowledge (*episteme*) of the human domain were possible, politics would immediately come to an end, and democracy would be both impossible and absurd: democracy implies that all citizens have the possibility of attaining a correct *doxa and* that nobody possesses an *episteme* of things political.

I think it is important to stress these connections because a great many of the difficulties of modern political thinking are related to the persisting dominant influence of theological (that is, Platonic) philosophy. The operative postulate that there is a total and "rational" (and therefore "meaningful") order in the world, along with the necessary implication that there is an order of human affairs linked to the order

21. The meaning of Anaximander's fragment (Diels, B, 1) is clear, and "classical" historians of philosophy have, for once, interpreted it correctly. Heidegger's "interpretation" of it ("Der Spruch des Anaximander," in *Holzwege*) is, as usual, Heidegger dressed up as Anaximander.

of the world—what one could call unitary ontology—has plagued political philosophy from Plato through modern liberalism and Marxism. The postulate conceals the fundamental fact that human history is creation—without which there would be no genuine question of judging and choosing, either "objectively" or "subjectively." By the same token, it conceals or eliminates the question of responsibility. Unitary ontology, in whatever disguise, is essentially linked to heteronomy. The emergence of autonomy in Greece was conditioned by the nonunitary Greek view of the world that is expressed from the beginning in the Greek "myths."

A curious but inevitable consequence of the "model/antimodel" mentality employed when examining Greece, and in particular Greek political institutions, is that these are taken, so to speak, "statically," as if there were *one* "constitution," with its various "articles" fixed once for all, that could and must be "judged" or "evaluated" as such. This is an approach for people who seek recipes—whose number, indeed, does not seem to be on the decrease. But, of course, what is important in ancient Greek political life—the *germ*—is the *historical instituting process:* the activity and struggle around the change of the institutions, the explicit (even if partial) self-institution of the *polis* as a permanent process. This process goes on for almost four centuries. The annual election of the *thesmothetai* in Athens is established in 683/2 B.C., and it is probably around the same time that the citizens in Sparta (9,000 of them) are instated as *homoioi* ("similar," i.e., equals) and the rule of *nomos* (law) affirmed. The widening of democracy in Athens continues well into the fourth century. The *poleis*—at any rate Athens, about which our information is most complete—do not stop questioning their respective institutions; the *demos* goes on modifying the rules under which it lives. This is, of course, inseparable from the hectic pace of creation during this period in all fields beyond the strictly political one.

This movement is a movement of explicit self-institution. The cardinal meaning of explicit self-institution is autonomy: we posit our own laws. Of all the questions arising out of this movement, I will briefly survey three: "Who" is the "subject" of this autonomy? What are the limits of his action? What is the "object" of autonomous self-institution?[22]

The community of citizens—the *demos*—proclaims that it is absolutely sovereign (*autonomos, autodikos, autoteles,* self-legislating, self-judging, self-governing, in Thucydides' words). It also affirms the political equality (equal sharing of activity and power) of all free men. This is the self-position, self-definition, of the political body, which contains an element of arbitrariness—and always will. *Who* posits the *Grundnorm*—in Kelsen's terminology, the norm ruling the positing of norms—is a *fact.* For the Greeks, this "who" is the body of adult, male, free citizens (which means, in principle, [those men born] of other citizens, though naturalization is known and practiced). Of course, the exclusion of women, foreigners, and slaves from citizenship is a limitation we do not accept. This limitation was never lifted in practice in ancient Greece (at the level of ideas, things are less simple, but I will not discuss this aspect here). But indulging for a moment in the absurd "comparative merits" game, let us remember that slavery was present in the United States until 1865 and in Brazil until the end of the nineteenth century. Further, in most "democratic" countries, voting rights were granted to women only after World War II; that no country today grants political rights to foreigners, and that in most cases naturalization of resident foreigners is by no means automatic (a quarter of the resident population of very "democratic" Switzerland are *metoikoi*).

Equality of the citizens is of course equality in respect of the law (*isonomia*), but it is essentially much more than that. It is not the granting of equal passive "rights," but active general participation in public affairs. This participation is not left to chance, but actively promoted both through formal rules and through the general *ethos* of the *polis.* According to Athenian law, a citizen who will not take sides

22. Given the contraints of space, I will have to speak "statically" myself, ignoring the movement and considering only some of its most significant "results." I beg the reader to bear in mind this inevitable limitation.

while the city is in civil strife becomes *atimos*—deprived of political rights.[23]

Participation materializes in the *ecclesia,* the Assembly of the people, which is the acting sovereign body. All citizens have the right to speak (*isegoria*), their votes carry the same weight (*isophephia*), and they are under moral obligation to speak their minds (*parrhesia*). Participation also materializes in the courts. There are no professional judges, virtually all courts are juries with their jurors chosen by lot.

The *ecclesia,* assisted by the *boule* (Council), legislates and governs. This is *direct democracy.* Three of its aspects deserve further comment.

1. *The people versus "representatives."* Direct democracy has been rediscovered or reinvented in modern history every time a political collectivity has entered a process of radical self-constitution and self-activity: town meetings during the American Revolution, *sections* during the French Revolution, the Paris Commune, the Workers' Councils, or the Soviets in their original form. Hannah Arendt has repeatedly stressed the importance of these forms. In all these cases, the sovereign body is the totality of those concerned; whenever delegation is inevitable, delegates are not just elected but subject to permanent recall. One should remember that for classical political philosophy, the notion of "representation" is unknown. For Herodotus as well as for Aristotle, democracy is the power of the *demos,* unmitigated in matters of legislation, and the designation of magistrates (not "representatives"!) by sortition or rotation. Scholars merely repeat today that Aristotle's preferred constitution, what he calls *politeia,* is a mixture of democracy and aristocracy, and forget to add that for Aristotle the "aristocratic" element in this *politeia* is the *election* of the magistrates—for Aristotle clearly and repeatedly defines election as an aristocratic principle. This is also clear for Montesquieu and Rousseau. It is Rousseau, not Marx or Lenin, who writes that Englishmen believe that they are free because they elect their Parliament, but in reality are only free one day every five years. When Rousseau says that democracy is a

23. Aristotle, *Constitution of the Athenians,* VIII, 5.

regime too perfect for men, suitable only for a people of gods, what he means by democracy is the identity of the *souverain* and the *prince*—that is, there are no *magistrates*. Serious modern liberals—in contradistinction to contemporary "political philosophers"—knew all this perfectly well. Benjamin Constant did not glorify elections and "representation" as such; he defended them as lesser evils on the grounds that democracy was impossible in modern nations because of their size *and* because people were not interested in public affairs. Whatever the value of these arguments, they are based upon the explicit recognition that representation is a principle alien to democracy. This hardly bears discussion. Once permanent "representatives" are present, political authority, activity, and initiative are expropriated from the body of citizens and transferred to the restricted body of "representatives," who also use it to consolidate their position and create the conditions whereby the next "election" becomes biased in many ways.

2. *The people versus the "experts."* Linked to the principle of direct democracy is the Greek view of "experts." Not only legislative decisions but important political ones—on matters of *government*—are made by the *ecclesia* after it has listened to various speakers, possibly including those who claim some specific knowledge about the affairs at hand. There are not and cannot be "experts" on political affairs. Political expertise—or political "wisdom"—belongs to the political community, for expertise, *techne,* in the strict sense is always related to a specific, "technical" occupation, and is, of course, recognized in its proper field. Thus, Plato says in the *Protagoras,* the Athenians will listen to technicians when the building of proper walls or ships is discussed, but will listen to anybody when it comes to matters of politics. (The popular courts embody the same idea in the domain of justice.) War is, of course, a specific field entailing a proper *techne,* and thus the war chiefs, the *strategoi,* are elected—as are the technicians in other fields charged by the *polis* with a particular task. So Athens was, after all, a *politeia* in Aristotle's sense since some (and very important) magistrates were elected.

Now the *election* of the experts entails another principle central to the Greek view, clearly formulated and accepted not only by Aristotle, but despite its massive democratic implications, even by that archenemy of democracy, Plato. The proper judge of the expert is not another expert, but the *user:* the warrior and not the blacksmith for the sword, the horseman and not the saddler for the saddle. And evidently, for all public (common) affairs, the user, and thus the best judge, is the *polis*. From the results—the Acropolis, or the tragedy prizes—the judgment of this user appears to have been quite sound.

One can hardly overemphasize the contrast between this view and the modern one. The dominant idea that experts can be judged only by other experts is one of the conditions for the expansion and the growing irresponsibility of the modern hierarchal-bureaucratic apparatus. The prevalent idea that there exist "experts" in politics, that is, specialists of the universal and technicians of the totality, makes a mockery of the idea of democracy: the power of the politicians is justified by the "expertise" they would alone possess, and the, inexpert by definition, populace is called upon periodically to pass judgment on these "experts." It also—given the emptiness of the notion of a specialization in the universal—contains the seeds of the growing divorce between the capacity to attain power and the capacity to govern—which plagues Western societies more and more.

3. *The community versus the "State."* The Greek polis is *not* a "State" in the modern sense. The very term "State" does not exist in ancient Greek (characteristically, modern Greeks had to invent a word, and they used the ancient *kratos,* which means "sheer force"). *Politeia* (e.g., in the title of Plato's work) does not mean *der Staat* as in the standard German translation (the Latin *respublica* is less opposed to the meaning of *politeia*). It means both the political institution/constitution and the way people go about common affairs. It is a scandal of modern philology that the title of Aristotle's treatise, *Athenaion Politeia,* is everywhere translated "The Constitution of Athens," both a straightforward linguistic error and the inexplicable sign of ignorance or incomprehension on the part of very erudite men. Aristotle wrote *The Constitution of the Athenians.* Thucydides is perfectly explicit about this: *Andres gar polis,* "for the *polis* is the men." For example, before the Battle of Salamis, when Themistocles has to resort to a last-ditch argument to impose his tactics, he threatens the other allied chiefs that the Athenians will take their families and their fleet and found anew their city in the

West. This notwithstanding the fact that for the Athenians—even more than for the other Greeks—their land was sacred and they took pride in their claim to autochthony.

The idea of a "State" as an institution distinct and separated from the body of citizens would not have been understandable to a Greek. Of course, the political community exists at a level which is not identical with the concrete, "empirical" reality of so many thousands of people assembled in a given place at a given time. The political community of the Athenians, the *polis,* has an existence of its own: for example, treaties are honored irrespective of their age, responsibility for past acts is accepted, etc. But the distinction is not between a "State" and a "population"; it is between the continuous corporate body of perennial and impersonal Athenians and the living and breathing ones.

No "State" and no "State apparatus." There is, of course, in ancient Athens a technical-administrative mechanism, but it does not possess any political function. Characteristically, this administration, up to and including its higher echelons—police, keepers of the public archives, public finance—is composed of slaves (possibly Treasury Secretary Donald Regan and certainly Federal Reserve Chairman Paul Volcker would have been slaves in Athens). These slaves were supervised by citizen magistrates usually drawn by lot. "Permanent bureaucracy," the task of *execution* in the strictest sense, is left to the slaves.

The designation of magistrates through lot or rotation in most cases insures participation by a great number of citizens in official tasks—and knowledge of those tasks. That the *ecclesia* decides all important governmental matters insures the control of the political body over elected magistrates, as does the fact that they are subject to what amounts in practice to the possibility of recall at any time: conviction in a judicial procedure entails *inter alia* that they lose their office. Of course all magistrates are responsible for their performance in office as a matter of routine (*euthune*); accounts are given, in the classical period, to the *boule.*

In a sense, the unity and very existence of the political body is "prepolitical," at least insofar as explicit political self-institution is concerned. The community "receives itself," as it were, from its own past, with all that this past entails. (In part, this is what the moderns call the question of "civil society" versus the "State.") Elements of this given may be politically irrelevant or nontransformable. But *de jure,* "civil society" is itself an object of instituting political action. This is strikingly exemplified by some aspects of Cleisthenes' reform in Athens (506 B.C.). The traditional division of the population among tribes is superseded by a redivision having two main objects. First, the number of tribes is changed. The traditional (Ionian) four *phulai* become ten, each subdivided into three *trittues,* all sharing equally in all magistratures through rotation (which entails what is in fact the creation of a new, "political" year and calendar). Second, each tribe is formed by a balanced composition of agricultural, maritime, and urban people. Thus, the tribes—which henceforth have their "headquarters" in the city of Athens—become neutral as to territorial or professional particularities; they are clearly political units.

What we have here is the creation of a properly political social space, founded on social (economic) and geographical elements, but not *determined* by these. No phantasm of "homogeneity" here: an articulation of the citizen body within a political perspective is created and superimposed on the "prepolitical" articulations without crushing them. This articulation obeys strictly political imperatives: equality of power-sharing on the one hand, unity of the body politic (as against "particular interests") on the other.

The same spirit is exemplified by a most striking Athenian disposition (Aristotle, *Politics,* 1330 a 20): when the *ecclesia* deliberates on matters entailing the possibility of a conflict such as a war with a neighboring *polis,* the inhabitants of the frontier zone are excluded from the vote. For they could not vote without their particular interests overwhelming their motives, while the decision must be made on general grounds only.

This again shows a conception of politics diametrically opposed to the modern mentality of defense and the assertion of "interests." Interests have, as far as possible, to be kept at bay when political decisions are made. (Imagine the following disposition in the U.S. Constitution: "Whenever questions pertaining to agriculture are to be decided, senators and representatives from predominantly agricultural States cannot participate in the vote.") At this point one may comment on the ambiguity of Hannah Arendt's position concerning what she calls "the social." She rightly saw that politics is destroyed when it becomes a mask for the defense and assertion of "interests." The political space is then hopelessly fragmented. But *if* society is, in reality, strongly divided along conflicting "interests"—as it is today—insistence on the autonomy of politics becomes gratuitous. The answer, then, is not to ignore the "social," but to change it so that the conflict of "social"—that is, economic—interests ceases to be the dominant factor in shaping political attitudes. If this is not done, the present situation among Western societies results: the decomposition of the body politic and its fragmentation into lobbies. In this case, as the "algebraic sum" of opposing interests is very often zero, the consequence is political impotence and aimless drift, such as is observed today.

The unity of the body politic has to be preserved even against extreme forms of *political* strife. This is, to my mind, the meaning of the Athenian law on ostracism (not the usual interpretation, which sees in it a safeguard against would-be tyrants). In Athens political division and antagonism should not be allowed to tear the community apart; one of the two opposing leaders must go into temporary exile.

General participation in politics entails the creation for the first time in history of a *public space*. The emphasis Hannah Arendt has put on this, her elucidation of its meaning, is one of her outstanding contributions to the understanding of Greek institutional creation. I will confine myself, therefore, to a few additional points.

The emergence of a public space means that a political domain is created which "belongs to all" (*ta koina*).[24] The "public" ceases to be a "*private*" affair—of the king, the priests, the bureaucracy, the politicians, and the experts. Decisions on common affairs have to be made by the community.

But the essence of the public space does not refer only to "final decisions"; if it did, it would be more or less empty. It refers as well to

24. Something similar can be found in some savage societies, but it is confined to the handling of "current" affairs, since in these societies the (traditional) law cannot be called into question.

the presuppositions of the decisions, to everything that leads to them. Whatever is of importance has to appear publicly. This is, for example, effectively realized in the *presentation* of the law: laws are engraved in marble and publicly exposed for everybody to see. But much more importantly, law materializes in the discourse of the people, freely talking to each other in the *agora* about politics and about everything they care about before deliberating in the *ecclesia*. To understand the tremendous historical change involved, one only has to contrast this with the typical "Asiatic" situation.

This is equivalent to the creation of the possibility—and actuality—of free speech, free thinking, free examination and questioning without restraint. It establishes *logos* as circulation of speech and thought within the community. It accompanies the two basic traits of the citizen already mentioned: *isegoria,* the right for all equally to speak their minds, and *parrhesia,* the commitment for all to really speak their minds concerning public affairs.

It is important to stress here the distinction between the "formal" and the "real." The existence of a public space is not just a matter of legal provisions guaranteeing rights of free speech, etc. Such provisions are but conditions for a public space to exist. The important question is: What are the people actually doing with these rights? The decisive traits in this respect are courage, responsibility, and shame (*aidos, aischune*). Lacking these, the "public space" becomes just an open space for advertising, mystification, and pornography—as is, increasingly, the case today. Against such development, legal provisions are of no avail, or produce evils worse than the ones they pretend to cure. Only the education (*paideia*) of the citizens as citizens can give valuable, substantive content to the "public space." This *paideia* is not primarily a matter of books and academic credits. First and foremost, it involves becoming conscious that the *polis* is also oneself and that its fate also depends upon one's mind, behavior, and decisions; in other words, it is participation in political life.

Equally important, hand in hand with the creation of a public space goes the creation of a *public time*. By this I do not mean just "social," "calendar" time, a system of socio-temporal benchmarks which, of course, already exists everywhere. I mean the emergence of a dimension where the collectivity can inspect its own past as the result of its own actions, and where an indeterminate future opens up as domain for its activities. This is the meaning of the creation of historiography in Greece. It is a striking fact that historiography properly speaking has existed only during two periods of human history: in ancient Greece, and in modern Europe—that is, in the cases of the two societies where questioning of the existing institutions has occurred. In other societies, there is only the undisputed reign of tradition, and/or simple "recording of events" by the priests or the chroniclers of the kings. But Herodotus starts with the declaration that the traditions of the Greeks are not trustworthy. The disruption of tradition and critical inquiry into "true causes" of course go together. Moreover, this knowledge of the past is open to all. Herodotus, for example, is reported to have read his *Histories* to the Greeks assembled for the Olympic games (*si non e vero, e ben trovato*). And the Funeral Speech of Pericles contains a survey of the history of the Athenians from the viewpoint of the spirit of the activities of the successive generations—a survey leading up to the present and clearly pointing toward new things to be done in the future.

What are the limits of political action—the limits of autonomy? If the law is God-given, or if there is a philosophical or scientific "grounding" of substantive political truths (with Nature, Reason, or History as ultimate "principle"), then there exists an extrasocial standard for society. There is a norm of the norm, a law of the law, a criterion on the basis of which the question of whether a particular law (or state of affairs) is just or unjust, proper or improper, can be discussed and decided. This criterion is given once and for all and, *ex hypothesi,* does not depend upon human action.

Once it is recognized that no such ground exists, either because there is a separation between religion and politics, as is, imperfectly, the case in modern societies, or because, as in Greece, religion is kept strictly at bay by political activities, and once it is also recognized that there is no "science," no *episteme* or *techne,* of political matters, the question of what a just law is, what justice is—what "the proper" institution of society is—opens up as a genuine, that is, interminable, question.

Autonomy is only possible if society recognizes itself as the source of its norms. Thus, society cannot evade the question: Why this norm rather than that?—in other words, it cannot evade the question of justice by answering, for example, that justice is the will of God, or the will of the Czar, or the reflection of the relations of production. Neither can it evade the question of *limits* to its actions. In a democracy, people *can* do anything—and must know that they *ought not* to do just anything. Democracy is the regime of self-limitation; therefore it is also the regime of historical risk—another way of saying that it is the regime of freedom—and a tragic regime. The fate of Athenian democracy offers an illustration of this. The fall of Athens—its defeat in the Peloponnesian War—was the result of the *hubris* of the Athenians: *Hubris* does not simply presuppose freedom, it presupposes the absence of fixed norms, the essential vagueness of the ultimate bearings of our actions. (Christian sin is, of course, a heteronomous concept.) Transgressing the law is not *hubris,* it is a definite and limited misdemeanor. *Hubris* exists where self-limitation is the only "norm," where "limits" are transgressed which were nowhere defined.

The question of the limits to the self-instituting activity of a community unfolds in two moments. Is there any intrinsic criterion of and for the law? Can there be an effective guarantee that this criterion, however defined, will not be transgressed?

With the move to fundamentals, the answer to both questions is a definite *no.* There is no norm of norms which would not itself be a historical creation. And there is no way of eliminating the risks of collective *hubris.* Nobody can protect humanity from folly or suicide.

Moderns have thought—have pretended—that they have found the answer to these two questions by fusing them into one. This answer would be the "Constitution" as a fundamental Charter embodying the norms of norms and defining particularly stringent provisions for its revision. It is hardly necessary to recall that this "answer" does not hold water either logically or effectively, that modern history has for two centuries now in all conceivable ways made a mockery of this notion of a "Constitution"; or that the oldest "democracy" in the liberal West, Britain, has no "Constitution" at all. It is sufficient to point to the shallowness and duplicity of modern thinking in this respect, as exemplified both in the field of international relations and in the arena of changes in political regimes. At the international level, despite the rhetoric of professors of "International Public Law," there is in fact no law but the "law of force," that is, there is a "law" as long as matters are not really important—as long as you hardly need a law. The "law of force" also rules concerning the establishment of a new "legal order" within a country: "A victorious revolution creates right" is the dictum which almost all teachers of international public law avow, and all countries follow in practice. (This "revolution" need not be, and usually is not, a revolution properly speaking; most of the time, it is a successful *Putsch*.) And, in the European experience of the last sixty years, the legislation introduced by "illegal" and even "monstrous" regimes has always been maintained in its bulk after their overthrow.

The very simple point here is of course that in the face of a historical movement which marshals *force*—be it by actively mobilizing a large majority or a passionate and ruthless minority in the forefront of a passive or indifferent population, or be it even just brute force in the hands of a group of colonels—legal provisions are of no avail. If we can be reasonably certain that the reestablishment of slavery tomorrow in the United States or in a European country is extremely improbable, the "reasonable" character of our forecast is *not* based on the existing laws or constitutions (for then we would be simply idiotic), but on a judgment concerning the active response of a huge majority of the people to such an attempt.

In Greek practice and thinking the distinction between "constitution" and "law" does not exist. The Athenian distinction between laws and decrees of the *ecclesia* (*psephismata*) did not have the same formal character and in fact disappeared during the fourth century. But the question of self-limitation was dealt with in a different (and, I think, more profound) way. I will only consider two institutions related to this problem.

The first is an apparently strange but fascinating procedure called *graphe paranomon* (accusation of unlawfulness).[25] The procedure can

25. M. I. Finley has recently stressed the importance and elucidated the spirit of this procedure: *Democracy, Ancient and Modern* (New Brunswick, N.J.: Rutgers University Press, 1973). See also V. Ehrenberg, *The Greek State*, 2d ed. (London: Methuen, 1969), pp. 73, 79, 267—where two other important procedures or provisions similar in spirit are also discussed: *apate tou demou* (deceit of the *demos*) and the exception *ton nomon me epitedeion einai* (inappropriateness of a law).

be briefly described as follows. You have made a proposal to the *ecclesia,* and this proposal has been voted for. Then another citizen can bring you before a court, accusing you of inducing the people to vote for an unlawful law. You can be acquitted or convicted—and in the latter case, the law is annulled. Thus, you have the right to propose anything you please, but you have to think carefully before proposing something on the basis of a momentary fit of popular mood and having it approved by a bare majority. For the action would be judged by a popular court of considerable dimensions (501, sometimes 1,001 or even 1,501 citizens sitting as judges), drawn by lot. Thus, the *demos* was appealing against itself in front of itself: the appeal was from the whole body of citizens (or whichever part of it was present when the proposal in question was adopted) to a huge random sample of the same body sitting after passions had calmed, listening again to contradictory arguments, and assessing the matter from a relative distance. Since the source of the law is the people, "control of constitutionality" could not be entrusted to "professionals"—in any case, the idea would have sounded ridiculous to a Greek—but only to the people themselves acting in a different guise. The people say what the law is; the people can err; the people can correct themselves. This is a magnificent example of an effective institution of self-limitation.

Tragedy is another institution of self-limitation. People usually speak of "Greek tragedy," but there is no such thing. There is only *Athenian* tragedy. Only in the city where the democratic process, the process of self-institution, reached its climax, only there could tragedy (as opposed to simple "theater") be created.

Tragedy has, of course, many layers of signification, and there can be no question of reducing it to a narrow "political" function. But there is certainly a cardinal political dimension to tragedy, not to be confused with the "political positions" taken by the poets, not even with the much commented upon (rightly, if insufficiently) Aeschylean vindication of public justice against private vengeance in the *Oresteia.*

The political dimension of tragedy lies first and foremost in its ontological grounding. What tragedy, not "discursively" but through *presentation,* gives to all to see, is that Being is Chaos. Chaos is exhibited here, first, as the absence of order *for* man, the lack of positive correspondence between human intentions and actions, on one hand, and their result or outcome, on the other. More than that, tragedy shows not only that we are not masters of the consequences of our actions, but that we are not even masters of their *meaning*. Chaos is also presented as Chaos *in* man, that is as his *hubris*. And the ultimately prevailing order is, as in Anaximander, order through catastrophe—a "meaningless" order. From the universal experience of catastrophe stems the fundamental *Einstellung* of tragedy: universality and impartiality.

Hannah Arendt has rightly said that impartiality enters this world through the Greeks. This is already fully apparent in Homer. Not only can one not find in the Homeric poems any disparagement of the "enemy," the Trojans, for example, but the truly central figure in the *Iliad* is Hector, not Achilles, and the most moving characters are Hector and Andromach. The same is true for Aeschylus' *Persians*—a play performed in 472 B.C., seven years after the battle at Plataea, with the war still going on. In this tragedy, there is not a single word of hatred or contempt for the Persians; the Persian queen, Atossa, is a majestic and venerable figure, and the defeat and ruin of the Persians is ascribed exclusively to the *hubris* of Xerxes. And in his *Trojan Women* (415 B.C.), Euripides presents the Greeks as the cruelest and most monstrous beasts—as if he were saying to the Athenians: this is what you are. Indeed, the play was performed a year after the horrible massacre of the Melians by the Athenians (416 B.C.).

But perhaps the most profound play, from the point of view of tragedy's political dimension, is *Antigone* (442 B.C.). The play has been persistently interpreted as a tract against human and in favor of divine law, or at least as depicting an unsurmountable conflict between these two principles (or between "family" and "State," as in Hegel). This is indeed the manifest content of the text, repeated again and again. Since the spectators cannot fail to "identify" with the pure, heroic, helpless, and desperate Antigone against the hard-headed, authoritarian, arrogant, and suspicious Creon, they find the "thesis" of the play clear. But the meaning of the play is multilayered and the standard interpretation misses what I think is most important. A full justification of the interpretation I propose would require a complete analysis of the play, which is out of the question here. I will only draw attention to a few points. The insistence on the obvious—and rather shallow—opposition between human and divine law forgets that for the Greeks to bury their dead is *also* a human law, as to defend one's country is *also* divine law (Creon mentions this explicitly). The chorus oscillates from beginning to end between the two positions, always putting them on the same plane. The famous hymn (v. 332–75) to the glory of man, the builder of cities and creator of institutions, ends with praise for the one who is able to *weave together* (*pareirein*) "the laws of the land and the justice of gods to which he has sworn" (cf. also v. 725: "well said from both sides"). Antigone's upholding of "divine law" is remarkably weakened by her argument that she did what she did because a brother is irreplaceable when one's parents are dead, and that with a husband or a son the situation would have been different. To be sure, neither the divine nor the human law regarding the burial of the dead recognizes such a distinction. Moreover, what speaks through Antigone, here and throughout the play, more than respect for the divine law, is her passionate love for her brother. We need not go to the extremes of interpretation and invoke incestual attraction, but we certainly must remember that the play would not be the masterpiece it is if Antigone and Creon were bloodless representatives of principles and not moved by strong passions—love for her brother in Antigone's case, love for the city *and* for his own power, in Creon's case. Against this passionate background, the characters' arguments appear additionally as rationalizations. Finally, to present Creon as unilaterally "wrong" goes against the deepest spirit of tragedy, and certainly of Sophoclean tragedy.

What the final verses of the chorus (v. 1348–55) glorify is not divine law, but *phronein*, an untranslatable word, unbearably flattened in its Latin rendering by *prudentia*. The chorus lauds *phronein*, advises against impiety, and reverts again to *phronein*, warning against "big words" and the "*huperauchoi*," the excessively proud.[26] Now the content of this *phronein* is clearly indicated in the play. The catastrophe is

26. I must leave open here the question raised by Hannah Arendt's (and Hölderlin's) interpretation of these last verses (*The Human Condition*, p. 25, note 8), which does not, in any case, create difficulties for my comment. Curiously, Michael Denneny in his excellent paper does not mention the translation offered in *The Human Condition* and supplies instead a different (oral) rendering by Hannah Arendt, which is totally unacceptable, both philologically and from the point of view of the play's whole meaning. Denneny, *op. cit.*, pp. 268–69 and 274.

brought about because *both* Creon *and* Antigone insist on their own reasons, without listening to the reasons of the other. No need to repeat here Antigone's reasons; let us only remember that Creon's reasons are irrefutable. No city can exist—and therefore, no gods can be worshipped—without *nomoi;* no city can tolerate treason and bearing arms against one's own country in alliance with foreigners out of pure greed for power, as Polynices did. Creon's own son, Aimon, clearly says that he cannot prove his father wrong (v. 685–6); he voices the play's main idea when he begs Creon not to *monos phronein,* "not to be wise alone" (v. 707–9).

Creon's is a political decision, taken on very solid grounds. But very solid political grounds can turn out to be very shaky, if they are only "political." To put it in another way, precisely because of the totalistic character of the domain of politics (in this case, inclusive of decisions about burial and about life and death), a correct political decision must take into account all factors, beyond the strictly "political" ones. Even when we think, on the best of rational grounds, that we have made the right decision, this decision may turn out to be wrong, and catastrophically so. Nothing can guarantee a priori the correctness of action—not even reason. And above all, it is folly to insist on *monos phronein,* "being wise alone."

Antigone addresses itself to the problem of political action in terms which acquire their acute relevance in the democratic framework more than in any other. It exhibits the uncertainty pervading the field, it sketches the impurity of motives, it exposes the inconclusive character of the reasoning upon which we base our decisions. It shows that *hubris* has nothing to do with the transgression of definite norms, that it can take the form of the adamant will to apply the norms, disguise itself behind noble and worthy motivations, be they rational or pious. With its denunciation of the *monos phronein,* it formulates the fundamental maxim of democratic politics.[27]

---

27. An additional support for my interpretation can be found at the end (v. 1065–75) of Aeschylus' *Seven Against Thebes*. This is certainly an addition to the initial text, probably dating from 409–405 B.C. (Mazon, in the Budé edition, p. 103). This addition has been inserted to prepare for the performance of *Antigone* immediately afterward. It makes the *Seven* end with the two halves of the chorus divided, the one chanting that

What is the "object" of autonomous self-institution? This question may be rejected at the outset if one thinks that autonomy—collective and individual freedom—is an end in itself, or that once significant autonomy has been established in and through the political institution of society, the rest is no more a matter of politics but a field for the free activity of individuals, groups, and "civil society."

I do not share these points of view. The idea of autonomy as an end in itself would lead to a purely formal, "Kantian" conception. We will autonomy both for itself and in order to able *to do*. But to do what? Further, political autonomy cannot be separated from "the rest," from the "substance" of life in society. Finally, a very important part of that life concerns common objectives and works, which have to be decided in common and therefore become objects of political discussion and activity.

Hannah Arendt did have a substantive conception of what democracy—the *polis*—was about. For her, the value of democracy derived from the fact that it is the political regime in which humans can reveal who they are through deeds and speech. To be sure, this element was present and important in Greece—but not only in democracy. Hannah Arendt (after Jacob Burckhardt) rightly emphasized the agonistic character of Greek culture in general—not only in politics but in all spheres, and one should add, not only in democracy but in all cities, Greeks cared above all for *kleos* and *kudos* and the elusive immortality they represented.

However, the reduction of the meaning and purposes of politics and of democracy in Greece to this element is impossible, as the foregoing brief account, I hope, makes clear. Moreover, it is surely very difficult to defend or support democracy on this basis. First, though of course democracy more than any other regime allows people to "manifest" themselves, this "manifestation" cannot involve everybody—in fact not even anybody apart from a tiny number of people who are active

they will support those who are united with their blood (*genea*), because what the *polis* holds to be right is different at different times, i.e., the *polis's* laws change though blood right is perennial; and the other asserting their support for the *polis* and *dikaion*, i.e., right. A nonnegligible testimony of how Athenians at the end of the fifth century viewed the matter and the meaning of Antigone.

and deploy initiative in the political field as narrowly defined. Second, and more importantly, Hannah Arendt's position defers the crucial question of the content, the substance, of this "manifestation." To take it to extremes, surely Hitler and Stalin and their infamous companions have revealed who they were through deeds and speech. The difference between Themistocles and Pericles, on the one hand, and Cleon and Alcibiades on the other, between the builders and the gravediggers of democracy, cannot be found in the sheer fact of "manifestation," but in the content of this manifestation. Even more so, it is precisely because for Cleon and Alcibiades, the only thing that mattered was "manifestation" as such, sheer "appearance in the public space," that they brought about catastrophe.

The substantive conception of democracy in Greece can be seen clearly in the entirety of the *works* of the *polis* in general. It has been explicitly formulated with unsurpassed depth and intensity in the most important political monument of political thought I have ever read, the Funeral Speech of Pericles (Thuc. 2, 35–46). It will always remain puzzling to me that Hannah Arendt, who admired this text and supplied brilliant clues for its interpretation, did not see that it offers a *substantive* conception of democracy hardly compatible with her own.

In the Funeral Speech, Pericles describes the ways of the Athenians (2, 37–41) and presents in a half-sentence (beginning of 2, 40) a definition of what is, in fact, the "object" of this life. The half-sentence in question is the famous *Philokaloumen gar met'euteleias kai philosophoumen aneu malakias.* In "The Crisis of Culture" Hannah Arendt offers a rich and penetrating commentary of this phrase. But I fail to find in her text what is, to my mind, the most important point.

Pericles' sentence is impossible to translate into a modern language. The two verbs of the phrase can be rendered literally by "we love beauty . . . and we love wisdom . . .," but the essential would be lost (as Hannah Arendt correctly saw). The verbs do not allow this separation of the "we" and the "object"—beauty or wisdom—external to this "we." The verbs are not "transitive," and they are not even simply "active": they are at the same time "verbs of state." Like the verb *to live,* they point to an "activity" which is at the same time a way of being or rather *the* way by means of which the subject of the verb *is.* Pericles does not say we love beautiful things (and put them in museums), we love wisdom (and pay professors or buy books). He says we *are* in and by the love of beauty and wisdom and the activity this love brings forth, we live by and with and through them—but far from extravagance, and far from flabbiness.[28] This is why he feels able to call Athens *paideusis*—the education and educator—of Greece.

In the Funeral Speech, Pericles implicitly shows the futility of the false dilemmas that plague modern political philosophy and the modern mentality in general: the "individual" versus "society," or "civil society" versus "the State." The object of the institution of the *polis* is for him the creation of a human being, the Athenian citizen, who exists and lives in and through the unity of these three: the love and "practice" of beauty, the love and "practice" of wisdom, the care and responsibility for the common good, the collectivity, the *polis* ("they died bravely in battle rightly pretending not to be deprived of such a *polis*, and it is understandable that everyone among those living is willing to suffer for her" 2, 41). Among the three, there can be no separation; beauty and wisdom such as the Athenians loved them and lived them could exist only in Athens. The Athenian citizen is not a "private philosopher," or a "private artist," he is a citizen for whom philosophy and art have become ways of life. This, I think, is the real, materialized, answer of ancient democracy to the question about the "object" of the political institution.

When I say that the Greeks are for us a germ, I mean, first, that they never stopped thinking about this question: What is it that the institution of society ought to achieve? And second, I mean that in the paradigmatic case, Athens, they gave this answer: the creation of human beings living with beauty, living with wisdom, and loving the common good.

Paris and New York, March 1982–June 1983

28. I follow the usual translation of *euteleia*. Hannah Arendt's rendering of this word, ending with the interpretation "we love beauty within the limits of political judgment," while not strictly impossible, is extremely improbable.

6

The Nature and Value of Equality

In his invitation to this conference, Jean Starobinski noted quite rightly: "The question of equality is concerned with the representation that we ourselves make of human nature; it is connected therefore with a philosophical and religious interrogation. But this interrogation also is concerned with the model that we have in view for a just society: it therefore has a socio-political dimension." And one of the indices of the difficulty of our question, the question of the nature and value of equality, is the very existence of these two dimensions, the philosophical dimension and the political dimension, with their relative independence and at the same time their solidarity.

Philosophy and politics are born together, at the same moment, in the same country, and they are brought forth by the same movement, the movement toward individual and collective autonomy. Philosophy is not a matter of systems, of books, of scholastic arguments. It is a matter first and foremost of putting into question the instituted representation of the world, the idols of the tribe, within the horizon of an

---

This lecture was delivered at the *Rencontres Internationales de Genève* in 1981. The French text appears in *L'Exigence d'égalité* (Neuchâtel: Editions de la Baconnière, 1982), pp. 15–34 and has been reprinted in *Domaines de l'homme. Les Carrefours du labyrinthe II* (Paris: Seuil, 1986), pp. 307–24. Translated by David Ames Curtis in *Philosophy and Social Criticism*, 11:4 (Fall 1986), pp. 373–90.

unlimited interrogation. Politics is not a matter of municipal elections, nor even presidential ones. Politics, in the true sense of the term, puts into question the actual institution of society; it is the activity that tries to aim clearly at the social institution as such.

These two dimensions are born together, as I said, in Greece of course, and they are reborn together in Western Europe at the end of the Middle Ages. These two coincidences are in truth much more than coincidences. It is a matter of an essentially common birth [*co-nativité*], of a consubstantiality.

Consubstantiality, however, does not signify identity and still less a dependence of one of the terms on the other. It happens, in my view, that the inherited ontology, the central core of philosophy, has remained crippled and this infirmity has brought with it momentous consequences for what is called political philosophy, which itself really has never been anything but a philosophy talking about politics and external to the latter. This begins already with Plato.

But even if it had been otherwise, it still would not have been possible to deduce a politics from philosophy. There is no passage from ontology to politics. A banal affirmation, indeed. Yet we must repeat it in face of the confusion that perpetually springs up between the two domains. It is not simply that one can never legitimately pass from facts to laws, which is true. Much more is at stake: the ultimate schemata employed in philosophy and in politics, as well as their respective positions in relation to the world, are in the two cases radically different despite the fact that, as I said, the two proceed from the same movement of putting into question the established order of society.

Let us try briefly to explicate this difference. Philosophy cannot found a politics—indeed, it cannot "found" anything at all. In political matters in particular, all that philosophy can say is: if you want philosophy, you also must will a society in which philosophy is possible. That is quite true, and there are societies—they exist today—where philosophy is not possible, where, at best, it can be practiced only in secret. In order to accept this line of reasoning, however, we still must want philosophy; and we are not able to justify this will for philosophy rationally since such a rational justification would presuppose again philosophy: it would invoke as a premise that which is to be demonstrated.

We also know that philosophy cannot, as it always wanted to do, "found" itself. Every "foundation" of philosophy proves to be either straightforwardly fallacious or else based upon circular arguments. These circles are vicious from the point of view of simple formal logic, but in another respect they are the circles entailed by genuine social-historical creation. I speak of creation here as an idea whose absence as a matter of fact marks what I have just called the infirmity of the inherited ontology. Creation in general, as well as social-historical creation, is incomprehensible for the established logic quite simply because in creation the result, the effect of the operations in question, is presupposed by these operations themselves.

Let us take an example from our sphere: society's self-creation—I will come back to this right away—is possible only if *social* individuals exist. Its self-transformation is possible only if there exist some individuals who aim at this transformation and are able to effectuate it. But where then do these individuals come from?

Philosophical creation, as well as political creation, has a meaning only for those who are downstream from this creation. This is why we encounter the following limit: not only is it impossible for philosophy to be founded upon logic, but also it could not prevail against the attitudes and beliefs which ignore this philosophical world, which are upstream from this world. Likewise, and I also will come back to this right away, the political ideas to which we appeal are not demonstrable contrary to individuals who are brought up in other societies and for whom these ideas do not represent a part of their tradition or of their representation of the world.

Philosophy, itself a social-historical creation, depends of course upon the social-historical world in which it is created: this does not mean, however, that it is determined by this world. This dependence, in the same way as the freedom of philosophical creation, finds its limit as well as its counterweight in the existence of a referent of thought, of a term to which thought refers itself, at which it aims, and which is other than thought itself. To philosophize or to think, in the strong sense of the word, is this supremely paradoxical enterprise which consists in creating forms of thought in order to think that which is beyond thought—that which, simply, *is*. To think is to aim at the other of thought, knowing all along that this other can never be grasped except in and by thought; and knowing that the question—What, in that which is thought, comes from the one who thinks, and what comes from that which is thought?—will forever remain undecidable as an ultimate question. And this paradox is itself, paradoxically, the ballast, the only ballast, of thought.

But political thinking/willing, the thinking/willing of a different institution of society, does not have a referent external to itself. Certainly, if it is not delirious, it also finds its ballast or a certain ballast, in any case certainly its source, in the will and activity of a collectivity to which it addresses itself and from which it proceeds. As it happens, however, the collectivity, or the part of the collectivity which acts politically, deals in this context only with itself. Thought and philosophy have no assured foundation, but they find some bearings in that which is, in a certain manner, external to themselves. No bearings of this type exist for political thinking/willing. Thought *ought* to aim at its independence—paradoxical and finally impossible—against its social-historical grounding. But political thinking/willing *cannot* aim at such an independence, in an absolute way. The peculiarity of thought is its will to encounter something other than itself. The peculiarity of politics is its will to make itself other than it is, starting from itself.

There is an infirmity in the inherited ontology, as I said. It consists, briefly speaking, in the occultation of the question, or rather of the *fact,* of creation and of the radical imaginary at work in history. And it is this ontology which ought to be surpassed since it continues to overdetermine, consciously or not, what is thought in all domains. This ontology is what ought to be surpassed if we want to confront the question of politics on its own terrain. And this is manifestly clear in the question which concerns us today, the question of equality, just as it is with another question closely tied to the first, that of freedom.

Indeed, ever since they first occurred, discussions on equality as well as those on freedom have been mortgaged to an anthropological ontology, to a metaphysics of the human being which makes of this human being—of this singular example of the species *Homo sapiens*—an *individual-substance,* an individual of divine right, of natural law, of rational law. God, Nature, Reason, posed in each case as supreme and paradigmatic existing beings [*êtres-étants*], which function at one and the same time as being and meaning, always also have been posited in the framework of the inherited ontology as sources of a being/meaning of society, a derived and inferior being/meaning; and they have been parceled out in each case in the guise of fragments or molecules of the divine, the natural, or the reasonable, which in turn define, or ought to define, the human as individual.

These metaphysical foundations of equality among humans are untenable in themselves, and, in fact, we no longer hear them spoken of as such. We hardly ever hear it said anymore that the exigency of equality or the exigency of freedom is founded upon the will of God, who created us all equal, or upon the fact that we are naturally equal, or that reason requires [*exige*] that . . . And it is entirely characteristic, in this regard, that all the contemporary discussions on the rights of man are marked by a bashfulness, not to say false modesty, not to say philosophical pusillanimity, which is altogether clear-cut.

But also, these philosophical or metaphysical "foundations" of equality are, or become in their utilization, more than equivocal. By means of a few logical slips or a few hidden, supplementary premises, the defense of equality as well as its contrary can be derived.

Christianity, for example, in proper theology, is concerned only with equality before God, not social and political equality. Similarly, in its proper historical practice, Christianity almost always has accepted and justified terrestrial inequalities. The metaphysically equal status of all humans insofar as they are children of God who are promised redemption, etc., is concerned only with a single important matter: the "eternal" destiny of souls. This says nothing, and *ought* to say nothing, of the destiny of human beings down here during this infinitesimal fraction of earthly time of their life which is, as the mathematician would say, of null measure in the face of eternity. Christianity, at least original and primitive Christianity, was completely consistent and coherent on this subject: Render unto Caesar that which is Caesar's, my Kingdom is not of this world, all power comes from God (Paul, *Epistle to the Romans*), etc. This attitude was formulated when Christianity still was a firmly acosmic faith. When it ceased to be so in order to become an instituted religion, and even legally obligatory for the inhabitants of the Empire (with the decree of Theodosius the Great), it perfectly accommodated itself to the existence of social hierarchies and it justified them. Such was its social role for the overwhelming majority of countries and epochs.

It is strange sometimes to see otherwise serious thinkers wanting to make of the transcendent equality of souls as professed by Christianity the precursor of modern ideas about social and political equality. To do this, one must forget, or erase in the most incredible fashion, twelve centuries of Byzantium, ten centuries in Russia, sixteen Iberian centuries, the sanctification of serfdom in Europe (and that beautiful German name for serfdom, *Leibeigenschaft,* the ownership of the body: evidently, the soul is the property of God), the sanctification of slavery outside of Europe, Luther's postures during the Peasant War, and I omit many other examples.

It is true that our equality insomuch as we are all descendants of the same Adam and Eve could be evoked frequently by some sects and socio-religious movements and, indeed, by these very same sixteenth-century peasants. But this shows only that we finally have entered once again, and after 1,000 years of a religiously confirmed and ratified reign of social hierarchy, into a new period of putting into question the institution of society, a putting into question which at its start made use of whatever was at hand and utilized whatever appeared useful in the established representations while giving to it a *new* signification. The advancement of the democratic and egalitarian movement, starting from the seventeenth century and especially from the eighteenth century onward, did not occur in all Christian countries; far from it. This movement took place only in a few countries, and in those ones it was dependent upon other factors; it expresses the action of new historical elements, requires fresh expenditures, represents a new social creation. It is in this context that the famous statement by Grotius from the beginning of the seventeenth century acquires its genuine meaning (I cite it from memory), "Even to grant what could not be expressed without the greatest blasphemy, that God does not exist, or that He is not at all interested in human affairs, it still would be possible to found the Social Contract upon natural law." What Grotius thus said, with these precautions—which for him certainly were not just oratorical, because he was a believer, a good Protestant—is that in the end divine law is not needed in order to found human law. And besides, we hardly need recall that in this town of Geneva even the metaphysical status of the "equality" of souls is in itself more than equivocal, since Christianity is perfectly compatible with the most extreme doctrine of predestination, which creates social-metaphysical classes, or social-transcendental ones, in the beyond and for eternity.

Just as equivocal in this domain are the invocations of "nature" and "reason." It is characteristic that the only Greek philosopher who undertook the task of "founding" slavery (which was for the Greeks a pure *fact* resulting from an unequal *power* and which no one had tried to *justify*), I mean Aristotle, invokes at the same time "nature" and "reason" in order to do so. When Aristotle says that there exist *physei douloi,* slaves by nature, the *physis* for him here, as always, is not a "nature" in the modern scientific sense; it is the form, the norm, the purpose, the *telos,* the finality, the essence of a thing. A slave "by nature" is, according to Aristotle, one who is incapable of governing himself; this is, when one reflects upon it, almost a tautology on the level of *concepts,* and we continue to apply it, for example, in the case of the legal deprivation of civil rights or of psychiatric confinement. And it is striking to discover that one of the most eminent representatives of modern liberalism, Benjamin Constant, in his defense of a restricted and income-based suffrage, restated almost word for word Aristotle's argument, which leads to depriving those who practice the banausic professions[1] (the *banausoi*) of their political rights.

Modern scientific arguments are just as inadequate and equivocal. The "nature" of "natural science" (in the case of biology) creates at the same time an "equality" of humans in certain respects—for example, save in the case of an abnormality, all men and women are capable of intraspecies fertilization—and an "inequality" in other respects, in a multitude of somatic characteristics, for example. Not only racism, but also even "biological" antiracism seems to me to rest upon some logical slips. That there are human traits that are genetically transmit-

1. Translator's Note: The "banausic professions" are those devoted to the making of money and are engaged in by those who practice artisanal trades. A *banausos* is, simply, an artisan.

ted is a truism; it is incontestable. Beyond this truism, the question of knowing *which* traits are genetically transmitted is an empirical question. The answer to this question, however, will never tell us what *we want* and what *we should want.* If we thought that the supreme goal [*valeur*] of society, the goal to which all others should be subordinated, was to run the 100 meter dash in less than nine seconds, or to weight-lift 300 kilograms, we would breed pure human clones capable of performing these feats—as we breed Leghorn hens for their prolific egg-laying capacities or Rhode Island hens for their very tender meat.

Similar confusions usually surround discussions about the "intelligence quotient." I simply will make two remarks. First, even if IQ heritability were successfully "demonstrated," for me there would be neither a scientific scandal nor a motive for changing my political attitude one iota. For, if the "intelligence quotient" measures something—which may be seriously doubted—and if we suppose that what it measures is separable from all the postnatal influences experienced by the individual—which appears to me still more doubtful—it would measure in the end man's intelligence only insofar as he is purely an *animal.* Indeed, it would measure rather the "intelligence" which consists in the capacity to combine and integrate facts, you might as well say the more or less lofty perfection of the individual insomuch as he is examined as an ensemblistic-identitarian automaton, that is, in that which she shares with the monkey, it would measure the degree to which she is a particularly successful hyper-monkey. No test measures or ever will be able to measure what makes up properly human intelligence, what marks our departure from pure animality: the creative imagination, the capacity to propose or to bring into being something new. Such a "measure" would be, by definition, deprived of any sense.

On the other hand, no *political* conclusions can be drawn from any measurement like an intelligence quotient. To do that, one would have to add supplementary premises that generally one makes no mention of and perfectly arbitrary if not frankly absurd ones at that, such as, for example: the most intelligent should have more money (one wonders if Einstein was less intelligent than Henry Ford or if, in case he had been given more money, he would have made additional scientific discoveries). Or else: the most intelligent should govern. This conclusion seems at first to run contrary to the consensus of contemporary societies, which demonstrate repeatedly during elections that they do not deem it especially important to have very intelligent governors; and, on the other hand, this would involve taking a political position which is at once very specific and supremely vague: the most intelligent should govern with a view to what? And in order to do what?

We cannot draw political conclusions from these kinds of considerations. We belong to a tradition which takes its roots in the will to freedom, to a tradition of individual and collective autonomy—the two being inseparable. We assume this tradition explicitly (and critically) by a *political choice* whose nondelirious character is demonstrated by the occasions in our European tradition where the movement toward equality and toward freedom has forged ahead as well as, indeed, by the simple fact that we are able today to hold this discussion here freely. Despite the provisional inequality of our positions—me speaking to you, you simply listening—it is in our power to reverse these roles, and to have a discussion, for example, tomorrow morning with no one being allowed to speak more than anyone else. This tradition and this political choice have an anchorage in the anthropological structure of Greco-Western man, of European man such as he has been created. This choice finds expression under the circumstances found in the following affirmation: we want everyone to be autonomous, that is to say, we want all people to learn to govern *themselves*, individually and collectively: and one is able to develop one's capacity to govern oneself only by participating on an equal footing, in an equal manner, in the governance of common business, of common affairs. The second affirmation certainly contains an important factual or "empirical" component—but seems to be one which is not easily contestable. Every human being has in his genes the capacity to talk—which serves no purpose if he does not learn a language.

The attempt to found equality as well as freedom, that is, human autonomy, on an extrasocial basis [*fondement*], is intrinsically antinomic. It even is a manifestation of heteronomy. If God, Nature, or Reason have decreed freedom (or, moreover, slavery), we always will be, in this case, submissive and enslaved to this pretended decree.

Society is a form of self-creation. Until now, however, its institution has been a self-institution which is occulted from itself. This self-occultation is, as a matter of fact, the fundamental characteristic of heteronomy in societies. In heteronomous societies, that is to say, in the overwhelming majority of societies that have existed up to the present time—almost all of them—we find, institutionally established and sanctioned, the representation of a source of the institution of society that only can be found *outside* of this society: among the gods, in God, among the ancestors, in the laws of Nature, in the laws of Reason, in the laws of History. In other words, we find imposed upon individuals in these societies a representation to the effect that the institution of society does not depend upon them, that they cannot lay down for themselves their own law—for that would mean *autonomy*—but rather that this law already is given by someone else. There is therefore a self-occultation of the self-institution of society and this is an integral part of the society's heteronomy.

But there also is considerable confusion in contemporary discussions, and already in those since the eighteenth century, about the idea or the category of the individual. The individual that is always being talked about in this context is social creation. The individual is a total part, as mathematicians say, of the institution of society. The individual incarnates an imposition of this institution on the psyche which is, by its nature, asocial. The individual is social creation as form in general: in the savage forest, the individual does not develop if not tended to by someone; the result will be a wolf-child, a wild child, a crazed person, or whatever you like, but not an individual. But the individual also is, in each period and in each given type of society, a fabrication. I say fabrication expressly, a specific social production—virtually a mass production. This creation is always going on. Every society in the process of becoming established [*s'instituant*] presupposes the individual as an instituted form and no society, even if it were to practice the most extreme form of "totemism," really confuses a human individual, whatever its social status, with a leopard or a jaguar. In each period, however, this creation also is creation of a historically *specific type* (*eidos*) of individual and "mass fabrication" of copies of this type: what French, Swiss, American, or Russian society fabricates as individual has very little relation, apart from characteristics so general that they are empty, to the individual that Roman,

Athenian, Babylonian, or Egyptian societies, not to mention primitive societies, fabricate.

This creation and this fabrication always involve the abstract and partial form of equality because the institution always operates in and through the universal, or what I call the ensemblistic-identitarian: it operates by classes, properties, and relations. As soon as society first is instituted, it creates straight off a supernatural "equality" among human beings which is different from their biological similarity, for society cannot become established [*s'instituter*] without establishing [*établir*] relations of equivalence. Society has to say: *the* men, *the* women, *those* who are between 18 and 20 years old, *those who* live in such and such a village . . . ; society operates necessarily by classes, relations, properties. But this segmentary and logical "equality" is compatible with the most acute substantive inequalities. It is always an equivalence with respect to a *certain* criterion, or as mathematicians say, to the *modulus* of something. In an archaic society, the members of a given "age class" are "equal" among themselves—*insofar as* they are members of this class. In a slave society, slaves are equal among themselves—*insofar as* they are slaves.

What is there beyond all this? Aside from their biological animal constitution, do human beings have a universal endowment which asserts itself [*s'impose*] in all societies? The sole universal endowment which human beings have is the psyche insofar as it is radical imagination. But this psyche can neither manifest itself, nor even subsist and survive if the form of the social individual is not imposed [*imposée*] upon it. And this individual is "endowed" with whatever the institution of the society to which it belongs in each case grants to it.

To see this, it suffices to reflect upon this shocking fact: in the majority of instances and in the majority of historical periods, the individual is fabricated by society in such a manner that it carries within itself the exigency of *inequality* in relation to others, and not of equality. And this is no accident. For, an institution of society which institutes inequality corresponds much more "naturally"—though the term here is completely misplaced—to the exigencies of the originary psychical core, of the psychical monad which we carry within us and which always dreams, whatever our age, of being all-powerful and at the center of the world. Of course, this feeling of all-powerfulness and of centeredness in relation to the universe is not realizable; a simulacrum of it can be found, however, in a petty power and in a centeredness relative to a petty universe. And it is obvious that a fundamental correlate of the exigencies of the individual's psychical economy is created, invented by society precisely under the form of social hierarchy and inequality.

The idea of a substantive social and political equality of individuals is not, and cannot be, either a scientific thesis or a philosophical thesis. It is a *social imaginary signification,* and more precisely an idea and a political will, an idea that concerns the institution of society as political community. It is itself historical creation and a creation, if it may be said, which is extremely improbable. Contemporary Europeans ("European" here is not a geographical expression, it is an expression of civilization) do not take account of the enormous historical improbability of their existence. In relation to the general history of humanity, this history, this tradition, philosophy itself, the struggle for democracy, equality, and freedom are as completely improbable as the existence of life on Earth is in relation to the existence of solar systems in the Universe. Still today, the caste system remains extremely powerful for people in India: no one contests this system. Recently, newspaper articles told how, in a State of India, pariahs who wanted to free themselves from their lot did not set in motion a political movement for equal rights for pariahs, but began to convert to Islam because Islam does not recognize castes.

The exigency of equality is a creation of *our* history, this segment of history to which we belong. It is a historical fact, or better a *meta-fact* which is born in this history and which, starting from there, tends to transform history, including also the history of *other* peoples. It is absurd to want to found equality upon any particular accepted sense of the term since it is equality that founds us insomuch as we are Europeans.

The situation in this regard is profoundly analogous to the exigencies of rational inquiry, of unlimited interrogation, of *logon didonai*—to account for and to explain. If I try to "found" equality rationally, I am able to do this only in and through a discourse which addresses itself to all and refuses all "authority," a discourse therefore which has *already presupposed* the equality of humans as reasonable beings. And the latter obviously is not an empirical fact; it is the hypothesis of all rational discourse since such a discourse presupposes a public space for thought and a public time for thinking, both of which are open to anybody and everybody. Just like the ideas—the social imaginary significations—of freedom and justice, the idea of equality also has animated for centuries the social and political struggles of European countries (in the broad sense just indicated) and their process of self-transformation. The culmination of this process is the project of setting up [*instauration*] an *autonomous society:* that is to say, a society capable of explicitly self-instituting itself, capable therefore of putting into question its already given institutions, its already established representation of the world. This society also could be described as one which, in living entirely under laws and knowing that it cannot live without law, does not become a slave to its own laws; a society, therefore, in which the question, "What is a just law?," always remains effectively open.

Such an autonomous society is inconceivable without autonomous individuals and vice versa. It is a gross fallacy to oppose here, once again, society and individuality, autonomy of the individual and social autonomy, since when we say individuality, we speak of an inclination [*versant*] of the social institution and when we speak of social institution, we speak of something whose sole positive, effective, and concrete support is the collectivity of individuals. Free individuals cannot exist in a serf society. Perhaps there may be some philosophers who reflect in their garret; but these philosophers were made possible in this historical space because autonomous collectivities preceding them already had created in the same stroke both philosophy and democracy. Descartes can say to himself expressly that he prefers to change himself rather than the order of the world. To be able to say this to himself, however, he needs the tradition of philosophy. And this philosophical tradition *was not* founded by persons who thought that it would be better to change themselves rather than the order of the world. It was founded by persons who began by changing the order of the world, rendering possible by that very act the existence, in this changed world, of philosophers. Descartes, as a philosopher who "retires from society," or any other philosopher, is possible only in a society in which freedom and autonomy already are open options. A Babylonian Socrates is inconceivable. This he knows and he says it in the *Crito*, or Plato has him say it: he cannot transgress the laws that made him what he is. In the same way, an Egyptian Kant (Pharaonic, I mean) is completely impossible, although we may doubt whether he himself really knew that.

The autonomy of individuals, their freedom (which involves, of course, their capacity to put themselves back into question) also and especially has as a context the *equal participation of all in power*, without which there is obviously no freedom, just as there is no equality without freedom. How could I be free if other people than myself decide on what concerns me and yet in this decision I cannot take part? It must be affirmed vigorously, against the platitudes of a certain liberal tradition, that there is not an antinomy but rather reciprocal implications between the exigencies of freedom and of equality. These platitudes, which continue to be repeated everyday, acquire a semblance of substance only by starting off with a degraded conception of freedom as restrained, defensive, and passive freedom. In this conception, it is a matter simply of "defending" the individual against power: this presupposes that one already has accepted alienation or political heteronomy, that one is resigned in the face of the existence of a statist sphere *separated* from the collectivity, that, ultimately, one has adopted a view of power (and even of society) as a "necessary evil." This view is not only false: it represents a distressing ethical degradation. No one has expressed this degradation better than Benjamin Constant, one of the greatest spokesmen for [classical] liberalism, when he wrote that, in contrast to the individual of antiquity, all that the modern individual asks of the law and of the State is, I quote, "the guarantee of his enjoyments." We may admire the elevation of his thought and his ethics. But must we recall that this idea so sublime—the guarantee of our enjoyments—even this is impossible to realize if we maintain a passive attitude toward power? And need we recall, since there necessarily are in our social life some rules which affect everyone and which are indispensable for everyone, that there is only one guarantee for this famous freedom to choose which has again been drummed into our ears for some time now [by Milton Friedman and others] and this is the active participation in the formation and definition of these rules?

There is another monstrous circular fallacy current today. Some people pretend to demonstrate that freedom and equality are completely separable, and even antinomic, by invoking the example of Russia or the countries called, by antiphrasis, socialist. We hear it said: you easily can see that total equality is incompatible with freedom and goes hand in hand with slavery. As if there were any equality whatsoever in a regime like that of Russia! As if, in this regime, there were not a portion of the population which is privileged in every way, which manages production, which, especially, has in its hands the direction of the party, of the state, of the army, etc. What sort of "equality" exists when I can put you in prison without you being able to do likewise?

We can, we should even, go further. Let us make a quick allusion to Tocqueville and point out that the "despotic democracy" in which he believed and of which he prophesied the possibility if not even the probability, cannot be realized. "Despotic democracy" cannot exist. Tocqueville caught a glimpse, in effect, of something that prepared the way for what was later on to become totalitarianism: he saw in his time something that went on to furnish one of the components of totalitarianism and he called this "democracy" in a language that was his own and which is quite nebulous, the limit of which he named the equality of conditions, of the tendency toward equality. But, to tell the truth, the idea of a "despotic democracy" is a nonconcept, it is a *nichtiges Nichts* as Kant would say. There can be no "despotic democracy," a total equality of all in servitude, which would be realized for nobody's (*personne, niemand*) particular profit. This "despotic democracy" always is realized for the benefit at least of someone, and this someone never can rule alone in society. Therefore, it always is established for the benefit of some portion of society; it implies inequality. Let us avail ourselves of this remark in order to emphasize that the traditional distinctions between equality of rights, equality of opportunities, and equality of conditions should be extremely relativized. It is vain to want a democratic society if the possibility of equal participation in political power is not treated by the collectivity as a task whose realization concerns it. And this takes us from equal rights to the equality of conditions for the *effective exercise* and even *assumption* of these rights. This, in its turn, sends us right back to the problem of the total institution of society.

I take again the same example from Constant already cited. When Benjamin Constant says, repeating in fact an idea of Aristotle's, that modern industry renders those who work there unfit to occupy themselves with politics, that therefore an income-based suffrage is absolutely indispensable, the question for us to answer is whether we want this modern industry such as it is and with its supposed consequences, among which is political oligarchy, for this is what is in fact at stake and this, indeed, is what exists. Or else, do we want a genuine democracy, an autonomous society? In the second hypothesis, we take the organization of modern industry, and this type of industry itself, not as a natural fatality or an effect of a divine will, but as one component, among others, of the social life which, in principle, can and should itself also be transformed in terms of our political and social aims and exigencies.

Quite obviously the question of knowing what is implied and required in each case by the equal participation of all in power remains open. There is nothing astonishing about this: it is the very essence of genuine political debate and struggle. For, like justice, like freedom, like social and individual autonomy, equality is not an answer, a solution which could be given once and for all to the question of the institution of society. It is a signification, an idea, a will which opens up questions and which does not go without question.

Aristotle defined the just, or justice, as the legal and the fair [*le légal et l'égal*]. But he also knew that these terms, the legal and the fair, open up the interrogation process rather than closing it. What is fair [*l'égal*]? Is it the "arithmetically" equal [*égal*], to give the same thing to everyone—or the "geometrically" equal, to give to each *according to . . . , in proportion to . . . .* In proportion to what? According to what? What is the criterion? These questions always are with us. In fact, even in the contemporary situation of society, these two types of equality are, in part at least, recognized and applied. For example, there is an "arithmetical" equality of adults in the right to vote; but there is also, somehow or other, and whatever may be the reservations that can be made on top of that, a "geometrical" equality according to our health expense needs, at least in countries where social security at least roughly functions.

What line can we draw here, between the "arithmetical" and the "geometrical," and starting with what criterion? These questions cannot be avoided. The idea that there could be an institution of society in which they would disappear or would be automatically resolved once and for all, as in the mythic phase of Marx's higher communism, is worse than fallacious. It is a profoundly mystifying idea, for the shining light of a promised land becomes, as we have been able to confirm for half a century, the source of the most profound alienations.

It is vain to try to evade our own will and responsibility in the face of these questions. That still is obvious and it is still one facet of the question of equality as found in the problem of the *constitutive positing* of the political community. When it is said that all people should be equal as regards participation in power, it still has not been said *who* these "all" are, nor *what* they are. The body politic, such as it is in each case, self-defines itself on a basis which must recognize that it exists *in fact* and that in a certain sense it rests upon *force*. Who *decides* who the *equal ones* are? Those who, in each case, are *considered as equals*. We should not evade the importance of the principle of this question. We are taking upon ourselves, for example, to settle upon an age of majority starting from which alone political rights can be exercised, we take upon ourselves, also, to declare that such and such individuals are—for valid, conjectured, or false medical reasons and with the possibility of who knows what possible deceptions—incapable of exercising their political rights. We cannot shun doing it. But we must not forget that it is *we* who do it.

Likewise we cannot ignore—it's the least that can be said—that *what* these equal individuals, whom we want to participate equally in power, are is in each case codetermined in a decisive manner by society and by its institution, by means of what I called before the social fabrication of individuals, or to utilize a more classical term, their *paideia,* their education in the largest sense of the word. What are the implications of an education which aims at rendering all individuals fit, to the greatest extent possible, to participate in a common government? We must come back once again to Aristotle, who was acquainted quite well with this form of education, calling it the *paideia pros ta koina*—civic education—and considering it the essential dimension of justice.

I do not want to close without alluding to another enormous problem which appears in the context of equality and which is not simply concerned with the relations among the individuals of a given community and with their connections to political power in this community, but which also is concerned with the relations between communities, that is, in the contemporary world, between nations. It is useless to recall the hypocrisy which reigns from the point of view of the brute and brutal relations of force, of the possibility of certain nations imposing their will on others; but there is hypocrisy also in the flight before a much more substantial problem of the necessity and the impossibility of reconciling what follows from our exigency of equality, namely: the affirmation that all human cultures are, from a certain point of view, equivalent; and the discovery from another point of view that they are not since a great number among them *actively deny* (in any case they do so in their deeds) equality between individuals as well as the idea of an equivalence between differing cultures. This is, in its substance, a paradox analogous to the one which confronts us in the existence of totalitarian parties in more or less democratic regimes. Here the paradox consists in the following: we affirm that all cultures have equal rights whereas we also must recognize that there are cultures which, themselves, do not admit that all cultures have equal rights and affirm their right to *impose* their "right" on others. It is a paradox to affirm that the point of view of Islam, for example, is as worthy of being valued as any other culture—when the main point of view of Islam is to affirm that the point of view of Islam *alone* is worthy of being valued. And *we* ourselves do the same thing: we affirm that only our point of view, according to which there is an equivalence of cultures, is worthy of being valued—denying in the same way, from an eventually "imperialist" point of view, the value of such another culture.

There is therefore this paradoxical peculiarity of European culture and tradition (again, in a nongeographical sense), which consists in affirming the equal rights of all cultures when other cultures reject this equivalence and when European culture itself rejects it in a certain sense by the very fact that it alone affirms it. And this paradox is not simply theoretical and philosophical. It poses a political problem of the first order since there exist, in superabundance, societies, regimes, States which constantly, systematically, and massively violate the principles that we consider as constitutive of a human society. Should we consider the excision and infibulation of women, the mutilation of thieves, police tortures, concentration camps, and "psychiatric" confinement for political reasons as some interesting ethnological peculiarities of the societies which practice them?

It is obvious, as Robespierre said, that "the people do not like armed missionaries," it is obvious that the answer to these kinds of questions cannot be given by force; but it also is obvious that these questions, at an international and world level, not only remain but acquire at the present time a renewed importance which runs the risk of becoming critical.

To all these questions we must, in each case, give a response which does not have and cannot have a scientific basis, but rather is one which is based upon our political opinion, our political *doxa,* our political will, our political responsibility. And in this responsibility, whatever it is that we do, we *all* share *equally.* The exigency of equality implies also an equality in our responsibilities for the formation of our collective life. The exigency of equality would undergo a radical perversion if it concerned itself with passive "rights" alone. Its meaning is also and especially one of an equal activity, of an equal participation, of an equal responsibility.

7

Power, Politics, Autonomy

The Social-Historical, the Psyche, the Individual

The radical imaginary deploys itself as society and as history: as the social-historical. This it does, and it can only do, in and through the two dimensions of the *instituting* and the *instituted*.[1] The *institution* is an originary creation of the social-historical field—of the collective-anonymous—transcending, as form (*eidos*), any possible "production" of individuals or of subjectivity. The individual, and individuals, is an institution, both once and for all and different in each different

1. Cornelius Castoriadis, "Marxism and Revolutionary Theory," *Socialisme ou Barbarie* 36–40 (April 1964–June 1965), since reprinted as the first part of *The Imaginary Institution of Society* (1975), tr. Kathleen Blamey (Oxford: Polity Press, and Cambridge, Mass.: M.I.T., 1987). Cited here as *MRT* for the first part and *Institution* for the second part. See in particular *MRT*, pp. 111–14 as well as *Institution*, passim.

First published in French as "Pouvoir, politique, autonomie," in *Revue de Métaphysique et de Morale*, 93 (January 1988). Reprinted in *Le Monde morcelé. Les Carrefours du Labyrithe III* (Paris: Seuil, 1990), pp. 113–39. My English translation first appeared in *Zwischenbetrachungen Im Prozess der Aufklärung. Jürgen Habermas zum 60. Geburtstag* (Frankfurt am Main: Suhrkamp, 1989). [Editor's Note: I have reedited Castoriadis' typescript English translation, restoring footnotes omitted from the published English version and translating passages left out of the abridged typescript and published versions.]

society. It is the pole of regulated social imputation and allocation, without which society is impossible.[2] Subjectivity, as agent of reflection and deliberation (as thought and will) is a social-historical *project;* its origins, repeated twice with different modalities in Greece and in Western Europe, can be dated and located.[3] The nucleus of both, of the individual and of subjectivity, is the psyche or psychical monad, which is irreducible to the social-historical but susceptible to almost limitless shaping by it, on condition that the institution satisfies certain minimal requirements of the psyche. Chief among these is that the institution must offer to the psyche *meaning for its waking life.* This is done by inducing and forcing the singular human being, during a period of schooling that starts with birth and which is reinforced till death, to invest (cathect) and make meaningful for him/herself the emerged parts of the magma of social imaginary significations instituted each time by society and which hold society together.[4]

Manifestly, the social-historical immensely transcends any "intersubjectivity." This term is the fig leaf used to conceal the nudity of inherited thought and its inability to confront the question of the social-historical. It fails in this task. Society is irreducible to "intersubjectivity"—or to any sort of common action by individuals. Society is not a huge accumulation of face-to-face situations. Only already socialized individuals can enter into face-to-face, or back-to-back, situations. No conceivable "cooperation," or "communicative action" of individuals could ever create language, for instance. Language, though leaning on biological properties of the human being, is not a biological datum either, it is a fundamental institution. And an assembly of unsocialized human beings, acting solely according to their deep psychical drives, would be unimaginably more Boschian than any ward for the mentally disturbed in an old psychiatric asylum. Society, as *always already instituted,* is self-creation and capacity for self-

2. *Institution,* ch. 6.

3. Cornelius Castoriadis, "The State of the Subject Today" (1986), tr. David Ames Curtis, *Thesis Eleven,* 24 (1989), pp. 5–43.

4. *Institution,* ch. 6 and *passim;* also, "Institution de la société et religion," *Esprit,* May 1982, reprinted in *Domaines de l'homme. Les Carrefours du labyrinthe II* (Paris: Seuil, 1986), pp. 364–84.

alteration. It is the work of the radical imaginary as instituting, which brings itself into being as instituted society and as a given, and each time specified, social imaginary.

The individual as such is not, however, "contingent" in relation to society. Society can exist concretely only through the fragmentary and complementary incarnation and incorporation of its institution and its imaginary significations in the living, talking, and acting individuals of that society. Athenian society is, in a sense, nothing but the Athenians; without them, it is only the remnants of a transformed landscape, debris of marble and vases, indecipherable inscriptions, worn statues fished out some place in the Mediterranean. But the Athenians are Athenians only by means of the *nomos* of the *polis*. In this relationship between an instituted society—which infinitely transcends the totality of the individuals that "compose" it, but which can actually exist only by being "realized" in the individuals it manufactures—on the one hand, and these individuals, on the other hand, we witness an original, unprecedented type of relationship which cannot be thought under the categories of the whole and its parts, the set and its elements, the universal and the particular, etc. In and through its own creation, society creates the individual as such and the individuals in and through which alone it can actually exist. But society is not a property of composition; neither is it a whole containing something more than and different from its parts, if only because these "parts" are made to be, and to be thus and not otherwise, by this "whole" which, nevertheless, can only be in and through its "parts." This type of relationship, which has no analogy elsewhere, has to be reflected upon for itself, as principle and model of itself.[5]

In this respect, one can never be too careful. This state of affairs has nothing to do with "systems theory" or with "self-organization," "order from noise," etc. And it would be erroneous to say, as some do, that society produces individuals, which in turn produce society. Society is the work of the *instituting* imaginary. The individuals are made by the *instituted* society, at the same time as they make and remake it. The two mutually irreducible poles are the radical instituting

5. *MRT;* and *Institution,* ch. 4.

imaginary—the field of social-historical creation—on the one hand, the singular psyche, on the other. Starting with the psyche, using it, as it were, as a material, the instituted society each time makes the individuals—which, as such, can henceforth only make the society which has made them. It is only insofar as the radical imagination of the psyche seeps through the successive layers of the social armor, which cover and penetrate it up to an unfathomable limit-point, and which constitute the individual, that the singular human being can have, in return, an independent action on society. Let me note, in anticipation of what follows, that such an action is extremely rare and, at any rate, imperceptible wherever *instituted heteronomy*[6] prevails—that is, in fact, in almost all known societies. In this case, apart from the bundle of predefined social roles, the only *ascertainable* ways in which the singular psyche can manifest itself are transgression and pathology. Things are different in the rare case of societies where the bursting of complete heteronomy makes a true *individuation of the individual* possible and thus allows the radical imagination of the singular psyche to find or create the social means of publicly expressing itself in an original manner and to contribute perceptibly to the self-alteration of the social world. A third aspect of this relation appears during manifest and marked epochs of social-historical alteration when society and individuals alter themselves together, those alterations entailing each other in this case.

Validity of Institutions and Primordial Power

The institution, and the imaginary significations borne by it and animating it, create a world. This is the world of the particular society considered: it is established in and through the articulation it performs between a "natural" and "supranatural"—more generally, an "extra-social"—world and a "human" world in a narrow sense. This articulation can take on an extraordinary variety of forms: from an imaginary virtual fusion of the two to their utmost separation, from the submission of society to the cosmic order or to God to the utmost frenzy of

6. *MRT*, pp. 108–10; and "Institution de la société et religion," in *Domaines*.

control of and domination over nature. In all cases, "nature" and the "supranatural" are instituted in their meaning as such and in the innumerable articulations of this meaning; and these articulations maintain a complex network of relations with the articulations of society itself as they are posited each time by its institution.[7]

Society creates itself as form (*eidos*) and each time as a singular form. (To be sure, influences, historical transmissions, continuities, similarities, etc., are always there. They are tremendous, and so are the questions they raise; but they do not modify in the least the essence of the situation, and their discussion need not detain us here.) In creating itself, society deploys itself in and through a multiplicity of particular organizing and organized forms. It deploys itself as creation of its own space and its own time (of its own spatiality and temporality), populated by innumerable objects and entities of "natural," "supranatural," and "human" character, all of them categorized and brought into relations posited each time by the given society. This work always leans on immanent properties of the being-thus of *the* world; but these properties are recreated, isolated, chosen, filtered, brought into relation, and, above all, *endowed with meaning* by the institution and the imaginary significations of the given society.[8]

Trivialities apart, a general discourse about these articulations is almost impossible. They are, each time, the work of the given society and permeated by its imaginary significations. In its "materiality," or "concreteness," this or that institution as found in two different societies may appear identical or highly similar; however, this apparent material identity is each time *immersed* in a different magma of different significations, and this suffices to transform such an apparent identity into an actual alterity from the social-historical point of view (for example, writing, with the same alphabet, in Athens, 450 B.C., and in Constantinople, 750 A.D.). Universals stretching across the boundaries of different societies—such as language, the production of material life, the regulation of sexual life and reproduction, norms and

7. *MRT*, pp. 149–50; and *Institution*, ch. 5.

8. *Ibid.*

values, etc.—certainly do exist; by no means, however, can their existence found a "theory" of society and history with substantive content. And, within these "formal" universals, more specific universals also exist (e.g., concerning language and certain phonological laws). But, like writing with the same alphabet, they work only at the border of the being of society, which deploys itself as meaning and signification. As soon as one considers "grammatical" or "syntactic" universals, much more redoubtable questions arise. For instance, Chomsky's enterprise must face this impossible dilemma: either grammatical (syntactical) forms are totally indifferent as to meaning—a statement whose absurdity any translator would readily acknowledge—or they contain and carry with them potentially *since the advent of the first human language* and God knows how, all the significations which will ever appear in history—which entails a metaphysics of history both overladen and naive. To say that in each and every language it must be possible to express the idea "John gave an apple to Mary" is certainly true but also regrettably meager.

There is, however, one universal we can "deduce," *once we know what society is and what the psyche is*. It concerns the effective validity (*Geltung*), the positive validity (in the sense of "positive law") of the immense instituted edifice of society. How is it possible for the institution and for institutions (language, the definition of "reality" and "truth," ways of doing things, work, sexual regulation, licit/illicit, calls to die for the tribe or the nation which are almost always greeted with enthusiasm, and so on) to compel recognition and acceptance on the part of the psyche, which in its essence can only ignore all this hodgepodge and would, if ever it perceived it, find it highly inimical and repugnant? There are two sides to this question: the psychical and the social.

From the psychical point of view, the social fabrication of the individual is the historical process by means of which the psyche is coerced (smoothly or brutally; in fact, the process always entails violence against the proper nature of the psyche) into giving up its initial objects and its initial world (this renunciation is never total, but almost always sufficient to fulfill social requirements) and into investing (cathecting) socially instituted objects, rules, and the world. This is the true meaning of the process of sublimation.[9] The minimal requirement for this process to unfold is that the institution provide the psyche with *meaning*—another type of meaning than the protomeaning of the psychical monad. The social individual is thus constituted by means of the internalization of the world and the imaginary significations created by society; it internalizes explicitly vast fragments of this world, it internalizes implicitly its virtual totality by virtue of the interminable reciprocal referrals which link, magmatically, each fragment of this social world to the rest of it.

The social side of this process concerns the whole complex of institutions in which the human being is steeped as soon as it is born and, first of all, the Other—generally, but not inevitably, the mother—who, already socialized in a determinate manner, takes care of the newborn and speaks a determinate language. More abstractly speaking, there is a "part" of almost all institutions that aims at the nurturing, the rearing, the education of the newcomers—what the Greeks called *paideia:* family, age groups, rites, school, customs, laws, etc.

The effective validity of the institutions is thus ensured, first and foremost, by the very process which makes a social individual out of the little screaming monster. The latter can only become an individual if it internalizes the institutions of its society.

If we define *power* as the capacity for a personal or impersonal instance (*Instanz*) to bring someone to do (or to abstain from doing) that which, left to him/herself, s/he would not necessarily have done (or would possibly have done), it is immediately obvious that the greatest conceivable power lies in the possibility of preforming someone in such a way that, *of his/her own accord,* s/he does what one wants him/her to do, without any need for *domination* (*Herrschaft*) or of *explicit power* (*Macht/Gewalt*) to bring him/her to . . . (do or abstain from doing something). Equally obvious, a being subject to such shaping will present at the same time the appearances of the fullest

9. Cornelius Castoriadis, "Epilegomena to a Theory of the Soul which has been presented as a Science" (1968), now in *Crossroads in the Labyrinth* (1978), tr. Martin H. Ryle and Kate Soper (Brighton: Harvester, and Cambridge, Mass.: M.I.T., 1984); see pp. 34–40, and also *Institution,* pp. 311–20.

possible spontaneity, and the reality of a total heteronomy. Compared to this absolute power, any explicit power and any form of domination can be seen as deficient, for they betray the markings of an irreparable failure. (Henceforth, I will speak of "*explicit power*"; the term "domination" is better used for the specific social-historical situations in which an *asymmetric and antagonistic division* of the social body is instituted.)

Thus, before any explicit power and, even more, before any "domination," the institution of society wields over the individuals it produces a *radical ground-power.* This ground-power, or primordial power, as manifestation of the instituting power of the radical imaginary, is not locatable. It is never the power of an individual or of a nameable instance. It is carried out by the instituted society, but in the background stands the instituting society; and "once this institution is set in place, the social as instituting slips away, puts itself at a distance, is already somewhere else."[10] In turn, the instituting society, however radical its creation may be, always works by starting from something already instituted and on the basis of what is already there. It is always historical—save for an inaccessible point of origin. It is always, and to an unmeasurable degree, also recovery of the given, and therefore burdened with an inheritance, even if under *beneficium inventorii,* the limits of which cannot be fixed either. We will discuss later the implications of this fundamental situation for the project of autonomy and for the idea of *effective* human freedom. Before that, however, we must come to understand that, to begin with, the institution of society wields a radical power over the individuals making it up, and that this power itself is grounded upon the instituting power of the radical imaginary and of the whole preceding history which finds, each time, in the institution as it is posited its transient outcome. Ultimately, therefore, we are dealing with the power of the social-historical field itself, the power of *outis,* of Nobody.[11]

---

10. *MRT,* p. 112; *Institution,* pp. 369–73.

11. "Epilegomena," in *Crossroads,* p. 40.

Limits of the Instituting Ground-Power

Considered in itself, therefore, the instituting ground-power and its realization by the institution should be absolute and should shape the individuals in such a fashion that they are bound to reproduce eternally the regime which has produced them. And this is, almost always, almost everywhere, manifestly the strict intention (or finality) of existing institutions. If this finality were strictly fulfilled, there would be no history. We know, however, that this is not true. Instituted society never succeeds in wielding its ground-power in an absolute fashion. The most it can attain—as we see in primitive societies and, more generally, in the whole class of what we must call traditional societies—is the instauration of a temporality of apparently essential repetition, beneath which its insurmountable historicity continues to work imperceptibly and over very long periods.[12] Seen as absolute and total, the ground-power of the instituted society and of tradition is therefore, sooner or later, bound to fail. This is a sheer fact which we are compelled to recognize: *there is* history, *there is* a plurality of essentially different societies. Nevertheless, we can try to elucidate it.

For this elucidation, four factors have to be taken into account.

1. Society creates its world; it invests it with meaning; it provides itself with a store of significations designed in advance to deal with whatever may occur. The magma of the socially instituted imaginary significations resorbs, potentially, whatever may present itself, and it could not, in principle, be taken unawares or find itself helpless. In this respect, the role of religion and the essential function it fulfills for the *closure of meaning* have always been central.[13] (For instance, the Holocaust becomes a proof of the singularity and the divine election of the Jewish people.) The "world in itself" bears within itself an ensemblistic-identitary organization that is sufficiently stable and "systematic" in its first layer to allow humans to live socially and at the same time sufficiently lacunar and incomplete to bear an

12. *Institution*, pp. 185–86 and 202–15.

13. *MRT*, pp. 130–31, 139–40, 143–44, and 147–48; *Institution*, pp. 361–62; and "Institution de la société et religion," in *Domaines*.

indefinite number of social-historical creations of signification. *Both* aspects relate to ontological dimensions of the world in itself, which no transcendental subjectivity, no language, no pragmatics of communication could ever bring into existence.[14] But also the world *qua* "presocial world"—a limit for any thought—though in itself signifying nothing, is always there as inexhaustible provision of alterity and as the always imminent risk of laceration of the web of significations with which society has lined it. The *a-meaning* of the world is always a possible threat for the meaning of society. Thus the ever-present risk that the social edifice of significations will totter.

2. Society fabricates individuals with the psyche as raw material. I do not know which of the two is more amazing: the almost total plasticity of the psyche with respect to the social formation that shapes it or its invincible capacity to preserve its monadic core and its radical imagination and to thwart, at least partially, the incessant schooling imposed upon it. However rigid or watertight the type of individual into which it has been transformed, the irreducible being proper to the singular psyche always manifests itself in the form of dreams, "psychical" illnesses, transgressions, contentions and querulent expressions, but also in the form of singular contributions to the more than slow alteration of our social modes of making/doing and representing. (In traditional societies, these singular contributions are rarely, if ever, locatable.)
3. Society is but exceptionally—or never—unique or isolated. *It just so happens* (*sumbainei*) that *there is* an indefinite plurality of human societies as well as synchronic coexistence and contact among them. The institution and the significations of the others are always a deadly threat to our own; what is sacred for us is for them abominable, what is meaning for us is for them the very figure of nonsense.[15]
4. Finally, and principally, society can never escape itself. The instituted society is always subject to the subterranean pressure of insti-

14. *Institution*, ch. 5; also, "Portée ontologique de l'histoire de la science," in *Domaines*, pp. 419–55.

15. Cornelius Castoriadis, "Notations sur le racisme," *Connexions*, 48 (1986), pp. 107–18.

> tuting society. Beneath the established social imaginary, the flow of the radical imaginary continues steadily. Indeed, this primordial and raw fact of the radical imaginary allows us not to "solve," but to phrase differently, the question implied by our previous expressions, *it just so happens,* and *there is.* That *there is* an essential plurality, synchronic and diachronic, of societies means just that: there is an instituting imaginary.

All these factors threaten society's stability and self-perpetuation. And against all of them, the institution of society establishes in advance and contains defenses and protections. Principal among these is the virtual omnipotence, the capacity of universal covering, of its magma of significations. Any irruption of the raw world becomes for it *sign of* something, is interpreted away and thereby exorcised. Dreams, illnesses, transgressions, and deviance are also explained away. Alien societies and people are posited as strange, savage, impious. The enemy against which the defenses of society are feeblest is its own instituting imaginary, its own creativity. This is also why it is against this danger that the strongest protection has been set up; strongest, that is, as long as it lasts, and for all we know it has lasted at least 100,000 years. It is the denial and the covering up of the instituting dimension of society through the imputation of the origin of the institution and of its social significations to an extrasocial source.[16] "Extrasocial" here means external to the actual, living society: gods or God, but also founding heroes or ancestors who are continually reincarnated in the newborn humans; in the latter case, society posits itself as literally *possessed* by another "itself," one infinitely close and infinitely distant. In more agitated historical worlds, supplementary lines of defense are established. The denial of the alteration of society, or the covering up of the new by means of its attribution to mythical origins, may become impossible. In such cases, the new can be subjected to a fictitious but nevertheless efficient reduction with the help of "commentary" on and "interpretation" of the tradition. This is, typically, the case of the *Weltreligionen,* in particular of the Jewish, Christian, and Islamic worlds.

---

16. *MRT,* p. 131; *Institution,* pp. 213–15 and 371–73.

Explicit Power and the Political Dimension of the Institution of Society

All these defenses can fail, and, in a sense, they always eventually fail. Crimes, violent insuperable contentions, natural calamities destroying the functionality of existing institutions, wars are always there. This fact is one of the roots of *explicit power.* There always has been, and there always will be, a dimension of the social institution in charge of this essential function: to reestablish order, to ensure the life and the operation of society against whatever, actually or potentially, endangers them.

There is another, perhaps even more important, root of explicit power. The social institution, and the magma of imaginary significations it embodies, are much more than a heap of representations (or of "ideas"). Society institutes itself in and through the three inseparable dimensions of representation, affect, and intention. The "representational" (not necessarily representable and expressible) part of the magma of social imaginary significations is the least difficult to approach. But this approach would remain critically inadequate (as is, indeed, the case in almost all philosophies and theories of history and even in historiography) if, aiming only at a history and a hermeneutics of "representations" and "ideas," it ignored the *magma of affects* proper to each society—its *Stimmung,* its way of living itself and of living the world and life itself—or if it ignored the *intentional vectors* which weave together the institution and the life of society, what one may call its proper and characteristic *push and drive,* which are never reducible to its simple conservation.[17] It is by means of this push and drive that the past/present of society is always inhabited by a future which is, perpetually, *to be made* and *to be done.* It is this push and drive that invest with meaning the biggest unknown of all: that which is not yet but will be, the future, by giving to those who are living the means to participate in the preservation or the constitution of a world that perpetuates the established meaning. It is also because of this push and drive that the innumerable plurality of social activities always transcends the sim-

17. *Institution,* passim.

ple biological "preservation" of the species and is, at the same time, subject to a hierarchization.

This unavoidable dimension of push and drive toward that which is to be made and done introduces another type of "disorder" within the social order. Even within the most rigid and repetitive setup, the facts of ignorance and uncertainty as to the future forbid a complete prior codification of *decisions*. *Explicit power* is thus also rooted in the necessity to decide what is and is not to be done with respect to the more or less explicit ends which are the objects of the push and drive of the society considered.

Therefore, what we call "legislative" and "executive" power can be buried in the institution as custom and internalization of supposedly intangible norms. "Judicial" power and "governmental" power, however, must be explicitly present, under whatever form, as soon as there is society. The question of *nomos* (and of its, so to speak, "mechanical" implementation, the so-called executive power) may be covered up by a society; but this cannot be done as regards *dike*—the judiciary—and *telos*—the governmental.

Whatever its explicit articulation, explicit power can never, therefore, be thought exclusively in terms of "friend-foe" (Carl Schmitt). Neither can it (nor can domination) be reduced to the "monopoly of legitimate violence" (Engels). Beneath the monopoly of legitimate violence lies the monopoly of the legitimate word, and this is, in turn, ruled by the monopoly of the valid signification. The throne of the Lord of signification stands above the throne of the Lord of violence.[18] The voice of the arms can only begin to be heard amid the crash of the collapsing edifice of institutions. And for violence to manifest itself effectively, the word—the injunctions of the existing power—has to keep its magic over the "groups of armed men" (Engels). The fourth company of the Pavlovsky regiment, guards to His Majesty the Czar, and the Semenovsky regiment, were the strongest pillars of the throne, until those days of February 26 and 27, 1917 when they fraternized with the crowd and turned their guns against their own officers. The mightiest army in the world will not protect you if it is not loyal to

18. *Institution*, pp. 308–09.

you—and the ultimate foundation of its loyalty is its imaginary belief in your imaginary legitimacy.

There always is, thus, and there always will be, an *explicit power,* that is, unless a society were to succeed in transforming its subjects into automata that had completely internalized the instituted order and in constructing a temporality that took into account, in advance, all future time. Both aims are impossible to achieve, given what we know about the psyche, the instituting imaginary, the world.

On Some Confusions: "The Political"

There is, thus, a dimension of the institution of society pertaining to *explicit power,* that is, to the existence of *instances capable of formulating explicitly sanctionable injunctions.* This dimension is to be called the dimension of "*the political.*" It matters little, at this level, whether the instances in question are embodied by the whole tribe, by the elders, by the warriors, by a chief, by the *demos,* by a bureaucratic apparatus, etc.

We must try here to clear up three confusions.

The first is the identification of explicit power with the State. "Societies without the State" are by no means "societies without power." Not only can we observe in these societies, as everywhere, the enormous ground-power of the established institution (which becomes that much the greater as explicit power is reduced), we also always find an *explicit power* of the collectivity (or of the males, the warriors, etc.) pertaining to *dike* and *telos*—to jurisdiction and to decisions. Explicit power *is not* identical to the State. We have to restrict the term and the notion of State to a specific *eidos,* the historical creation of which can almost be dated and localized. The State is an instance *separated from* the collectivity and it is instituted in a way that it continuously ensures this separation. The State is, typically, what I call an *institution of the second order,* belonging to a specific class of societies.[19] I would insist, moreover, that the term "State" be restricted to the cases where there

19. On this term, see *Institution,* p. 371, and "The First Institution of Society and Second-Order Institutions" (1985), tr. David Ames Curtis, *Free Associations,* 12 (1988), pp. 39–51.

is an institution of a *State Apparatus,* which entails a separate civilian, military or priestly "bureaucracy," even if it be rudimentary, that is, a hierarchal organization with a delimition of regions of competence. This definition can cover the immense majority of known Statelike organizations; there are of course some rare borderline cases which can be left to the quibblings of those who forget that, in the social-historical domain, definitions are valid only *os epi to polu,* as Aristotle would say, only "for the most part and in most cases." In this sense, the Greek democratic *polis* is not a "State," since in it explicit power—the positing of *nomos, dike* and *telos*—belongs to the whole body of citizens. This explains also the difficulties encountered by a mind as powerful as Max Weber's when faced with the democratic *polis,* difficulties rightly underlined and correctly commented upon in one of M. I. Finley's last writings.[20] Hence the impossibility of grasping Athenian democracy by means of the ideal types of "traditional" or "rational" domination (remember that for Max Weber "rational domination" and "bureaucratic domination" are almost interchangeable terms), and his infelicitous attempts to present the Athenian "demagogues" as holders of charismatic power. Marxists and feminists would, no doubt, reply that the *demos* wielded power over slaves and women, and therefore "was the State." Should one then say that in the South of the United States whites "were the State" vis-à-vis blacks until 1865? Or that French adult males "were the State" vis-à-vis women until 1945? Or that today, everywhere, adults "are the State" vis-à-vis nonadults? Neither explicit power, nor domination need take the form of the State.

The second confusion involves mixing up *the political,* the dimension of explicit power, with the overall institution of society. As is well known, the term "the political" was introduced by Carl Schmitt (*Der Begriff des Politischen,* 1928) with a restricted meaning which, if we accept the foregoing, should be found wanting. We witness today an attempt in the opposite direction, an attempt to expand the meaning of

20. M. I. Finley, *Ancient History: Evidence and Models* (New York: Viking Press, 1986), ch. 6: "Max Weber and the Greek City-State," pp. 88–103, and Epilogue, pp. 106–8. See also my article, "The Greek *Polis* and the Creation of Democracy," ch. 5 of this book, pp. 109–10.

the term until it resorbs the overall institution of society. The distinguishing of the political from other "social phenomena" would stem, it seems, from a positivist attitude. (Of course, what we are dealing with here are not "phenomena" but rather ineliminable dimensions of the social institution: language, work, sexual reproduction, the raising of new generations, religion, mores, "culture" in the narrow sense, etc.) In this attempt, "the political" is presented as that which generates the relations of humans among themselves and with the world, the representation of nature and time, the mutual positions of religion and power. This is, of course, exactly what I have defined since 1965 as the imaginary institution of society.[21] Personal tastes aside, the gains to be made by calling the overall institution of society "the political" are hard to see, but the damages are obvious. Either, in calling "the political" that which everybody would naturally call the institution of society, one merely attempts a change in vocabulary without substantive content, creating only confusion and violating the maxim *nomina non sunt praeter necessitatem multiplicanda,* or one attempts to preserve in this substitution the connotations linked with the word "political" since its creation by the Greeks, that is, whatever pertains to explicit and at least partially conscious and reflective decisions concerning the fate of the collectivity; but then, through a strange reversal, language, economy, religion, representation of the world, family, etc., have to be said to depend upon political decisions in a way that would win the approval of Charles Maurras as well as of Pol Pot. "Everything is political" either means nothing, or it means: everything ought to be political, ought to flow from an explicit decision of the Sovereign.

Politics

The root of the second confusion is perhaps to be found in a third one. One frequently hears it said nowadays: the Greeks invented (or "discovered") the political.[22] One may credit the Greeks with many things—

---

21. *MRT,* pp. 115–64; and *Institution,* passim.

22. The French translator of M. I. Finley's *Politics in the Ancient World* was quite right not to give in to facile fashion, when she entitled her translation *L'Invention de la Politique*—"the invention of politics," not "the invention of the politic*al*."

and, mostly, with things other than the ones they are usually credited with—but certainly not with the invention of the institution of society, or even of explicit power. The Greeks did not invent "the" politi*cal,* in the sense of the dimension of explicit power always present in any society. They invented—or, better, created—politic*s,* which is something entirely different. People sometimes argue about whether and to what extent politics existed before the Greeks. A vain argument, framed in vague terms, muddled thinking. Before the Greeks (and after them) one sees intrigues, plots, machinations, conspiracies, influence peddling, silent or open struggles over explicit power. One observes an art of managing, or of "improving," established power (fantastically developed in many places, e.g., in China). One can even observe explicit and deliberate changes in some institutions—or even, in rare cases, radical reinstitutions ("Moses," or, certainly, Mohammed); but in these cases, the legislator, whether prophet or king, invokes an instituting power of divine origin, he produces or exhibits sacred books. Now, if the Greeks were able to create politics, democracy and philosophy it is also because they had neither sacred books nor prophets. They had poets, philosophers, legislators and *politai*—citizens.

Politics, such as it was created by the Greeks, amounts to the explicit putting into question of the established institution of society. This presupposes that at least important parts of this institution had nothing "sacred" or "natural" about them, but rather that they represented *nomos*. The democratic movement in the Greek cities took aim at the explicit power and tried to reinstitute it. As is known, in about half the *poleis* it failed (or did not succeed even in making a real start). Despite this, its emergence acted upon the totality of the *poleis,* since even the oligarchical or tyrannical regimes, in being confronted with it, had to define themselves as such and therefore *appear such as they were*. But the democratic movement is not confined to the struggle around explicit power, it aims potentially at the overall reinstitution of society, and this is materialized through the creation of philosophy. Greek thought is not a commentary on or an interpretation of sacred texts, it amounts *ipso facto* to the putting into question of the most important dimension of the institution of society: the representations and the norms of the tribe, and the very notion of *truth*. To be sure, there is in all societies a socially instituted "truth," which amounts to the canonical conformity of representations and statements to what is socially instituted as the equivalent of "axioms" and "procedures of validation." This "truth" ought, properly speaking, to be called *correctness* (*Richtigkeit*). But the Greeks *create the truth* as the interminable movement of thought which constantly tests its bounds and looks back upon itself (reflectiveness), and they create it as democratic philosophy. Thinking ceases to be the business of rabbis, of priests, of mullahs, of courtiers, or of solitary monks, and becomes the business of citizens who want to discuss within a public space created by this very movement.

Greek politics, and politics properly conceived, can be defined as the explicit collective activity which aims at being lucid (reflective and deliberate) and whose object is the institution of society as such. It is, therefore, *a coming into light,* though certainly partial, of the instituting in person; a dramatic, though by no means exclusive, illustration of this is presented by the moments of revolution.[23] The creation of politics takes place when the established institution of society is put into question as such and in its various aspects and dimensions (which rapidly leads to the discovery and the explicit elaboration, but also *a new and different articulation,* of solidarity), that is to say, when *another relation,* previously unknown, is created between the instituting and the instituted.[24]

True politics, therefore, is from the start potentially radical as well as global, and the same is true about its offspring, classical "political philosophy." I say "potentially" because, as is known, many explicit institutions in the democratic *poleis,* including some particularly repugnant to us (slavery, the inferior status of women), were never put into question on a practical basis. But this is irrelevant to our discussion. The creation of democracy and philosophy is truly the creation of *historical movement* in the strong sense—a movement which, in this

---

23. *MRT,* p. 112.

24. *MRT,* pp. 95–114. See also the General Introduction (1972) in the first volume of my *Political and Social Writings,* tr. David Ames Curtis, 2 vols. (Minneapolis: University of Minnesota Press, 1988), pp. 29–36; and *Institution,* pp. 371–73.

phase, deploys itself from the eighth to the fifth century, and is in fact brought to an end with the defeat of Athens in 404.

The radicality of this movement should not be underestimated. Leaving aside the activity of the legislators (*nomothetes*), on which trustworthy information is scant (though many reasonable inferences about it, especially in relation to the founding of colonies, starting in the eighth century, remain to be drawn), suffice it to mention the boldness of the Cleisthenean revolution, which subjected the traditional Athenian society to a far-going reorganization aimed at the equal and balanced participation of all citizens in political power. The discussions and projects to which the dispersed and mutilated torsos of the sixth and fifth century bear witness (Solon, Hippodamos, the Sophists, Democritus, Thucydides, Aristophanes, etc.) present a dazzling picture of this radicality. The institution of society is clearly seen in the fifth century as a human work (Democritus, the *Mikros Diakosmos* as handed down to us by Tzetzes, the Sophists, Sophocles in *Antigone*). The Greek also know from very early on that the human being will be such as the *nomoi* of the *polis* will make it (the idea, clearly formulated by the poet Simonides, is still repeated many times as obvious by Aristotle). They know, therefore, that there is no worthy human being without a worthy *polis*, without a *polis* ruled by the proper *nomos*. They also know, contrary to Leo Strauss, that there is no "natural" law (the expression would be self-contradictory in Greek). And the discovery of the "arbitrariness" of the *nomos* as well as of its constitutive character for the human being opens the interminable discussion about right, wrong, justice, and the "correct *politeia*."[25]

This same radicality, along with the awareness of the fabrication of the individual by the society in which it lives, stands behind the philosophical works of the period of decadence—of the fourth century, those of Plato and Aristotle—forces itself upon them as a self-evidence, and nourishes them. Thanks to it, Plato is able to think a radical utopia; because of it, Plato as well as Aristotle emphasizes the importance of *paideia* even more than of the "political constitution" in the narrow sense. And it is no accident that the renewal of political

---

25. Cornelius Castoriadis, "Value, Equality, Justice, Politics: From Marx to Aristotle and from Aristotle to Ourselves" (1975), in *Crossroads*, pp. 278–330.

thought in Western Europe is quickly accompanied by the resurgence of radical "utopias." These utopias manifest, first and foremost, awareness of this fundamental fact: institutions are human works. And it is no accident either that, contrary to the poverty in this respect of contemporary "political philosophy," grand political philosophy from Plato to Rousseau has placed the question of *paideia* at the center of its interests. Even if, practically considered, the question of education has always remained a concern of modern times, this great tradition dies in fact with the French Revolution. And it takes a good deal of philistinism and hypocrisy to display surprise at the fact that Plato thought it proper to legislate about the musical *nomoi* or about poetry—forgetting that the State today decides about the poems children will learn in school. We will discuss later whether Plato was right to do it *as* he did and *to the degree* that he did.

The Greeks' creation of politics and philosophy is the first historical emergence of the project of collective and individual autonomy. If we want to be free, we have to make our own *nomos*. If we want to be free, nobody should have the power to tells us what we should think.

But free how, and up to what point? These are the questions of true politics—preciously absent from the contemporary discourses about "the political," "human rights," or "natural law"—to which we must now turn.

Heteronomy and Autonomy

Almost always, almost everywhere societies have lived in a state of *instituted heteronomy*.[26] An essential constituent of this state is the instituted representation of an extrasocial source of *nomos*. In this respect, religion plays a central role. It supplies a representation of this source and of its attributes, it ensures that all significations—those pertaining to the world as well as those pertaining to human affairs—spring from the same origin, it cements the whole by means of a belief that musters the support of essential tendencies of the psyche. Let me add parenthetically that the contemporary fashion—for which Max

26. *MRT*, pp. 108–10, and the texts cited in note 24.

Weber is partly responsible—of presenting religion as a set of "ideas" or as a "religious ideology" leads to a catastrophic misunderstanding, for it fails to recognize that the religious *affect* and the religious *drive* are as important, and as variable, as religious "representations."

The denial of the instituting dimension of society, the covering up of the instituting imaginary by the instituted imaginary, goes hand in hand with the creation of true-to-form individuals, whose thought and life are dominated by repetition (whatever else they may do, they do very little), whose radical imagination is bridled to the utmost degree possible, and who are hardly truly individualized. To see this, it is enough to compare the similitude of sculptures dating from the same Egyptian dynasty to the difference between Sappho and Archilochus or Bach and Handel. It also goes hand in hand with the peremptory exclusion of any questioning about the ultimate grounds of the beliefs and the laws of the tribe, thus also of the "legitimacy" of the instituted explicit power. In this sense, the very term "legitimacy" becomes anachronistic (and Eurocentric, or Sinocentric) when applied to most traditional societies. *Tradition means that the question of the legitimacy of tradition shall not be raised.* Individuals in these societies are fabricated in such a way that this question remains for them mentally and psychically inconceivable.

As a germ, autonomy emerges when explicit and unlimited interrogation explodes on the scene—an interrogation that has bearing not on "facts" but on the social imaginary significations and their possible grounding. This is a moment of creation, and it ushers in a new type of society and a new type of individuals. I am speaking intentionally of *germ,* for autonomy, social as well as individual, is a *project.* The rise of unlimited interrogation creates a new social-historical *eidos:* reflectiveness in the full sense, or self-reflectiveness, as well as the individual and the institutions which embody it. The questions raised are, on the social level: Are our laws good? Are they just? Which laws *ought we* to make? And, on the individual level: Is what I think true? Can I know if it is true—and if so, how? The moment of philosophy's birth is not the appearance of the "question of Being" but rather the emergence of the question: *What is it that we ought to think?* The "question of Being" is only a component of this more general question: What ought we to think about Being (or about justice, or about ourselves, etc.)? The "question of Being" has been, for instance, both raised and solved in the Pentateuch, as in most sacred books. The moment of democracy's birth, and that of politics, *is not* the reign of law or of right, nor that of the "rights of man," nor even the equality of citizens as such, but rather the emergence of the questioning of the law in and through the actual activity of the community. Which are the laws we ought to make? At that moment *politics* is born; that is to say, freedom is born as social-historically *effective* freedom. And this birth is inseparable from the birth of philosophy. (Heidegger's systematic and not accidental blindness to their inseparability is the main factor distorting his view of the Greeks and of all the rest.)

Autonomy comes from *autos-nomos:* (to give to) oneself one's laws. After what has been said about heteronomy it is hardly necessary to add: to make one's own laws, knowing that one is doing so. This is a new *eidos* within the overall history of being: a type of being that reflectively gives to itself the laws of its being.

Thus conceived, autonomy bears little relation to Kant's "autonomy" for many reasons, of which it will suffice to mention one. Autonomy does not consist in acting according to a law discovered in an immutable Reason and given once and for all. It is the unlimited self-questioning about the law and its foundations as well as the capacity, in light of this interrogation, *to make, to do* and *to institute* (therefore also, *to say*). Autonomy is the reflective activity of a reason creating itself in an endless movement, both as individual and social reason.

Autonomy and Politics

Let us return now to politics, and start, so as to facilitate understanding, with what is *proteron pros hemas,* first with respect to ourselves: the individual. In what sense can an individual be autonomous? There are two sides to this question, the internal and the external.

The internal side: the nucleus of the individual is the psyche (the Unconscious, the drives). Any idea of eliminating or "mastering" this nucleus would be plainly ridiculous; that task is not only impossible, it would amount to a murder of the human being. Also, at any given moment, the individual carries with itself, in itself, a history which cannot and should not be "eliminated," since the individual's very reflectiveness and lucidity are the products of this history. The autonomy of the individual consists in the instauration of an *other* relationship between the reflective instance and the other psychical instances as well as between the present and the history which made the individual such as it is. This relationship makes it possible for the individual to escape the enslavement of repetition, to look back upon itself, to reflect on the reason for its thoughts and the motives of its acts, guided by the elucidation of its desire and aiming at the truth. This autonomy can effectively alter the behavior of the individual, as we positively know. This means that the individual is no longer a pure and passive product of its psyche and history and of the institution. In other words, the formation of a reflective and deliberative instance, that is, of true *subjectivity,* frees the radical imagination of the singular human being as source of creation and alteration and allows this being to attain an effective freedom. This freedom presupposes, of course, the indeterminacy of the psychical world as well as its permeability to meaning. But it also entails that the simply given meaning has ceased to be a cause (which is also always the case in the social-historical world) and that there is the effective possibility of the *choice of meaning* not dictated in advance. In other words, once formed, the reflective instance plays an active and not predetermined role in the deployment and the formation of meaning, whatever its source (be it the radical creative imagination of the singular being or the reception of a socially created meaning).[27] In turn, this presupposes again a specific psychical mechanism: to be autonomous implies that one has *psychically invested* freedom and the aiming at truth.[28] If such were not the case, one could not understand why Kant toiled over the *Critiques* instead of having fun with something else. And this psychical investment—"an empirical determination"—does not diminish in the least the possible validity of the ideas in the *Critiques,* the deserved admiration we feel

27. *MRT,* pp. 101–7; "The State of the Subject Today," *Thesis Eleven,* pp. 24–43.

28. "Epilegomena," in *Crossroads,* pp. 36–40.

toward the daring old man, the *moral* value of his endeavor. Because it neglects all these considerations, the "freedom" of the inherited philosophy is bound to remain a sheer fiction, a fleshless phantom, a *constructum* void of interest *fur̈ uns Menschen,* to use the same phrase Kant obsessively repeats.

The external side of the question throws us into the deepest waters of the social-historical ocean. I cannot be free alone; neither can I be free in each and every type of society. Here again we encounter philosophical self-delusion, exemplified this time by Descartes—though he is far from alone in this respect—when he pretends that he can forget he is sitting upon twenty-two centuries of interrogation and doubt and that he lives in a society where, for centuries, Revelation as well as naive faith by no means suffice any longer, since a "proof" of the existence of God is henceforth required by those who think, even if they believe.

The important point in this respect is not the existence or nonexistence of formal coercion ("oppression") but the inescapable internalization of the social institution, without which there can be no individuals. Freedom and truth cannot be objects of investment if they have not already emerged as social imaginary significations. Individuals aiming at autonomy cannot appear unless the social-historical field has already altered itself in such a way that it opens a space of interrogation without bounds (without an instituted or revealed truth, for instance). For someone to be able to find in him/herself the psychical resources and, in his environment the actual possibility, to stand up and say: "Our laws are unjust, our gods are false," a self-alteration of the social institution is required, and this can only be the work of the instituting imaginary. For instance, the statement: "The Law is unjust" is linguistically impossible, or at least absurd, for a classical Hebrew, since the Law is given by God and Justice is but one of the names and attributes of God. The institution must have changed to the point that it allows itself to be put into question by the collectivity it enables to exist and by the individuals belonging to it. But the concrete embodiment of the institution are those very same individuals who walk, talk, and act. It is therefore essentially with the same stroke that a new type of society and a new type of individual, each presupposing the other, must emerge, and do emerge, in Greece from the eighth century B.C. onward and in Western Europe from the twelfth to thirteenth centuries onward. No phalanx without hoplites, no hoplites without phalanx. No Archilochus capable of boasting, soon after 700 B.C., that in flight he threw away his shield and that little damage was done because he could always buy another one, without a society of warrior-citizens capable of honoring above all else both bravery and a poet who holds this quality up, for once, to derision.

The necessary simultaneity of these two elements during a social-historical alteration produces a state of affairs which is unthinkable from the point of view of the inherited logic of determinacy. How could one compose a free society unless free individuals are already available? And where could one find these individuals if they have not already been raised in freedom? (Could freedom be inherent in human nature? Why then has it been sleeping over millennia of despotism, whether oriental or otherwise?) But this apparent impossibility has been surmounted several times in actual history. In this we see, once more, the creative work of the instituting imaginary, as radical imaginary of the anonymous collectivity.

Thus, the inescapable internalization of the institution refers the individual to the social world. He who says that he wants to be free and, at the same time, proclaims his lack of interest in his society's institutions (or, another name for the same thing, in politics), should be sent back to grammar school. But the same link can also be established starting from the very meaning of *nomos,* of the law. To posit one's own law for oneself has meaning for certain dimensions of life only, and it is totally meaningless for many others: not only the dimensions along which I meet the others (I can reach an understanding with them, or fight them, or simply ignore them), but those along which I encounter society as such, the social law—the institution.

Can I say that I posit my own law when I am living, necessarily, under the law of society? Yes, if and only if I can say, reflectively and lucidly, that *this law is also mine.* To be able to say this, I need not approve of it; it is sufficient that I have had the effective possibility of participating actively in the formation and the implementation of the law.[29] If I accept the idea of autonomy *as such* (and not only because "it is good for me")—and this, obviously, no proof can force me to do, no more than any proof can force me to square my words with my deeds—then the existence of an indefinite plurality of individuals belonging to society entails immediately the idea of democracy defined as the effective possibility of equal participation of all in instituting activities as well as in explicit power. I will not delve here into the necessary reciprocal implication of equality and freedom when the two ideas are thought rigorously, nor into the sophistries by means of which, for a long time now, various people have tried to make the two terms appear antithetical.

And yet, we seem now to be back at square one, for the fundamental "power" in a society, the prime power upon which all the others depend, what I have already called the ground-power, is the *instituting power.* And unless one is under the spell of the "constitutional delusion," this power is neither locatable nor formalizable, for it pertains to the instituting imaginary. Language, family, mores, "ideas," "art," a host of social activities as well as their evolution are beyond the scope of legislation in their essential part. At most, to the degree that this power can be participated in, it is participated in by all. Everybody is, potentially, a coauthor of the evolution of language, of the family, of customs, and so on.

To make our ideas on this matter clear, let us revert for a moment to the Greek case and ask: What was the radical character of the political creation of the Greeks? The answer is twofold:

1. A part of the instituting power has been made explicit and has been formalized: this is the part concerning legislation properly speaking, public—"constitutional"—legislation as well as private law.

29. The speech of the Laws in the *Crito*—which I take to be a simple, though certainly admirable, transcription of the *Topoi* of the democratic thinking of the Athenians—says everything that there is to say about the matter: *e peithein e poiein a an keleuei* (51b), either persuade it (the country, the collectivity which posits the laws) or do that which it commands. The Laws add: you are always free to leave, with all that you possess (51 d–e), which, strictly speaking, is not the case in *any* modern "democratic" State.

2. Specific institutions were created in order to render the explicit part of power (including "political power" in the sense defined earlier) *open to participation*. This led to the equal participation of all the members of the body politic in the determination of *nomos*, of *dike* and of *telos*—of legislation, of jurisdiction, and of government. Rigorously speaking, there is no such thing as "executive power." (Its functions, which were in the hands of slaves in ancient Athens, are performed today by people acting more or less as "vocal animals," and they may one day be performed by machines.)

As soon as the question has been posed in these terms, politic*s* has absorbed, at least *de jure*, "*the*" politic*al*. The structure and the operation of explicit power have become, in principle and in fact, in Athens as well as in the European West, objects of collective deliberation and decision. This collectivity is self-posited and, *de facto* and *de jure*, *always necessarily self-posited*. But more than that, and much more importantly, the putting into question of the institution *in toto* became, potentially, radical and unbounded. When Cleisthenes reorganizes, for political purposes, the Athenian tribes, this can perhaps be laid to rest as ancient history. But we are supposed to be living in a republic. Presumably, therefore, we need a republican education. But where does "education"—republican or not—start, and where does it end? The modern emancipatory movements, notably the workers' movement but also the women's movement, have raised the question: Is democracy possible, is it possible for all those who want it to obtain the equal effective opportunity to participate in power, when they live in a society where tremendous inequalities of economic power, which are immediately translatable into political power, prevail? Or in a society where women, though granted some decades ago "political rights," continue in fact to be treated as "passive citizens"? Are the laws of property (whether private or "State-owned") and of sex God-given, where is the Sinai on which they have been delivered?

Politics is a project of autonomy. Politics is the reflective and lucid collective activity that aims at the overall institution of society. It pertains to everything in society that is participable and shareable.[30]

30. See the text cited in note 25.

De jure, this self-instituting activity does not take into account and does not recognize any limit (physical and biological laws are not of concern to us here). Nothing can escape its interrogation, nothing, in and of itself, stands outside its province.

But can we stop at that?

The Limits of Self-Institution and the Object of Politics

The answer is in the negative, both from the ontological point of view—before any *de jure* consideration—and from the political point of view—after all such considerations.

The ontological point of view leads to the most weighty reflections, ones which, however, are almost totally irrelevant from the political point of view. In all cases, the explicit self-institution of society will always encounter the bounds I have already mentioned. However lucid, reflective, willed it may be, the instituting activity of society and individuals springs from the instituting imaginary, which is neither locatable nor formalizable. Every institution, as well as the most radical revolution one could conceive of, must always take place within an already given history. Should it have the crazy project of clearing the ground totally, such a revolution still would have to use what it finds on the ground in order to make a clean sweep. The present, to be sure, always transforms the past into a *present past,* that is, a past relevant for the now, if only by continually "reinterpreting" it by means of that which is being created, thought, posited *now;* but it is always *that given past,* not a past in general, that the present shapes according to its own imaginary. Every society must project itself into a future which is essentially uncertain and risky. Every society must socialize the psyche of the human beings belonging to it; but the nature of this psyche imposes upon the modes and the content of this socialization constraints which are as indefinite as they are decisive.

These considerations carry tremendous weight—and no political relevance. The analogy with personal life is very strong—and this is no accident. I am making myself within a history which has always already made me. My most maturely reflected projects can be ruined in a second by what just happens. As long as I live, I must remain for myself one of the mightiest causes of astonishment and a puzzle not comparable to any other—because so near. I can—a task by no means easy—come to an understanding with my imagination, my affects, my desires; I cannot master them, and I ought not to. I ought to master my words and my deeds, a wholly different affair. And all these considerations cannot tell me anything of substance about what I ought to do—since I can do whatever I can do, but I ought not to do whatever crosses my mind. On the question: "What ought I to do?", the analysis of the ontological structure of my personal temporality does not help me in the least.

In the same way, the possibility for a society to establish another relationship between the instituting and the instituted is confined within bounds, which are at once indisputable and undefinable, by the very nature of the social-historical. But this tells us nothing about what we ought to will as the effective institution of the society in which we live. It is certain, for instance, that, as Marx remarked, "*le mort saisit le vif*"—the dead take hold of the living. But no politics can be drawn from that. The living would not be living if they were not in the hold of the dead—but neither would they be living if this hold were total. What can I infer from this concerning the relationship a society *ought to will* to establish with its past, in as far as this relationship is subject to willing? I cannot even say that a politics that would try to ignore the dead totally, and even to obliterate their memory, and thus a politics so contrary to the nature of things, would be "bound to fail" or "crazy"; its total self-delusion, its complete inability to attain its proclaimed aim, would not wipe it out of reality. To be crazy does not prevent one from existing. Totalitarianism has existed, it still exists, it still tries to reform the "past" according to the "present." Let us recall, in passing, that in this it has only pushed to the extreme, systematically and monstrously, an operation which everybody performs every second and which is done every day by the newspapers, the history books, and even the philosophers. And if you were to say that totalitarianism could not succeed because it is contrary to the nature of things (which here can only mean "to human nature"), you would only be mixing up the levels of discourse and positing as an essential necessity that which is a sheer fact. Hitler has been defeated, communism has not succeeded, for the time being. *That is all.* These are sheer facts, and the partial explanations one could supply for them, far from unveiling a transcendental necessity or a "meaning of history," also have to do only with sheer facts.

Things are different, from the political point of view and once we have accepted that we are unable to define on a principled basis nontrivial bounds for the explicit self-institution of society. For, *if* politics is a project of individual and social autonomy (these being two sides of the same coin), consequences of substantive import certainly do follow. To be sure, the project of autonomy has to be posited ("accepted," "postulated"). The idea of autonomy can be neither founded nor proved since it is presupposed by any foundation or proof. (Any attempt to "found" reflectiveness presupposes reflectiveness itself.) Once posited, it can be *reasonably argued for* and *argued about* on the basis of its implications and consequences. But it can also, and more importantly, be *made explicit.* Then, substantive consequences can be drawn from it, which give a *content,* albeit partial, to a politics of autonomy, but which also subject it to *limitations.* For, from this perspective, two requirements arise: to open the way as much as possible to the manifestation of the instituting imaginary; but, *equally important,* to introduce the greatest possible reflectiveness in our explicit instituting activity as well as in the exercise of explicit power. We must not forget, indeed, that the instituting imaginary *as such* as well as its works are neither "good" nor "bad"—or rather that, from the reflective point of view, they can be either the one or the other to the most extreme degree (the same being true of the imagination of the singular human being and its works). It is therefore necessary to shape institutions that make this collective reflectiveness effectively possible as well as to supply it with the adequate instruments. I will not delve here into the innumerable consequences that follow from these statements. And it is also necessary to give to all individuals the maximal effective opportunity to participate in any explicit power, and to ensure for them the greatest possible sphere of autonomous individual life. If we remember that the institution of society exists only insofar as it is embodied in its social individuals, we can evidently, on the basis of the project of autonomy, justify (found, if you prefer) "human rights," and much more. More importantly, we can also abandon the shallow discourses of contemporary "political philosophy," and, remembering Aristotle—for whom the law aims at the "creation of total virtue" by means of its prescriptions *peri paideian ten pros to koinon,* relative to the *paideia* pertaining to public affairs (civic education)[31]—understand that *paideia,* education from birth to death, is a central dimension of any politics of autonomy. We can then reformulate, by correcting it, the problem posed by Rousseau: "Some form of association must be found as a result of which the whole strength of the community will be enlisted for the protection of the person and property of each constituent member, in such a way that each, when united to his fellows, renders obedience to his own will, and remains as free as he was before."[32] No need to comment upon Rousseau's formula nor upon its heavy dependence upon a metaphysics of the individual–substance and its "properties." But here is the true formulation, the true object of politics:

> *Create the institutions which, by being internalized by individuals, most facilitate their accession to their individual autonomy and their effective participation in all forms of explicit power existing in society.*

This formulation will appear paradoxical only to those who believe in thunderlike freedom and in a free-floating being-for-itself disconnected from everything, including its own history.

It also becomes apparent—this is, in fact, a tautology—that autonomy is, *ipso facto, self-limitation.* Any limitation of democracy can only be, *de facto* as well as *de jure,* self-limitation.[33] This self-limitation can be more than and different from exhortation if it is embodied in the creation of free and responsible individuals. There are no "guarantees" for and of democracy other than relative and contingent ones. The least contingent of all lies in the *paideia* of the citizens, in the formation (always a *social* process) of individuals who have internalized both the necessity of laws and the possibility of putting the laws into question, of individuals capable of interrogation, reflec-

31. *Nicomachean Ethics* E, 4, 1130 b 4–5, 25–26.

32. Jean Jacques Rousseau, *The Social Contract,* bk. I, ch. 6. English translation taken from *Social Contract. Essays by Locke, Hume, Rousseau* (London and New York: Oxford University Press, 1948).

33. Castoriadis, "La Logique des magmas et la question de l'autonomie," in *Domaines,* pp. 417–18; also "The Greek *Polis* . . ." ch. 5 of this book, pp. 114–20.

tiveness, and deliberation, of individuals loving freedom and accepting responsibility.

Autonomy is, therefore, the project—and now we are adopting both the ontological and the political point of view—that aims:

- in the broad sense, at bringing to light society's instituting power and at rendering it explicit in reflection (both of which can only be partial); and
- in the narrow sense, at resorbing *the* politic*al,* as explicit power, into politic*s,* as the lucid and deliberate activity whose object is the explicit institution of society (and thus, also, of any explicit power), and its working as *nomos, dike, telos*—legislation, jurisdiction, government—in view of the *common ends* and the *public endeavors* the society deliberately proposes to itself.

Burgos, March 1978–Paris, June 1988

8

Reflections on "Rationality" and "Development"

Posing the Question

For some time now, "development" has been simultaneously the motto and theme of the official and "professional" ideology—as well as government policies. It is perhaps useful to recall briefly the genealogy of the notion.

Despite the ascerbic and bitter critique of those who opposed a triumphant capitalism, the nineteenth century glorified "progress."

Text of a lecture presented to the Figline-Valdarno Colloquium on "The Crisis of Development" (September 13–17, 1974). Originally written in English, translated into French by Mme. de Venoge and printed in this form in *Esprit* (May 1976), then published in *Le Mythe du développement,* ed. Candido Mendès (Paris: Seuil, 1977), a volume containing the proceedings of the colloquium, it was retranslated into English, in consultation with me, by John Murphy and published in *Thesis Eleven,* 10/11 (1984–85), pp. 18–36. The French version of this 1974 lecture that was published in my *Domaines de l'homme. Les Carrefours du labyrinthe II* (Paris: Seuil, 1986), pp. 131–54 includes my comments during a round-table discussion held two years later in Paris at the initiative of Jean-Marie Domenach; this discussion focused on "socialist models" of development, a topic which had hardly been broached at all at Figline-Valdarno (cf. now, *Le Mythe du développement,* pp. 111–40) and *Domaines,* pp. 155–74. I was thus led to restore some of the comments of the participants at the round-table discussion, without which what I said would have been incomprehensible; I thank them for their understanding, and I refer the interested reader to the full discussion found in the collective volume cited above. Translation of these comments by David Ames Curtis.

World War I and, after a short interlude, the Depression, the rise of Fascism and Nazism in Europe, and the obvious inevitability of another world war, all seemed to demonstrate that the system was ungovernable, and led to a collapse of the official ideology. The theme of the 1930s was "the crisis of progress."

In the postwar world, the great powers were above all and mostly preoccupied with reconstruction, and with the new problems created by the struggle between the United States and Russia. For the West, the success of economic reconstruction surpassed all hopes, beginning a long phase of expansion. When, with the end of the Korean war, Russo-American tensions seemed to be diminishing, and when, despite some bloody exceptions, the "colonial question" seemed to be being settled more or less peacefully, official minds began to dream that they had finally found the key to all human problems. That key was economic growth, which was easily achievable thanks to the new methods of demand regulation, and the rate of growth of gross national product (GNP) per capita, which contained the solution to all problems. True, a potential conflict with the East remained a threat; but the idea gained ground that, as these countries grew to industrial maturity and were invaded by consumerism, their masters would be induced to follow a less aggressive foreign policy and perhaps to introduce a degree of internal "liberalization." It was also true that hunger was (as it still is) a daily reality for a huge part of the population of the globe, and that the Third World had *not* achieved economic growth, or that its growth remained too feeble and too slow. But the reason for this was that the countries of the Third World had not "developed" themselves. The problem was thus one of developing them, or of making them develop themselves. So the official international terminology has been adjusted accordingly. These countries, formerly called, with a sincere brutality, "backward," and then "underdeveloped," were politely designated "less developed" and finally "developing countries"—a nice euphemism, signifying in fact that these countries had *not* developed themselves. As the official documents put it time and again, to develop them meant to make them capable of entering a stage of "self-sustaining growth."

But this new ideology was no sooner in place than it was attacked from several sides; the established system began being criticized not because it could not guarantee growth, nor because it distributed the "fruits of growth" unequally—traditional critiques of the left—but because it concerned itself *only* with growth and could deliver *only* growth—and growth of a given type, with a specific content, involving determinate human and social consequences. Limited initially to a confined circle of heterodox social and political thinkers, these critiques became widespread, in the space of a few years, among the young and began to influence the student movements of the 1960s as well as the actual behavior of various groups and individuals, who decided to give up the "rat race" and try to establish for themselves new forms of communal life. More and more pointedly, the question of the "price" which human beings and communities "paid" for growth was being raised. Almost simultaneously, it was "discovered" that this "price" contained a huge component which until then had been passed over in silence and whose consequences did not directly concern present generations. This additional cost factor was the massive and perhaps irreversible accumulation of damage inflicted upon the global biosphere as a result of the destructive and cumulative interaction of the effects of industrialization; effects triggering environmental reactions which, beyond a certain point, remain unknown and unforeseeable and which could eventually end in a catastrophic avalanche spinning out of all "control." From Venice sinking beneath the waters to the possibly imminent death of the Mediterranean; from the entrophication of lakes and rivers to the extinction of dozens of living species; from the silent spring to the possible melting of the polar icecaps; from the erosion of the Great Barrier Reef to the thousandfold multiplication of acidity in the rains—the immense actual or virtual consequences of unbridled "growth" and industrialization began to emerge. The "energy crisis" and the depletion of world resources arose at an appropriate time to remind humans that it was not even certain whether they could for much longer continue their destruction of the Earth.

As could have been foreseen, the powers that be reacted in a manner conforming to their natures. Since the system was being criticized for being solely preoccupied with quantities of goods and productive services, new bureaucratic organs were established to take care of the "quality of life." Since there seemed to be an environmental problem,

Ministries, Commissions, and international Conferences were organized to resolve it. Such organizations have indeed resolved efficiently some pressing problems, such as, for example, finding ministerial posts for politicians who had to be found a place without political importance, or inventing good reasons for maintaining or increasing the budgetary credits for various moribund or idle national and international organizations. Economists immediately detected a new and promising field for their delectable exercises in elementary algebra—without for one moment pausing to question their conceptual framework. Economic indices were supplemented with "social indices" or "indices of the quality of life," while new lines and columns were added to the matrices of interindustrial transactions. "Costs" and "returns," along with the potential impact of pollution control measures on the rate of growth of GNP, were the only angles from which the environmental question was discussed; while this impact was likely to be negative, it has been hopefully suggested that it might well be counterbalanced by the new growth of a "pollution control industry." Needless to say, the phrase "pioneering work in pollution control" has immediately taken a prominent place in the publicity of the main polluters, the giant industrial companies. The question which received the most earnest discussion was whether and how one could and should "internalize" the costs of pollution control.[1] The idea that the problem as a whole goes far beyond "costs" and "returns" did not so much as cross the minds of the economists and politicians.

Even the most "radical" reactions to have emerged from within the dominant strata have not, in reality, questioned the deepest premises of the official view. Since growth creates problems that are impossible to control, and, what is more, since all processes of exponential growth must inevitably run up against some physical limits sooner or later, the

---

1. Which is to say how was one to have these costs borne by the polluting firms rather than by the public (the State). "External economies" or "externalities" (positive or negative), which will be discussed again, comprise all the effects of a firm's activity on other firms and on society (as well as the effects of the activities of other firms, etc., on the given firm) which diminish or increase the costs of the firm considered. In the dominant economic conceptualization, the destruction of the environment appears—and can only appear—as an "external (negative) economy" resulting from the operations of the firm.

"radical" response has been "no growth" or "zero growth." No consideration has been given to the fact that, in the "developed" countries, growth and gadgets are all that the system can offer the people, and that to call a halt to growth was inconceivable (or could only be done with violent social upheavals) unless there were to be a radical transformation of social organization as a whole, including the psychic organization of men and women.

Nor were the dramatic international aspects of the question taken any more seriously. Should the gap be maintained between those countries with a GNP of $6,000 per capita per annum and those of only $200?[2] Would the latter accept the perpetuation of such a gap, given their pressing material needs, the "demonstration effect" continuously exercised on them by the example of the life-style of the rich countries, and, *last but not least,* given the politics of power and the desire for power among the ruling classes of all countries? (Is there any one single president of one single "developing" country who would not willingly sacrifice the lives of half his subjects in order to have his own nuclear bomb?) And if we should fill this gap, which is to say if, *grosso modo,* the entire population of the globe should be brought to a level of GNP per capita of $6,000 (at 1974 prices)—then how are we to reconcile the reasoning and conclusions underlying notions of "zero growth" with the tripling (and much more) of "gross world product" involved in such an equalization (a tripling requiring one more quarter century of world "growth" at a rate of four percent per annum, assuming a *static* population) and how are we to reconcile it with the ensuing indefinite continuation of a level of annual production around $25 trillion at 1970s values—that is, approximately, twenty-five times the current GNP of the United States and thus also some twenty-five times their present consumption of energy and raw materials? Finally, given existing social and political structures, would the "developed" countries accept becoming and remaining an impotent minority compared with the countries of Asia, Africa, and Latin America, equally "rich" and much more populous? (Would Russia tolerate the existence of a

2. These figures—roughly corresponding to the official statistical data for 1973 and 1974—have mainly an illustrative value, but they accurately represent the orders of magnitude of the variables in question.

China three times more powerful than herself? Would the United States accept a Latin America twice as strong as herself? As always, reformism pretends to realism, but when one comes to the crucial questions, it reveals itself as one of the most naive modes of wishful thinking.

The "Obstacles to Development"

Obviously, the questions discussed here are tightly bound up with the total social organization, as much at the national as the international level. Still more they are tied to the fundamental ideas and conceptions which have dominated and formed the life, action, and thought of the West for six centuries, and by means of which the West has conquered the world and would conquer it again even if it were to be materially destroyed. "Development," "economy" and "rationality" are only a few of the terms which one can use to indicate this complex of ideas and conceptions, of which the greatest part remain nonconscious, as much for politicians as for theorists.

Thus, almost nobody asks himself: What is "development," *why* "development," or "development" of *what* and *towards what?* As already indicated, the term "development" came into use when it became evident that "progress," "expansion" and "growth" were not intrinsic virtualities, inherent in all human societies, the realization (actualization) of which could be considered inevitable, but were specific properties of Western societies possessing a "positive value." Thus one could consider these societies as "developed," meaning by this that they were capable of producing "self-sustaining growth"; and the problem then seemed to consist simply in bringing the other societies to that famous stage of "take-off." So the West thought of itself, and proposed itself, as the model for the entire world. The normal state of a society, what one could consider as the state of "maturity" and designate with this apparently self-evident term, was the capacity for indefinite growth. Other countries or societies were considered to be naturally less mature or less developed, and their main problem was defined as the existence of "obstacles to development."

For some time, these obstacles were seen as purely "economic," and as negative in character; lack of growth was due to lack of growth—

which, for an economist, is not a tautology, since growth is a self-catalytic process (it suffices that a country enters into a process of growth for it to continue to grow more and more rapidly). Consequently, injections of foreign capital and the creation of "poles of development" were proposed as being necessary and sufficient conditions for bringing less developed countries to the stage of "take-off." In other words, the essential thing was to import and install machinery. Soon enough, one was compelled to discover that it is people who operate machines, and these people have to have suitable qualifications; and so "technical assistance," technical training, and the acquisition of professional qualifications became all the rage. But in the end, account had to be taken of the fact that machinery and qualified workers are not enough, and that a great many other things were "lacking." The people were not always and everywhere ready and able to give up all that they had been in order to become mere cogs in the process of accumulation—even when, gripped by famine, they "ought" to have done so. Something was going wrong with these "developing countries"; they had plenty of people who were not themselves "developing." In a quite natural and characteristic way, the "human factor" was equated with the absence of an "entrepreneurial class." This absence was profoundly regretted, but the economists had little advice to offer on how to proceed to develop such a class. And while the more cultivated among them had some vague memories relating to the Protestant ethic and the spirit of capitalism, they were not quite able to transform themselves from missionaries of growth to apostles of an inner-worldly asceticism.

And so it dawned upon the ruling strata that particular and separable "obstacles to development" did not exist, and that if the Third World was to "be developed," the social structures, attitudes, mentalities, significations, values, and psychic make-up of human beings would have to be changed. Economic growth was not something that could be "added" to these countries, as the economists had thought; nor could it simply be superimposed upon their other characteristics. If these countries were to "be developed" they would have to undergo a total transformation. The West had to assert not that it had discovered the trick of producing more cheaply and more quickly more commodities, but that it had discovered *the* way of life appropriate to all human society. Fortunately for the Western ideologues, the unease they could have felt on this score was allayed by the haste with which the "developing" nations tried to adopt the Western "model" of society—even if its economic "basis" was missing. By the same token, it was unfortunate for them that the crisis of "development policies," in a real but limited sense, the failure of "development" in the "developing" countries, has coincided with a much greater and deeper crisis in their own societies, with the internal collapse of the Western model and of all the ideas which it embodied.

"Development" As Social Imaginary Signification

What is development? An organism develops when it progresses toward its biological maturity. We develop an idea when we explicate as far as possible what we think it implicitly "contains." In short, development is a process of realization of the virtual, of the movement from *dunamis* to *energeia,* from *potentia* to *actus.* Obviously this implies that there is an *energeia* or *actus* which we can determine, define, assess, that there *is* a norm pertaining to the essence of what is developing; or, as Aristotle would say, that this essence *is* the becoming-adequate [*le devenir-conforme*] to a norm defined by a "final" form: the *entelecheia.*

In this sense, development entails the definition of "maturity," and beyond this, the definition of a *natural norm:* development is only another name for the Aristotelian *physis.* For nature contains its own norms, as *ends* toward which beings develop and which they effectively attain. "Nature is an end (*telos*)," said Aristotle. Development is defined by the fact of attaining this end, as the natural norm of the being considered. In this sense also, development was a central idea for the Greeks—and not only as regards plants, animals, and humans as simply living beings. *Paideia* (upbringing, training, education) is development; it consists of bringing the newborn little monster to the fit state of a human being. If this is possible, it is because such a fit state *exists,* as a norm, a limit (*peras*), a norm embodied in the citizen, or the *kalos kagathos,* which, if attained, *cannot* be exceeded (to exceed such norms would simply be to relapse). "Now die, Diagoras, for you will not ascend Olympus." How and on what basis could such a fit state be determined once the constitution of the *polis* (which defines the norm of development of individual citizens) has been questioned and perceived in its relative character; in what sense can one say that there is a *physis* of the *polis,* a fit state unique to the city? For the Greek philosophers, such a question necessarily had to remain an obscure point at the frontier of their thinking, despite or because of their constant preoccupation with the *dikaiosune* or *orthe politeia.* Similarly, and for the same deep-seated reasons, *techne* remained undefined, hovering somewhere between the simple imitation of nature (*mimesis*) and creation properly speaking (*poiesis*)—between the repetition of an already given norm and, as Kant put it twenty-five centuries later, the actual positing of a new norm embodied in the work of art.[3]

The limit (*peras*) defines simultaneously being and norm. Unlimitedness, infinity, the without-end (*apeiron*) is obviously incomplete, imperfect, a lesser-being. Thus, for Aristotle, there is only a virtual infinity, not an actual infinity; and reciprocally, inasmuch as any object contains unrealized virtualities, it is infinite, since it is, by the same token, incomplete, undefined, indeterminate. So it is not possible to have development without a reference point, a defined state which must be attained; and nature furnishes, for any being, such a "final" state.

With the Judeo-Christian religion and theology the notion of unlimitedness, of a without-ending, of infinity, acquired a positive sign—but one which remained, in a way, without social or historical relevance for over ten centuries. The infinite God is elsewhere, and *this* world is finite; there is for each being an intrinsic norm corresponding to its nature as it has been determined by God.

The transformation occurs when infinity invades *this* world. It would be ludicrous to attempt to compress here, within a few lines, the immense mass of well-known historical facts, some of them less well-known than we think, covering so many countries and centuries. I will attempt only to reassemble some of them into a particular perspective,

3. For a fuller discussion, see my "Value, Equality, Justice, Politics: From Marx to Aristotle and from Aristotle to Ourselves," in Cornelius Castoriadis, *Crossroads in the Labyrinth,* tr. Martin H. Ryle and Kate Soper (Brighton: Harvester, and Cambridge, Mass.: M.I.T., 1984). See also *The Imaginary Institution of Society,* tr. Kathleen Blamey (Oxford: Polity Press, and Cambridge, Mass.: M.I.T., 1987), pp. 196–98.

discarding the usual "rational" explanations/justifications of their succession (explanations and justifications which are, of course, a self-"rationalization" of Western rationalism, trying to prove that there are rational reasons explaining and justifying the triumph of the particular variety of "Reason" seen in the West).

What is of importance here is the "coincidence" and convergence which one can ascertain, beginning from, let us say, the fourteenth century, between the birth and expansion of the bourgeoisie, the obsessive and growing interest prompted by discoveries and inventions, the progressive collapse of the medieval representation of the world and of society, the Reformation, the transition "from the closed world to the infinite universe," the mathematization of the sciences, the perspective of an "indefinite progress of knowledge," and the idea that the correct use of Reason is the necessary and sufficient condition for us to become the "masters and possessors of Nature" (Descartes).

It would be uninteresting, and senseless, to try to explain "causally" the rise of Western rationalism by the expansion of the bourgeoisie, or the converse. We must consider the emergence of the bourgeoisie, its expansion and final victory in parallel with the emergence, propagation, and final victory of a new "idea," the idea that the unlimited growth of production and of the productive forces is *in fact* the central objective of human existence. This "idea" is what I call a *social imaginary signification*.[4] To it correspond new attitudes, values, and norms, a new social definition of reality and of being, of what *counts* and what does *not* count. In a nutshell, henceforth what counts is whatever can be counted. On the other hand, the philosophers and scientists apply a new and specific twist to thought and knowledge; there are no limits to the powers and possibilities of Reason, and Reason *par excellence* is mathematics, at least insofar as the *res extensa* is concerned: *Cum Deus calculat, fit mundus* (As God calculates, the world is being made—Leibniz). We should not forget that Leibniz equally cherished the dream of a calculus of ideas.

The marriage—probably incestuous—of these two currents gives birth, in diverse ways, to the modern world. It is revealed in the "ra-

4. Cf. *Institution, op. cit.*

tional application of science to industry" (Marx)—as much as in the (rational?) application of industry to science. It is expressed in all ideologies of "progress." Since there are no limits to the march of knowledge, there are no more limits to the march of our "power" (and of our "wealth"); or, to put it another way, limitations, where they present themselves, have a negative value and must be transcended. Certainly, whatever is infinite is inexhaustible, so that we will perhaps never achieve "absolute" knowledge and "absolute" power; but we ceaselessly draw nearer to them. From this comes the curious notion of an "asymptotic" march of knowledge toward an absolute truth which is, even today, still shared by the majority of scientists. Thus, there cannot be a fixed reference point to our "development," a defined and definitive state to be attained; this "development" is nevertheless a movement with a fixed *direction,* and of course, the movement itself can be measured along an axis upon which we occupy at every instant an abscissa of increasing value. In short, the movement is directed to more and more; more commodities, more years to live, more decimal points in the numerical values of universal constants, more scientific publications, more people with PhDs—and "more" is "better." "More" of something positive and, of course, algebraically, "less" of something "negative." (But what *is* positive or negative?)

Thus we reach the present situation. Historical and social development lies in starting out from *any* defined state, and in attaining a state which is defined by nothing except the capacity to attain new states. The norm is that there are no norms. Historical and social development is an unfolding which is indefinite, infinite, and without end (in both senses of the word *end*). And as far as we find the indefinite unbearable, definiteness is provided by the growth of quantities.

I repeat: I am not trying to compress centuries of thought and events into a few lines. But I argue that there is a layer of historical truth which can only be represented by the bizarre cross section attempted here, traversing Leibniz, Henry Ford, IBM, and the activities of some unknown "planner" in Uganda or Kazakhstan, who has never heard of Leibniz. Obviously, most philosophers and historians would severely criticize such a bird's-eye view. But we must renounce the spectacle of the valleys and the scent of the flowers if we want to "see" that the Alps and the Himalayas belong to the "same" mountain chain.

Ultimately, then, development has come to signify an indefinite growth, and maturity, capacity to grow without end. Thus understood, as ideologies, but also at a deeper level, as social imaginary significations, they were and are consubstantial with a group of (theoretical and practical) "postulates," of which the most important seem to be: (1) the virtual "omnipotence" of technique; (2) the "asymptotic illusion" relating to scientific knowledge; (3) the "rationality" of economic mechanisms; and (4) various assumptions about humanity and society, which have changed with time but which all imply either that humanity and society are "naturally" predestined to progress, growth, etc. (*homo economicus,* the "invisible hand," liberalism[5] and the virtues of free competition), or—what is much more appropriate to the essence of the system—that they can be manipulated by various means in order to be led to progress, growth, etc. (*homo madisoniensis Pavlovi,* "human engineering" and "social engineering," bureaucratic organization and planning as universal solutions applicable to any problem).

The crisis of development is obviously also the crisis of these "postulates" and of their corresponding imaginary significations; which is simply to say that the institutions which embody these imaginary significations in actual reality undergo a brutal shake-up. (The term "institution" is used here in the broadest possible sense: in the sense, for example, in which language is an institution, as is arithmetic, the ensemble of implements within society, the family, law, "values.") This shake-up, in turn, is essentially due to the struggle which those living under the system carry on against the system—which is to say that the imaginary significations referred to are accepted less and less within society. This is the principal aspect of the "crisis of development," which I am not able to go into here.[6] But these "postulates" also

5. Here and elsewhere "liberalism" is to be taken in the Continental sense. In American terms "conservative individualism" is what is intended. [1989 note]

6. See my works, *La Société bureaucratique,* 2 vols. and *L'Expérience du mouvement ouvrier,* 2 vols. (Paris: 10/18, 1973 and 1974). [*La Société bureaucratique,* 2d ed. in 1 vol. (Paris: Christian Bourgois, 1990).] Many of these articles now appear in my *Political and Social Writings,* tr. David Ames Curtis, 2 vols. (Minneapolis: University of Minnesota Press, 1988).

collapse in and by themselves. I will attempt to illustrate briefly this situation in the course of discussing some aspects of economic "rationality" and the "omnipotence" of technique.[7]

The Fiction of An Economic "Rationality"

Perhaps it is not difficult to understand why it is that the economy has for two centuries been considered as the realm and paradigm of "rationality" in human affairs. Its subject matter is what has become the central activity of society, its discourse to prove (and for opponents like Marx, to disprove) the idea that this activity is achieved in the best possible manner in the framework of, and by means of the existing social system. But also—by a happy "accident"—the economy provided the apparent possibility of mathematization, since it is the only field of human activity where phenomena appear to be measurable in a manner which is not trivial, and even where this "measurability" seems to be—and to a certain extent is—the essential aspect in the eyes of the human agents concerned. The economy deals in "quantities"; on this point the economists have always fallen into line (though from time to time they have been forced to discuss the question: Quantities of *what?*). So, economic phenomena seem to lend themselves to an "exact" treatment and one which is amenable to the application of mathematical tools, the tremendous effectiveness of which has been demonstrated day after day in physics.

Within this domain, identifying the maximum (or extremum) and the optimum seems the obvious thing to do—and it has quickly been done. There was a product to maximize, and costs to minimize. Thus there was a difference to maximize: the net saleable product for the firm, the net "surplus" for the overall economy ("surplus" appearing under the guise of "goods" or of the growth in "leisure" measured in

7. I have discussed elsewhere some aspects of the problem of modern science understood as an "asymptotic illusion": "*Le Monde morcelé,*" *Textures,* 4/5 (1972), subsequently expanded as "*Science moderne et interrogation philosophique,*" *Encyclopaedia Universalis,* vol. 17 (Paris: Organum, 1974); now in *Crossroads in the Labyrinth, op. cit.,* pp. 145–226.

"free time," without consideration of the use or content of this "free time").

But what is the "product," and what are the "costs"? Nuclear bombs are included in the net product—because the economist "is not concerned with use values." Equally included are the costs of publicity, by means of which the people are induced to buy the junk which otherwise they probably would not buy; and of course, this junk itself. There are also the expenses accrued from having Paris cleaned of industrial soot; and for every road accident, the net national product is increased on several scores. It is equally augmented every time that a firm decides to nominate an extra vice-president drawing a substantial salary (because, *ex hypothesi,* the firm would not have nominated him if his net marginal product was not at least equal to his salary). More generally, the "measure" of a product reflects the valuations of various objects and of various types of work performed in the existing social system—valuations which themselves, of course, in their turn reflect the existing social structure. GNP is what it is *also* because a business manager earns twenty times what a street-sweeper earns. But even if these valuations are accepted, the measurability of economic phenomena, trivialities apart, is only a misleading appearance. The "product," on any definition, is measurable "instantaneously," in the sense that one can always add up, for the whole of the economy and at a given moment, the quantity of produced goods multiplied by the corresponding prices. But if the relative prices and/or the composition of the goods changes (which, in fact, is always the case) the successive "measurements" taken at different moments in time cannot be compared (any more than they can be compared between different countries, for the same reason). Strictly speaking, the expression "growth in GNP" is nonsense, except, and only, in the fictional case where there is a similar expansion in all types of products. Particularly, in an economy undergoing technical change, "capital" cannot be measured in any way which makes sense, except by means of ad hoc hypotheses which are highly artificial and contrary to the facts.

All this immediately leads to the conclusion that it is equally impossible to really measure "costs" (since the "costs" for one are for the most part the "products" of another). There are other reasons why "costs" cannot be measured: because we cannot apply the classical idea of *imputing* one part of the net product to this or that "factor of production," and/or this product to this arrangement of the means of production. Imputing parts to "factors of production" (labor and capital) involves postulates and decisions which largely go beyond the domain of the economy. Imputing costs to a given product cannot be done because of various types of indivisibility (which the classical and neoclassical economists treat as exceptions, though they are present everywhere), and because of the existence of all sorts of "externalities." "Externalities" signify that the "cost for the firm" and the "cost for the economy" do not coincide, and that a nonattributable (positive or negative) surplus appears. What is even more important, these "externalities" are not confined within the economy as such.

We are accustomed to think of most of the environment (its totality, with the exception of land under private ownership) as a "free gift of nature." Similarly, the social framework, general learning, the behavior and motivations of individuals are implicitly treated as "free gifts of history." The environmental crisis has only made obvious something which was always true (as Liebig knew over a century ago): an "appropriate state" of the environment is *not* a "free gift of nature" in all circumstances and without regard to the type and to the expansion of the economy considered. Nor is it a "good" to which one can assign a "price" (real or "dual")—since, for example, no one knows the cost of refreezing the polar icecaps, should they melt. And the case of non-"developing" countries shows that we cannot treat Judaism, Christianity, and Shintoism as "free gifts of history"—since history made a "gift" to other peoples of Hinduism and fetishism, which up till now appear rather as "obstacles to development," given freely by history.

Behind all this can be found the hidden hypothesis of *total separability,* as much *within* the domain of economics as *between* this domain and historical, social, and even natural processes. Political economy always supposes that it is possible, without absurdity, to separate the consequences of action X of firm A from the total flux of economic processes internal and external to the firm; as it also supposes that the effects of the presence or absence of a given "total" of "capital" and of "labor" can be separated from the rest of human and natural life in a meaningful fashion. But the moment we abandon this hypothesis the notion of an economic calculus, in other than a trite sense, collapses—and with it, the notion of economic "rationality" in the accepted sense of the term (as the achievement of an extremum or a family of extrema) as much at the theoretical level (the comprehension of facts) as at the practical level (the definition of an "optimal" political economy).

What is at stake here is not simply the "market economy" or "private capitalism," but the "rationality," in the sense just indicated, of the economy as such (of any expanding economy). This is because the ideas underpinning what I have just said apply as much to "nationalized" and "planned" economies, literally or *mutatis mutandis*.

To illustrate this last point, I will use another example, which touches upon the fundamental question of *time*. Time is taken into account in political economy only inasmuch as it can be treated as non-time, as a neutral and homogeneous medium. An expanding economy implies the existence of ("net") investment, and investment is intimately related to time, since in investment the past, the present, and the future are brought into mutual relation. Now, decisions concerning investment can never be "rational," except at the level of the firm and providing one takes a particularly narrow point of view. There are many reasons for this, of which I will mention only two. First, not only is the future "uncertain," but *the present is unknown* (things are constantly happening everywhere, other firms are in the process of making decisions, information is partial and costly, and this to different degrees for different actors, etc.). Second, as already mentioned, the costs and the product cannot really be measured. The first factor may, in theory, be eliminated in a "planned" economy; the second could never be.

But, in any case, a much more important question arises: What is the correct *overall* rate of investment? Should society devote to ("net") investment 10, 20, 40, or 80 percent of the ("net") product? The classical response, for "private" economies, was that "the" interest rate constitutes the balancing factor between the supply and demand of savings, and is consequently the appropriate "regulator" of the rate of investment. As we know, this response is pure nonsense. ("The" interest rate does not exist; it is not possible to assume that the rate of interest is the main determinant of total savings, that price levels are stable, etc.) Von Neumann proved, in 1934, that, given certain hypotheses, the "rational" interest rate must be equal to the rate of growth of the economy. But what *should* the rate of growth be? Supposing that this rate of growth is a function of productive capacity, and knowing that this rate depends upon the rate of investment, we arrive back at the original question: What should the rate of investment be? We can make the additional hypothesis that the "planners" are set on maximizing "final consumption" for a given period. The question then becomes: What is the rate of investment which will maximize (under complementary hypotheses about the "physical productivity" of additional capital) in a "permanent" or "steady state" the integral of "final consumption" (be it individual or public, of "goods" or of "leisure")? The value of this integral depends, of course, upon the interval of integration—which is to say, upon the temporal horizon which the "planners" have decided to take into account. If it is "instantaneous" consumption that is to be maximized (temporal horizon at zero distance) then the appropriate rate of investment is obviously zero. If consumption to be maximized is "forever" (temporal horizon at infinite distance) the appropriate rate of investment is nearly 100 percent of ("net") product—assuming that the "marginal physical productivity" remains positive for all corresponding values of investment. Any answer which "makes sense" obviously lies between these two limits; but where exactly, and *why?* No "rational calculus" exists which can show that a temporal horizon of 5 years is (for society) less or more "rational" than one of 100 years. The decision would have to be made on the basis of considerations other than "economic" ones.

All this does not mean that everything that happens within the economy is "irrational" in the positive sense, still less that it is unintelligible; but it means that we cannot treat an economic process as a homogeneous flux of values, of which the only relevant aspect would be that they can be measured and ought to be maximized. *This* type of "rationality" is secondary and subordinate. We can make use of it in order to clear part of the terrain, to scotch some obvious absurdities. But the factors which today effectively fashion reality—among them, the decisions of governments, of firms, and of individuals—are not susceptible to this sort of treatment. And, in a new, alternative society, they would be of a completely different nature.

Modern Technique as Vehicle for the Illusion of Omnipotence

The question of technique has long been treated from within one or another of successive mythic frameworks. At first, "technical progress" was, of course, good and nothing but good. Then technical progress became good "in itself," but utilized badly (or for evil) by the existing social system; in other words, technique was considered as a pure means, in itself neutral as to ends. This remains, to this day, the position taken by scientists, liberals, and Marxists; for example, there is nothing to be said against modern industry as such, what is at fault is that it is utilized for the profit and/or power of a minority, rather than for the well-being of all. This position rests upon two intertwined fallacies: the fallacy of the total separability of means and ends, and the composition fallacy. The fact that we can use steel to make either ploughs or guns does *not* mean that the total system of machines and techniques existing today could be used, indifferently, to "serve" either an alienated or an autonomous society. Neither ideally nor in reality is it possible to separate the technological system of a society from what this society *is*. And today, we have more or less come to the exact opposite position of the initial one: more and more people believe that technique is an evil in itself.

We must try to fathom the question more deeply. The unconscious illusion of the "virtual omnipotence" of technique, the illusion which has dominated the modern epoch, rests upon another idea, concealed and not discussed: the idea of *power*. Once this is understood it is obvious that it is not enough to simply ask: Power to do *what*, power for *whom?* The question is: What is power, and even, in what meaningful sense can there ever really *be* power?

Behind the notion of power lurks the fantasy of total control, of our will or desire mastering all objects and all circumstances. Doubtless, this fantasy has always been present in human history, either "materialized" in magic, etc., or projected onto some divine image. But, curiously enough, there has also always been a consciousness of certain limits forbidden to humanity—as is shown in the myth of the Tower of Babel, or in Greek *hubris*. Everybody obviously agrees that the idea of total control, or total mastery, is intrinsically absurd. Nevertheless, the idea of total mastery *remains* the hidden motor of modern technological development. The blatant absurdity of the idea of total mastery is camouflaged behind the less obvious absurdity of an "asymptotic progression." Humanity in the West has lived for centuries with the implicit postulate that it is always possible and feasible to achieve more power. The fact that, in some particular domain, and to some particular end, we have been able to do "more," has been taken to signify that in all domains taken together and for all imaginable ends, "power" can be extended without limit.

As we now know for certain, the fragments of successively conquered "power" remain always localized, limited, insufficient, and, most probably, intrinsically inconsistent if not downright incompatible with each other. No major technical "conquest" can escape the possibility that it will be used other than originally intended, none is devoid of "undesirable" side effects, none can avoid interfering with the rest—in any case, none of those which result from the type of technique and science which *we* have "developed." In this sense, *increased "power" is also, ipso facto, increased powerlessness or even "anti-power," a power giving rise to the contrary of that which was the original aim;* and who is to calculate the final balance sheet, in what terms, on what hypotheses, and for what time horizon?

Here again, the illusion operates on the basis of the idea of separability. To "control" things consists of isolating separate factors and precisely circumscribing the "effects" of their action. This works, up to a certain point, with the ordinary objects of everyday life; that is how we go about repairing the engine of a car. But the further we go, the clearer it becomes that separability is only a "working hypothesis" with localized and limited validity. Modern physicists are beginning to realize the true state of things; they suspect that the apparently insurmountable impasses in theoretical physics are due to the idea that there exist things such as separate and singular "phenomena," and they are asking themselves if the Universe should not be considered primarily as a unique and unified entity.[8] In another way, ecological problems force us to recognize a similar situation as regards technique. Here also, beyond certain limits, we cannot think that separability

8. Cf. the excellent articles of Wigner, d'Espagnat, Zeh, and Bohm in *Foundations of Quantum Mechanics,* ed. d'Espagnat (New York and London: Academic Press, 1971).

goes without saying; and these limits remain unknown until the moment when a catastrophe threatens.

Pollution and the devices designed to combat it provide a prime example—easy, and easily contestable. For more than twenty years, antipollution devices have been installed on the chimneys of factories, and the like, to trap carbon particles contained in the smoke. These devices proved to be very effective, and actually the atmosphere around industrial cities contains a good deal less carbon dioxide than before. Yet, during the same period, the acidity of the atmosphere has multiplied a thousandfold and the rain falling on certain parts of Europe and North America today [1974] is as acidic as "pure lemon juice"—leading to serious effects on forest growth, already observable—because the sulphur contained in the smoke, which was previously fixed by the carbon, is now freely released and combines with oxygen and hydrogen in the atmosphere to form acids.[9] The fact that the engineers, the men of science, and the administrations should not have thought in advance that this would happen may seem ridiculous: this does not make it any less true. Their response would be: "Next time we will know and do better." Maybe.

Let us now consider the question of the contraceptive pill. The discussions and anxieties about its possible undesirable side effects have been centered on whether women using it would be susceptible to putting on weight or to contracting cancer. Let us grant for the moment that such effects do not exist, or that they can be countered. But let us also be brave enough to admit that these aspects of the problem are microscopic. Let us put aside that which is perhaps the most important aspect of the pill, the psychical aspect, of which nobody talks: What might happen to human beings should they begin to see themselves as absolute masters over the decision to bequeath or not bequeath life, without having to pay a thing for this "power" (beyond two dollars a month)? And what might happen to human beings if they cut themselves off from their animal condition and destiny, in relation to the production of the species? I am not saying that "ill" will necessarily come of it. I am saying that everyone considers it as self-evident that this supplementary

---

9. *International Herald Tribune,* 14 June 1974.

"power" can be nothing but "good"—or even simply, that it *is* really "power." Let us come now to the strictly biological aspect. The pill is "effective" because it interferes with fundamental regulatory processes, deeply tied to the most important functions of the organism, of which we "know" practically nothing. So with regard to its eventual effects, the relevant question is not: What can happen to a woman if she takes the pill for ten years? The relevant question is: What would happen to the species, if women took the pill for 1,000 generations, that is to say, for 25,000 years? This corresponds to an experiment on a strain of bacteria *for about three months*. Now obviously 25,000 years is for us a "meaningless" time span. Consequently, we act as if not caring about the possible results of what we are doing were "meaningful." In other words, given linear time and an infinite temporal horizon, we act as if the only significant interval of time was the very near future.

In the country of my birth, my grandparents' generation had heard nothing of long-term planning, of externalities, of the continental drift, or the expansion of the Universe. Yet, even into their old age, they continued to plant olive trees and cypresses, without considering costs or returns. They knew that they would die, and that they should leave the Earth in good order for those who would come after them, perhaps simply for the Earth itself. They knew that whatever "power" they had at their disposal could only produce beneficial results if they obeyed the seasons, paid heed to the winds, and respected the unpredictable Mediterranean, if they pruned the trees at the right moment and allowed the year's vintage sufficient time to mature. They did not think in terms of the infinite—perhaps they would not have understood the meaning of the word; but they acted, lived, and died in a time which was truly *without end*. Obviously, the country was not yet developed.

Concluding Questions

It so happened that, on this planet, and in the course of billions of years, a balanced biosystem made up of millions of different living species has unfolded, and that, for some hundreds of thousands of years, human societies have succeeded in creating for themselves a material and mental habitat, a biological and metaphysical niche, by changing the environment without damaging it. Despite misery, ignorance, exploitation, superstition, and cruelty, these societies managed to create for themselves at the same time both well-adapted modes of living and coherent worlds of imaginary significations of astounding richness and variety. If we look at the life of the thirteenth century, passing from Chartres to Borobudur and from Venice to the Mayas, from Constantinople to Peking and from Kublai Khan to Dante, from the house of Maimonides at Cordoba to Nara, and from the *Magna Carta* to the Byzantine monks copying Aristotle; compare this extraordinary diversity with the present state of the world, where countries are not really different from each other in terms of their present—which, as such, is everywhere *the same*—but only in terms of their past. *That* is what the developed world *is*.

The uses of the past are limited, however. Despite the sympathy one can feel for modern-day "back-to-nature" movements, and for what they are trying to express, it would obviously be illusory to think that we could reestablish a "preindustrial" society, or that those who presently hold power would spontaneously give it up if they found themselves confronted with a hypothetical desertion growing within industrial society. These movements are themselves caught in contradictions. There is scarcely any "commune" without taped music; and a tape recorder implies the totality of modern industry.

It would be equally disastrous to misunderstand, misinterpret, or underestimate what the Western world has brought. Through and beyond its industrial and scientific creations, and the corresponding impact on society and nature, it has destroyed the idea of *physis* in general and its application to human affairs in particular. The West did this by means of a "theoretical" and "practical" interpretation and realization of "Reason"—a specific interpretation and realization, pushed to their limit. At the end of this process, it has come to the point where there is no longer, and can no longer be, any reference point or fixed state, any "norm."

Insofar as this situation induces the vertigo of an "absolute freedom," it could cause a plunge into absolute slavery. Already, the West is a slave to the idea of absolute freedom. Freedom, perceived in the past as "the consciousness of necessity" or as the assumption of a capacity to act in accordance with a pure ethical norm, has become naked freedom, freedom as pure arbitrariness (*Willkur*). Absolute arbitrariness is the absolute void: the void must be filled, and it is filled, with "quantities." But the endless growth of quantities has its end—not only from an external point of view, since the Earth is finite, but from an internal point of view, because "more" and "greater" are henceforth no longer "different," and "more" becomes qualitatively *indifferent*. (Qualitatively, a growth in GNP of 5 percent signifies that the economy is in the same state as the year before; people calculate their condition as having worsened if their "standard of living" has not been raised, and do not calculate that it has been raised if this "standard" only goes up by the "normal" amount.) Aristotle and Hegel knew all this perfectly well. But, as is often the case, reality catches up with thought only after a considerable time lag.

However, barring a religious, mystic, or irrational backlash of some sort—which is improbable, but not impossible—the main result of this destruction of the idea of *physis* cannot henceforth be conjured away. For it is true that man is not a "natural" being—though he is not a "rational" animal either. For Hegel, man was "a sick animal." Rather, we must say that man is a mad animal who, by means of his madness, invented reason. Being a mad animal, he naturally made of his invention, reason, the most methodical expression and instrument of his madness. We can now see this, because it has taken place.

To what extent can this knowledge help us in our present plight? Very little, and very much. Very little, because the transformation of the current state of world society is not a matter of knowledge, of theory, or of philosophy. Very little also because we cannot reject reason—any more than we can freely separate "reason *qua* reason" from its actual historical realization. We would be mad to think, in our turn, that reason could be considered as an "instrument" which could be assigned to better use. A culture is not a menu from which we can chose what we like and ignore all the rest.

But this knowledge could help us very much if it enables us to renounce and destroy the rationalist ideology, the illusion of omnipotence, the supremacy of the economic "calculus," the absurdity and incoherence of the "rational" organization of society, the new religion of "science," and the idea of development for development's sake. This we could do if we do not renounce thought and responsibility, if we view reason and rationality in an appropriate perspective, if we are capable of recognizing them as historical creations of humanity.

For, the existing crisis is advancing toward a point where, either we will be confronted with a natural or social catastrophe or, before or after this, human beings will react in one way or another and try to establish new forms of social life making sense to them. We cannot do this for them, or in their place, any more than we can say how it could be done. What we can do is destroy the myths which, more than money or weapons, constitute the most formidable obstacles in the way of the reconstruction of human society.

Reflections on "Rationality" and "Development": *Presentation and Response to Critics*

First of all, let me remark on Candido Mendès's talk about Domenach's "imperial language" and about the "absence of language" among barbarians.[1] Such talk reminds me of a beautiful poem of Cavafis's entitled, in fact, *The Barbarians*. Having learned that the barbarians were going to arrive that very day, the townspeople of an Imperial city gathered in the Forum; they awaited the arrival of the barbarians, hoping that, at last, something was going to lift them out of their boredom, their *mal de siècle*. For the occasion, the consuls and praetors wore their embroidered togas and their most beautiful jewelry; it is fair to assume that the old men were expecting to be slaughtered and the women to be raped. But the day passed, night began to fall and, suddenly, the crowd scattered in malaise and confusion. For messagers had just arrived from the frontier to announce that the barbarians were no longer in the area. "And now, what will become of

1. After Jean-Marie Domenach made his oral presentation, Candido Mendès, one of the colloquium's organizers, reproached him for having adopted an "imperial language" vis-à-vis the "marginality of barbarians" and "that of the periphery."

This oral presentation to the colloquium is followed by my responses to some remarks formulated by other participants during the discussion period. The reader can easily reconstitute the content of these remarks from my responses.

us, without barbarians? These people were, in a way, a solution." These are the last two lines of the poem.

If I, too, were waiting for the barbarians—which is not the case—I would have to say that I do not see them—not here, in any case. I see only Candido Mendès, whom I am unable to distinguish from an ultradecadent Westerner, and who, by means of a language whose preciosity rests upon forty centuries of culture and all of whose resources he learnedly exploits, flatters himself by posing as a barbarian—which is obviously a "civilized" idea. But let us suppose that there are some barbarians around and that they were to present themselves to us here. What could we do? Either the barbarians really want to cut our throats, in which case the only question that would arise is that of the relation of forces—they slaughter us or we slaughter them—or else discussion is possible, and in that case one must obey certain rules for the use of language, seeking in this discussion not victory via violence, via the violence of one's discourse, but the elucidation of questions. And "civilization" is nothing other than that.

Candido Mendès was gently teasing Domenach about the West, and Domenach responded that he really thought that, in a certain sense, the West possessed a kind of superiority. For my part, I reject these terms (while noting that those who claim to be barbarians are in fact speaking a Western language). There is *one* peculiarity to the West of import for us; Western culture (Greco-Western, since this begins at least with Herodotus) is the only one to have taken an interest in the existence of other cultures, to have interrogated itself about them and, finally, to have put itself in question, to have relativized itself in terms of this knowledge bearing on other cultures. This is what the Greco-Westerners have done—and it is starting from this that we think. If today we can discuss the problem of development as a world problem—that is to say, one of interest to all those who live on this planet, independent of the particular culture to which they belong—it is thanks to this; this is, indeed, the *de facto* and *de jure* condition for our discussion. Beyond this, there is, in my view, no superiority, nor inferiority to the West. There is simply a fact: namely that the Earth has been unified by means of Western violence. Factually speaking, the West has been and remains victorious—and not only through the force of its weapons: it remains so through its ideas, through its "models" of growth and development, through the statist and other structures which, having been created by it, are today adopted everywhere.

A second remark, which bears on the relationship between philosophy and "science," must be made in reference to a statement made by [Jacques] Attali, who said: "Philosophy accompanies the scientist, who opens the doors." A grave error. The scientist opens the doors using keys which have been fabricated on the basis of a certain number of ideas, philosophical ideas. If you had told a physicist at the turn of the century that everything he was doing was based on the *idea* of causality, he would have laughed in your face. A few years later, the physicists' house exploded and the debris is still falling on their heads. The "self-evident" fact of causality has become problematic again, and physicists are obliged once again to discuss philosophy. The same goes for politics. It is painful to see young militants becoming alienated in unreflective activism, proclaiming that what matters for them is action, not philosophy. For, when one looks at what passes for action and what the ideas in their leaflets and wall posters are made of, one realizes that these are only by-products of the writings of a nineteenth-century German sociological philosopher named Karl Marx. And looking a little closer at Marx's writings, one finds Hegel and Aristotle.

I come now to the problem of "development." We must return to the origin of this term and of this idea. Development is the process by means of which the germ, the egg, the embryo unfolds, opens up, spreads out—whereby the living being in general attains its state of "maturity." To speak of development is to refer both to a "potential" that is already there *and* to a given, definite, determined accomplishment, achievement, act, *energeia;* it is to oppose a "matter," already rich in as yet unexplicit determinations, to the *form* it is going to become—and this form is a norm. Here we have the language of Aristotle, of Aristotelian ontology, but under one form or another this ontology underlies all Western thought. Thus, in the case of the present problem, one speaks of "development" of Third World countries by positing that there exists a definable state of maturity which these countries should attain. Thus also, when Marx spoke of the "faculties which initially lie dormant within man the producer," he was speaking Aristotle's language. Within this language, to say that something is is to say that its form corresponds to a norm, that its *eidos* is defined by its *telos* and that it "really" or "fully" *is* only to the extent that it is complete, determined, defined. And this is what, even today, guides the scientist when seeking knowledge from nature: the scientist tries to translate, into his/her own domain, this conception, namely that that which is must be perfectly determined.

But the content of this determination has changed from ancient Greek to modern times. For the Greeks, "determined" signifies "finite," "complete"; and "infinite" signifies "less-determined," "incomplete," therefore ultimately "less-of-a-being." With Christianity (and neo-Platonism), the signs are reversed: the genuine being is God, and God is infinite. But this infinite God is far off, He is elsewhere: the world down here remains, so to speak, Aristotelian. The real upheaval takes place when the infinite invades the world down here. How then can determinateness, the conception of being as being-determined, be saved if there is "actual" infinity? It can be saved if determinateness is thought in mathematical terms, and, in fact, as quantitative determination: the fixed point of reference is provided by the possibility of calculating what is at hand.

This upheaval is conditioned by the confluence, the convergence, the coincidence of two great historical factors, if indeed they can be separated at all. One is the birth and the development of the bourgeoisie, along with the instauration by the latter of a novel universe of social imaginary significations. The other is the philosophical and scientific revolution, which may be symbolized by citing a few names. For example, Descartes, for whom his philosophy and his mathematics are indissociable, and of whom it must be understood that the goal he assigned to knowledge—to make of us the masters and possessors of nature—is nothing other than the programmatic phantasy of modern times. For another example, Leibniz, who said: *Cum Deum calculat fit mundus*—a statement of decisive importance for the new onto-theology, but also for the economy today. Leibniz's God calculates *maxima* and *minima,* more generally *extrema* which always turn out to be *optima,* He thinks differential calculus and the calculus of variations, and it is while He is thinking them that the world takes form. These are also the *extrema* and the *optima* that modern economists claim to be calculating, these are the brachistochrones of development that they are trying to determine.

In this world, which is both infinite and (allegedly) calculable, no fixed forms/norms remain, save those to which quantity itself, inasmuch as it is calculable, give rise. Thus the very evolution of scientific knowledge comes to be seen more and more as a succession of "growing approximations" moving toward greater and greater precision (with respect to laws, universal constants, etc.). Thus, too, in human, in social affairs, growth and expansion, seen from the quantitative point of view, are becoming absolutely decisive: the form/norm that guides social and historical "development" is one of increasing quantities.

Why recall, so hastily and so perfunctorily, all that? In order to emphasize in the strongest possible fashion that the paradigm of "rationality," upon which everyone relies today and which dominates as well all discussions about "development," is only a particular, arbitrary, and contingent historical creation. I have tried to show this in a somewhat more detailed fashion in those paragraphs of my written report which relate to the economy, on the one hand, and those relating to technique, on the other. I will add here simply that if this paradigm has been able to "function," and to do so with a relative—but nevertheless, as one knows, terrifying—"effectiveness," it is because it is not totally "arbitrary": there is certainly a nontrivial aspect, in that which exists, which lends itself to quantification and to calculation; and there is in our language and in every language an ineliminable dimension that is necessarily "logico-mathematical," which in fact embodies what, in its pure mathematical form, is called set theory. We cannot think of a society that is incapable of counting, classifying, distinguishing, making use of the excluded middle, etc. And, in a sense, starting from the moment it is understood that one can count beyond any given number, all mathematics is there in virtuality, and thence the possibilities of applying it; in any case, this "virtuality" today has already been developed, deployed, realized, and we cannot turn back or act as if it had never existed. The problem, however, is to reinsert this into our social life in such a way that it will no longer be the decisive and dominant element, as it is today. We must challenge the grand folly of the modern West, which consists in positing "reason" as sovereign, in understanding rationalization when one hears "reason" and quantification when one hears rationalization. It is this spirit, still operant (even here, as our discussion has shown), that must be destroyed. We must understand that "reason" is only a moment or a dimension of thought, and that it becomes folly when it becomes autonomous.

What is to be done, then? That which is to be done, that which lies before us, is a radical transformation of world society, which does not and cannot concern simply the "underdeveloped" countries. It is illusory to believe that an essential change could ever be brought about in the "underdeveloped" countries if it did not also occur in the "developed" world; this is obvious when one considers basic military and economic relations as well as "ideological" relations. If an essential transformation is to take place, it has to concern both parts of the world. And such a transformation will necessarily be, first and foremost, a *political* transformation—which, for my part, I can only conceive of as the instauration of democracy. The sort of democracy I intend here exists nowhere today, for democracy does not consist in electing, in the best of cases, a president of the Republic every [four or] seven years. Democracy is the sovereignty of the *demos,* of the people, and to be sovereign is to be so twenty-four hours a day. And democracy excludes any delegation of powers; it is the direct power of men and women over all aspects of their social life and organization, beginning with work and production.

Thus conceived, and going beyond the present "national" forms of living, the instauration of democracy can come only from an immense movement of the population of the world, and it can only be conceived of as extending over an entire historical period. For, such a movement—which goes far beyond everything habitually thought of as "political movement"—will not come about unless it also challenges all instituted significations, the norms and values which dominate the present system and are consubstantial with it. It will come into existence only as a radical transformation in what people consider as important and unimportant, as valid and invalid—to put it briefly, as a profound psychical and anthropological transformation, with the parallel creation of new forms of living and new significations in all domains.

Perhaps we are very far from that. Perhaps not. The most important social and historical transformation of the contemporary era, one which we have all been able to observe over the last [two] decade[s]—since it was [in the 1960s] that it really became manifest, though it has been underway [since the turn of the century]—is neither the Russian Revolution nor the bureaucratic revolution in China but the changing situation of woman and of her role in society. This change, which was on no political party's platform (for the "Marxist" parties, such a change could only come about as the by-product, one of numerous secondary by-products, of a socialist revolution), was not brought about by these parties. It has been carried out collectively, anonymously, daily, by women themselves, without their even explicitly representing to themselves its goals; [since the turn of the century], twenty-four hours a day, in the home, at work, in the kitchen, in bed, in the street, in relation to their children, to their husbands, they have gradually transformed the situation. Not only could planners, technicians, economists, sociologists, psychologists, and psychoanalysts not have foreseen this, but they were not even able to see it when it began to take shape.

The same goes, *mutatis mutandis,* for the changes brought about in the situation and attitudes of youth—and now even of children—which were the result of no political program and which the politicians were incapable of recognizing when it began to explode in their faces. Let me add parenthetically that it is to this that the utility of our "human sciences" today amounts. For my part, I believe that in every domain of life, and in the "developed" part of the world as well as in the "undeveloped" part, human beings are presently engaged in the process of liquidating the old significations, and perhaps creating new ones. Our role is to demolish the ideological illusions hindering them in their efforts at creation.

RESPONSE: Of course, mathematics goes beyond mere quantification. This in no way prevents the near-totality of *applications* of mathematics to the real world from being based on those branches of mathematics that relate to quantity and measurement (algebra, analysis, etc.). And it is in these applications—in physics notably, and since Newton—that mathematics has proved what could be called its "unreasonable effectiveness." These successes are what have put social scientists, and above all, economists, off the track. For a century now, political economics has tried to imitate mathematical physics—with practically no results. As for more recent attempts to apply "nonquantitative" mathematical formalization to the social sciences, as in structuralism, we must note that the results have been extremely meager; the sole domain in which they seem to possess a certain validity is that of the most elementary aspects of language (phonology), where, moreover, one cannot even speak of genuine formalization, but rather of the working application [*mise en oeuvre*] of a rudimentary *ars combinatoria*. For my part, I think that the essential dimensions of social and historical phenomena outstrip the power of any mathematical tools, whichever ones they may be; I do not think, for example, that there can be any meaningful mathematization or formalization whatsoever of the Freudian Unconscious.

I am not making, and I have never made, any apology for inaction. *Here,* our action is speech. I am speaking in my own name, and I assert the right to criticize as well as to propose. And it is not because we have criticized the ideology surrounding the term "development" and its actual usage that governments will cease their aid (or their nonaid) to development. Governments will continue to do what they do for reasons of their own, and these reasons have nothing to do with the fact that people are dying of hunger: their reasons are solely concerned with power games on a worldwide scale.

I am not "confounding," as has been said, science and religion; what is happening is that science today is taking the place of religion. You say: "The crisis of development is a crisis of faith." You call this faith, then; that is perhaps your heritage, but it is not mine. Science is taking the place of religion today because religion is collapsing and because belief is becoming belief in science. Such as it exists today, this belief in science is just as irrational as any religious belief. The great majority of people today, including scientists, do not have a rational attitude toward science: they *believe* in it; this actually is a sort of faith. And it is this belief, which gains common currency via the idea that doctors, engineers, physicists, and economists have the answer to all the problems humanity faces, that must be shaken.

Finally, an idealization of the so-called underdeveloped world is implicit in several of the speeches given here. For my part, I say: You are like the others, neither better nor worse. You can just as easily slaughter each other, and in reality you do so very often. In France, I belonged to the feeble minority that tried to struggle against the Algerian War. But I always knew that, if the positions were reversed and if the Algerians dominated France, they would have behaved, on the whole, like the French behaved in Algeria. I therefore believe that we must abandon this kind of polemic and turn our discussion over to an examination of the basic questions facing us.

Discussion on the "Socialist Model" of Development

CORNELIUS CASTORIADIS: I would like to have a turn to speak right after Bianco. Without entering into a terminological or lexicographical, let alone philosophical discussion, I want to challenge the terminology being employed.[2] People seem to be swallowing the idea that there exists a "socialist model" of development as embodied in the "socialist countries." One can do what one wants with words, but ultimately socialism has always signified the abolition of exploitation. My claim is that there still exists, in the countries called by antiphrasis "socialist," the exploitation of man by man—or the reverse, as the well-known Czech joke has it. Consequently, I absolutely refuse them use of the qualifier "socialist." Let the journalists of *Le Monde* and other quite serious newspapers talk on and on about "socialism" and about "revolution" apropos of everything and anything. All a corporal in any country needs to do is to seize power and to call himself a "socialist" (and what else would he say?) and articles on "the new face of Senechadian socialism," for instance, will appear. The Greek colonels, too, spoke of "*the* National Revolution"—and Greek newspapers have reached the point today [1977] where the word "revolution"

2. The preceding speakers (Edgar Morin, René Dumont and Lucien Bianco) had not stopped to consider that the term "socialism" was being applied to Russia, China, etc. [Translator's Note: On Castoriadis's use of the term "socialism," see now, however, "Socialisme et société autonome," Castoriadis's introduction to *Le Contenu du socialisme* (Paris: 10/18, 1979), in which he abandons this term to the "really existing socialism" of the Brezhnev era, opting instead for the term "autonomous society." Translated by David J. Parent as "Socialism and Autonomous Society," *Telos*, 43 (Spring 1980), pp. 91–105, a new translation of this article is to appear in the third volume of Castoriadis's *Political and Social Writings* (Minneapolis: University of Minnesota Press, forthcoming).]

means the Papadopoulos regime. [In the early 1970s], everyone was talking about "Arab socialism": in fact, it was a matter of the regime of Citizen Nasser. Now things are somewhat clearer; with Citizen Sadat there is no more talk of "Arab socialism," and still I am not completely sure what it was.

RENE DUMONT: There is still, with Sadat, a party called the Arab Socialist Union.

C.C.: And also the "socialism" of the "revolution" of Idi Amin Dada. But let us turn to more important matters. The term "model" has also been used; I challenge it as well, for there is no model. There is an ideological/imaginary cluster, the only hard part of its core being the power of a bureaucratic apparatus. This is the sole characteristic that remains constant across all the countries in question. Without doubt, these bureaucratic apparatuses are structured differently from one country to another: the Russian CP [Communist party] and the Chinese CP are not exactly the same, and the situation is something else again in Cuba and again in Libya. Most often, however, this apparatus forms around a political party, but it can be, at the limit, the army itself. Not the army of Tamerlane, but the army such as we have known it since Roman times, and in any case such as it has been imposed upon all countries by Europe.

Obviously, bureaucracy does not signify "offices" [*bureaux*]—still less the employees behind the windows at the post office. It is a matter of a highly hierarchalized managerial-directorial apparatus, where the area of competence of each authority is delimited, where this competence diminishes as one descends the hierarchal ladder; where, therefore, there is an internal division of labor of direction and command. This ruling apparatus stands opposed to a mass of executants who, theoretically, form its "base" but who in reality remain outside it.

Now, what we find to be the characteristic common to all the countries in question is, on the one hand, this hard core of a bureaucratic apparatus ruling society, and, on the other hand, the ideology of development. For, we cannot talk as if there were something incontestable about the content of development and about its ultimate goals [*finalités*], which would be at the same time the Beautiful, the Good, and the True, and which would be Development with a capital D. What we notice when looking at these allegedly "socialist" countries is that they are pursuing development in a Western capitalist sense—even if this is done via "planning" that is centralized or "decentralized," etc. What I mean by this is that in these countries the type of civilization in the broadest sense of the term, their type of culture if you prefer, the type of individuals that society aims at producing, the types of products fabricated or tools utilized, the type of relationships people have with each other, whatever the ideological/imaginary cluster surrounding them, are the types that the capitalist West has been creating for the past five or six centuries.

That there is on the planet an immense problem with hunger and material poverty is an obvious point, a massive and tragic fact; that this is used to speak and to act as if the sole response was to implant in non-Western countries the Western capitalist model, whose substance—productivism, pseudorationalization, etc.—is masked by a "socialist" phraseology, is an entirely other matter. "Development" is development of a Western–capitalist type; until now there has been no other type, and none other is known.

In this regard, we might add a note about certain aspects of the policy of the Chinese bureaucracy, which at times has seemed to want to pursue different paths: fewer large factories, less urbanization, less centralized medicine—this was discussed a year ago with [Ivan] Illich. The discussion here would have to be deepened; for my part, I note on the one hand that, on all these points, the Chinese bureaucracy sooner or later returns to the traditional [bureaucratic–capitalist] paths and on the other hand that, in all this it is a matter simply of employing more flexible and more efficient methods, from the bureaucracy's point of view, for mobilizing the population and putting it into the service of a policy and a project which, after all, is the "development" of China in the sense that the United States and Russia are "developed." We know, indeed, that even the organization of Chinese concentration camps is much more "intelligent" and subtle, much rougher and more brutal than that of the Russian camps under Stalin. Likewise, the exploitation of the peasantry, the mobilization of citizens in the neighborhoods, etc., are carried out with more flexibility and "efficiency." The mobilizations of the public in Stalinist Russia during the

1930s, for example, were grotesque theatrical spectacles; in China, they really seem to possess a certain "effectiveness," provided one adopts the standpoint of the objectives of the regime. But these are in fact the objectives that are to be attained each time—and which are, moreover, the same ones, even if the Chinese bureaucracy allows them to be realized at a slower pace and does so with more astuteness.

R.D.: Now, beware, the society that China is building is thoroughly different from Western society, at least on one fundamental point, that of social inequalities. In China there still are privileges, inequalities, but their order of grandeur is fundamentally different from our own, and China is being built upon a consciously different model.

LUCIEN BIANCO: Yes, the material inequalities are infinitely smaller in China than in France or in the USSR, for example. But here again one should take the poverty of the country into consideration.

EDGAR MORIN: In poor countries there has always been the luxury of a tiny minority; that is not a decisive argument.

L.B.: That is true: if one compares India to China, one really must recognize that Chinese society is much more egalitarian. But even in prerevolutionary China, the "big" owners were in fact quite small and their income quite mediocre, to the point that Sun Yat-sen said: "In China there are only two social classes: the very poor and the less poor."

C.C.: The data I have at my disposal do not lead me to think that the inequalities are "infinitely less" in China than elsewhere. But the basic point does not lie there. When one speaks of India, a capitalist country—where, it is true, capitalism has had trouble developing—as well as when one speaks of France, it must not be forgotten that income inequalities have, within the framework of capitalism, a nonindividual function, a "social" function: the financing of accumulation, of investments. In Russia or in China, this function is not carried out via private incomes but by means of the direct levy on a part of the social product by the Plan, etc. What should be compared is not what [a capitalist industrialist like] Monsieur Dassault [or Mr. Ford] makes and what Messrs. Brezhnev and Mao make, for most of the income of Monsieur Dassault is invested, whereas Messrs. Brezhnev and Mao invest nothing. What is to be compared is what Monsieur Dassault consumes and what Messrs. Brezhnev and Mao consume. Now, the answer is easy: they consume the same thing, for they consume all that they want to consume.

JULIETTE MINCES: By employing the term "consumption," when applied to heads of State or of a Party, I think you are mixing up several things. Let me take an example which greatly impressed me when I was in Guinea in 1962. We knew Sékou Touré who, personally, consumed very little, relatively speaking. That was not of inordinate interest to him. What he consumed was power, and that was what was most important. So when you talk about consumption, that bothers me a great deal. Moreover, there is a distinction you are not making, which is that all state apparatuses are privileged, everywhere. But not all of them are characterized by their parasitic aspect.

C.C.: We were talking about economic inequalities. I do not believe that René Dumont meant that inequality from the standpoint of power is infinitely less in China than in France; on this point, we are all in agreement, I believe. But we were talking about "material" inequalities, we were trying to see how these inequalities are to be judged, and it is in this regard that I, taking the narrow viewpoint of an economist, said that, whatever political judgment one makes, when one is talking about the income of a capitalist in a liberal capitalist society, it must not be forgotten that it has two functions, the less important of which concerns accumulation. A capitalist is not essentially someone who consumes, it is someone who invests in factories. In Russia, in China, in the "people's democracies," these factories are built on the general budget account; the levy on social revenues is direct, it is not mediated by "individual" income as in the West, and that constitutes the difference. What remains to be done, therefore, is to compare Brezhnev's thirty-seven cars and his dachas to the Rolls Royces and Saint-Tropez villas of the rich here—and, of course, the number of privileged persons there and here.

But are we not still in the process of postulating what is to be proved?[3] We are talking about progress in the realm of production. I am quite willing to grant that progress has been more rapid in China than in

3. In the meantime, the discussion had turned to the "comparative merits" of development in India and China, in particular to the comparison of their rates of growth.

India. But can one make of such progress the supreme criterion or an indisputable criterion without swallowing the whole universe of capitalist life and thought? And this brings us to another aspect which has been neglected in these comparisons and which undermines them: people were talking as if the social and anthropological structure of the Chinese world and the Hindu world were identical from the start. Now, without entering into a facile culturalism, the immense importance of the difference between these worlds must be taken into account. For deep-seated historical reasons, numerous "undeveloped" countries have been infinitely "closer" to the capitalist world, or more "ready" for capitalist development, than others. For example, even in its poorest periods, Greece has always "belonged" to the West in a certain sense; and Greece is in the process of developing—whereas Turkey has encountered many more difficulties. The same thing goes for Spain. Spain is already almost France; whether one likes it or not, in fifteen years, Franco's Spain achieved "development" as rapidly as any other country. And I do not think the situation is essentially different in Latin America, though the difficulties encountered by capitalist "development" are much greater there. I view the present [1977] Brazilian regime with horror, but I see, in principle, nothing that would prevent a capitalist "take-off" from occurring in Brazil; this take-off is already happening, it has already been accomplished. But it happens that all the countries I have just mentioned belong to a certain anthropological, cultural, social-historical area. Now, in Asia, for example, there is such an area to which the Chinese and the Japanese (and undoubtedly, too, the Indochinese) belong—and another, completely different one, that of the Hindu people (and, moreover, the Indonesians). Three thousand years of Chinese history cannot so easily be forgotten. The Chinese are people who, as the Greek expression goes, have always known how to extract fat from flies.

R.D.: And to make use of excrement.

C.C.: Yes, and to make use of human excrement, a point which Victor Hugo referred to in his wonderful book, *Les Misérables,* where he was already denouncing the fact that the city of Paris alone was each day dumping, via its sewers, the then-equivalent of 500 million gold francs into the sea whereas, as he said, the Chinese soil is as rich as the first day of Creation because the Chinese pour their excrement onto it. Likewise, the Japanese: Does Japan represent a "socialist model"? In the past century Japan has become the second largest industrial power on Earth.

JEAN-MARIE DOMENACH: But Japanese taxi drivers sleep in their cars.

C.C.: That is exactly what I am saying: what matters is "economizing," "producing," "saving." It is the same thing in Hong Kong: arriving at the airport at midnight, you find salesmen from the tailors who will offer you a made-to-order suit, with a fitting at five and delivery at eight in the morning, thus allowing you to continue your flight at nine. These are artisans—and they are not starving. But when I was in India, I hired a Hindu taxi driver to visit the wonderful temples around Madras. After a long friendly conversation on a variety of topics, he happened to mention to me that he had been able to set aside a considerable amount of money. In all innocence, I asked him: "Of course, you are going to buy a second taxi?" "Not at all," he replied, "For five years we have been preparing a great pilgrimage for the whole family to a great temple (I think it was Rameswaram), and this money will be just enough." This may seem facile to say, but this illustrates in one sentence the anthropological structure of the Hindu people as well as the "obstacles" it places in the way of capitalist "development." And in this regard, the situation is the same in Africa—though India is a "historical" society and African societies are, as such, "prehistoric" societies.

J.-M. D.: The Chinese anthropological structure was that millions of people were dying of hunger. Now, it is no longer the same thing. So, what has changed?

C.C.: There was a period during which traditional Chinese society was decomposing, as has occurred periodically, but in an infinitely more aggravated way over the past century due to the invasion by Western imperialism. The new regime has "reorganized" the country, but it has been able to do so as a function of an already existing attitude, one deeply rooted in the Chinese people: produce, economize, arrange things, put them in order, make use of the tiniest bits possible. That is the attitude of the Chinese, that is the attitude of the Japanese; it is not that of the Hindus.

I wanted to speak on other points, but Bianco's last statements bring me back to what strikes me about this discussion.[4] People are talking as if creating a nation were simply "positive." For my part, I have fought against nationalism as soon as I entered upon active political life. Now, what is happening is what Edgar Morin so well described a moment ago when he spoke of the "shame" experienced by Western intellectuals. They feel guilty criticizing Western-style "development" because someone coming from the Third World—and we encountered this at Figline-Valdarno—might say: "Ah, but all that is just criticism coming from well-fed people." The same goes for the idea of the nation; everything happens as if you were afraid that people might tell you: "For you, perhaps, the nation is an obsolete idea, but for us the nation means no longer being under the heels of some French or English sergeant." But they remain under the heel of a sergeant right at home: Idi Amin Dada, Khadafi, or Boumedienne.

Second, to rid oneself of foreign oppression (which, certainly, also manifests itself as "national" oppression, more precisely as the oppression of the indigenous population *qua* indigenous people) is not at all equivalent to the creation of artificial "nations" such as have been produced these days in Africa—a point which I will make in front of any African. One need only look at a map to see the grotesqueness of it all: most of the time, the boundaries of these "nations" follow exactly along the meridians and parallels on the map, these are the frontiers fixed for territories previously conquered by England, France, etc., solely as a function of partition treaties or for the convenience of the respective administrations and thanks to the Cartesian mind, since it is easier to demarcate territories by means of straight lines coinciding with meridians and parallels. What this now gives for the populations in question has been quite visible to see for several years: it has given Nigeria and Biafra, it has given the bloody tribal struggles in the ex-Belgian Congo,

4. Lucien Bianco had just said (*Le Mythe du développement*, p. 134), "The creation and consolidation of the Chinese nation is . . . the most incontestable feature on the balance sheet of this revolution."

or Senegal today, with four or five ethnic groups, some of them overflowing into neighboring countries, who are ready to kill each other.

The idea of the "nation" is presently one of the essential ingredients of the bureaucratic ideology. By means of it, the struggle against exploitation and imperialist oppression has been confiscated by a nascent bureaucracy. The bureaucratic apparatus presents itself to the indigenous masses as the authority which is going to "create for them" as well as "give to them" a nation and which embodies this nation as well as guarantees its existence. This is also how the mass struggle against oppression slips into being a "national" struggle, that is to say, into a struggle for the creation of a "national" State, with all that the creation of a State implies. I have spoken at length on this point, for I am struck to see to what extent people like those gathered here today have been able to become saddled with this monstrous dialectic of the past hundred years of history, which has rendered all words and all significations ambiguous, which has made them, in their current usage, instruments of mystification.

E.M.: But this void left by the ebbing of colonialism, or by its being chased out, is filled by the nation, and under present conditions it is hard to see what else could have filled this void.

C.C.: Here we agree. But that something had to fill it does not mean that we have to swallow this something. The last philosopher of history died in 1831. If I were speaking as a philosopher of history, I would have said, as he did: all that has been real has been rational, period, there is nothing else to say. But I am speaking politically; that that which has been was so as a function of certain causes may serve for me as part of the discussion, but it does not close it. It was said a moment ago that in politics "illusions" count as much as "reality" does, if not more so—and this is obviously true: otherwise there would not have been, for example, two great wars. Now, to speak today of the so-called socialist so-called model of so-called development and to denounce it is not to do a work of philosophy, it is to do a work of politics, it is to denounce and to try to dissolve these "illusions" that are of such importance in their "real" actions; and this is precisely what one sees when one discovers that all these words and all these terms convey representations, motivate activities, and justify realities, radically contrary to those that we have in mind or those that we—in any case, I—would be ready to defend. Jean-Marie Domenach asked a minute ago: What are the reasons these countries adopt the "socialist model"? One of these reasons, and not the least of which, is to be found precisely in these "illusions" and their force. The same thing goes for the "nation."

I return to the question of bureaucracy, and my old quarrel with Edgar [Morin] on this score. In my view, there can be no doubt about the specificity, the originality of the contemporary bureaucratic organization, its belonging to the modern world, even if one can find many kernels, many germs in the past—in China, in Imperial Rome, the official Christian Church, etc. But the modern bureaucracy finds its true origin, its social-historical sources elsewhere—and these sources are three in number. First, there is the spontaneous evolution, *the internal logic, of Western capitalism:* concentration and centralization, factory organization, the increasingly close ties established between the economy and the State, etc. The second is *the degeneration of working-class organizations themselves* and of the Revolution of 1917: for reasons which cannot be discussed right now, the Russian working class did not succeed in assuming, in effectively exercising, power, either in production or in politics; the Bolshevik party, which prepared itself for this task, emerged, seized power for itself and became the dominant, exploiting stratum. The third source—which shows Marxism's inability to account for contemporary history, since the first two can be, to a greater or lesser extent, interpreted within Marxist bounds—is what I have called *the emergence of the bureaucracy within the void* and from the void: traditional, precapitalist society collapses when it comes into contact with capitalism; imperialism proves incapable of continuing to impose its will, either directly or via an intermediary, a national bourgeoisie; the crisis of society and the struggle of the masses each amplify the other. This situation may last for a long time—it lasted for at least fifty years in China, for example; but if and when it is transcended, we note that it always happens basically in the same way. The apparatus which, in these societies, offer the most appropriate (or the least foreign) "welcoming structures" for the creation of a capitalist bureaucratic society, which possesses the "organizational" and "informational" data in the biological sense, the DNA that allows it to carry out a process of social catalysis, this appartus starts to proliferate and to extend its influence and its power, finally becoming the instance which "resolves" this society's crisis. The apparatus that is in a privileged position to play this role is quite obviously a "Marxist," "communist," etc., party, since internally it already has a "modern" organization; a "message," as Edgar says, or an ideology and system of explanation of the world and, lastly, established strategic and tactical models (cf. Portugal after April 1974); it already exists, ready-made for this role.

But we note too that, in other countries, just as numerous, the "primordial soup" created by the decomposition of traditional society does not permit the birth or development of such a party. Such is the case in almost all African societies; such is also the case in India, where the Communist (or Marxist-Leninist) party or parties find themselves faced with a golden opportunity but succeed in accomplishing nothing at all. Why is that? The same goes, indeed, in almost all Moslem countries. I do not want to return to anthropology, but I am certain that that has a lot to do with it. In all these instances, when something happens, we can see that another apparatus plays—generally, of course, with much less effectiveness—the role of the Party apparatus: it is the military apparatus, or, in the extreme case, it is personified by Mr. Amin Dada and his soldiers. Of course, this appartus, too, has need of a "socialist" ideology—or phraseology—for reasons already discussed, and which, moreover, are quite obvious.

Now, a final word on the "positive" question of politics properly speaking, in the sense of: What is to be done? This is the really decisive question, but there is a preliminary one: From what standpoint are you speaking? In what capacity are you speaking? Are we partners in the firm of "Consultants for Development with Attenuated Horror"? Are we going to draw the curves that would maximize wheat production and minimize the concentration camp population? For my part, I say that I will not do it. I am not a consultant for development with minimum horror.

E.M.: Aren't you sometimes forced to be?

C.C.: I do not see what could force me to do so for an instant, and I will not enter into that kind of discussion. But let me return to what Edgar said: perhaps we need a little of this, a little of that, a little self-management, etc. I am not being ironic, clearly this is not "false," and it is preferable to be a worker in a Yugoslavian factory than in a Hindu factory. But these little doses of this and that cannot vanquish this terrible power of the totality of society, of society *qua* overall institution and, as things stand now, *qua* bureaucratic society. And this may be seen in Yugoslavia, for example, where the control exercised by the State and Party apparatus is quite effectively complete—precisely because of "decentralized self-management"—via the control of economic mechanisms, of demand, of the world market, etc.

What, in my view, has been for a very long time the key to the whole question of "development" is that the countries of the Third World contained, and perhaps still contain, the possibility of making a positive, original contribution to the necessary transformation of world society. It is this possibility that is totally conjured away in the usual discussions about development; and this is what is destroyed through the bureaucratic–capitalist "development" of these countries—and in this too the hate we can feel toward the bureaucracies being created there is so much the greater. Schematically speaking, we may say that in most of these countries traditional cultural forms had not yet and still have not been completely destroyed. It goes without saying that in most cases these traditional forms went hand in hand with exploitation, poverty, a whole series of negative factors; yet, they also preserved something that has been shattered in and through capitalist development in the West: a certain type of sociability and of socialization, and a certain type of human being. It has long been my opinion that the solution to the present problems of humanity will have to pass by way of a junction between this element and what the West can contribute; I mean by this a transformation of Western technique and knowledge so that they will be able to serve in the maintenance and the development of the authentic forms of sociability extant in "underdeveloped" countries—and, in return, the possibility for Western peoples to learn something there that they have forgotten, how to become inspired to revive truly communitarian forms of living.

9

The Crisis of Culture and the State

I take it that this is a working seminar, so please do not expect my lecture to be in an academic style. Mostly I will try to delineate some ideas and to assert many question marks. The questions emerge from some positions and vice versa. There is no such thing as pure interrogation; when we question something, we presuppose some other things as not being questionable for the time being. Concerning these things, we do have a point of view. Of course, if we are mentally free, we are able to come back and question our very presuppositions, the points of view with which we began.

Now I do have some points of view relative to our theme, the crisis of contemporary culture and its relation to the State. My central idea, to put it briefly, is, first, that there is a crisis of culture and that this crisis is but an aspect of the crisis of Western societies. Second, this crisis cannot be relieved through any sort of action by the present-day State. The State is part of the problem, not part of the answer. How-

---

This essay is a revised version of a lecture presented at the Center for Humanistic Studies on April 18, 1986 as part of a seminar series entitled "Culture and the State" published by the Center for Humanistic Studies, University of Minnesota as CHS Occasional Papers, 16 (1987). A previous French language version of this article, which has now been substantially expanded and revised, was published as "Transformation sociale et création culturelle" in *Sociologie et Sociétés,* April 1979, and reprinted in *Le Contenu du Socialisme* (Paris: 10/18, 1979), pp. 413–39.

ever, irrespective of the character of the States existing in different historical periods, this has not always been the case. There have been periods, even recent ones, when the intervention of the State in the cultural field can be said to have been positive. The present plight is due both to the character of present culture and to the nature of the contemporary State, its bureaucratic character, and the fact that it is an object of massive indifference.

What do we mean by the term "culture"? You certainly have already discussed definitions of this term. What I mean by this word is something between the meaning which most American anthropologists give to it, namely, practically the totality of a social world, and the habitual French sense (not so different from the German *Kultur*), meaning the works of the spirit, what Hegel would call *objektiver Geist;* the works of the spirit, the knowledge of these works and an anonymous but living public aware of these works, capable of appreciating and judging them, capable of serving as the concrete, historical bearer of this culture. To put it more precisely, culture is whatever goes beyond the strictly instrumental or functional in a given institution of a society and in the works of this society, and that which presents an invisible dimension cathected or invested positively as such by the individuals in the given society. For example, a Gothic cathedral is certainly much more than the stones which compose it; apart from its sacred character, people continue to invest it with something which is more than the stones, more than shelter, more than a place where priests can perform their functions. They invest it, they cathect it because they positively value it in some invisible and noninstrumental, nonfunctional dimension.

Why speak about "crisis"? I am not using the term in its proper, original sense. The word comes from the Greek, meaning separation, judgment, decision (< the verb *krino*), and is intimately linked with the word *kairos,* meaning a moment of opportunity or of necessity for acting. Adhering to this original sense, one would say that there is a crisis when a process has reached a point where, implicitly or potentially, a moment of decision arises between opposing alternatives. For instance, in the evolution of a sickness, a crisis is a moment or a stage when the physician can say: either the patient will pass away in the next few hours or he will begin to get better. The word is frequently used in this sense in the old Hippocratic writings. But I am using the word in the present context to denote a protracted period of wear and tear, of corrosion of the world of imaginary significations which animate society's institutions and which hold society together. The existence of such a protracted corrosion points to an important deterioration of a society's capacities for self-repair, to use a biological metaphor. Society is not, of course, an organism, but societies always possess the equivalent of self-repair capacities.

Regarding present society, this means that the two poles, the two nuclei of imaginary significations which have coexisted in Western societies for centuries are in a state of crisis. One of these nuclei is the capitalistic nucleus properly speaking, the imaginary signification of unlimited expansion of pseudorational mastery over nature and over humans. To this is opposed the other nucleus, the project of social and individual autonomy (or the emancipatory project, or the democratic movement, or the revolutionary movement). The latter is not something which has appeared only in the last two centuries. The emancipatory project has dominated Western European history since the end of the Middle Ages, beginning in fact with the new cities founded by a new category of individuals, the first "bourgeois," *Bürger,* the protobourgeoisie which arose out of the feudal order. This protobourgeoisie built political communities which tended toward self-government and maneuvered between the feudal lords, the Church, and the new monarchies to obtain a degree of independence.

The key characteristic of our society is this dual institution: it is not *just* a capitalist society, nor is it a democratic society, as journalists, politicians, and "political philosophers" would have it. Politically, our society is a liberal oligarchy, with a well-entrenched ruling minority, and with various institutions which embody residues of age-old struggles for freedom, for emancipation, for autonomy. And, of course, these residues suffice in establishing a tremendous difference between this type of society and a totalitarian or stratocratic society like the one in Russia.

Concomitant with the erosion of these significations and deeply linked with it, is the waning of political and social conflict. This type of conflict has been characteristic of European history. Incidentally, when I speak of "Europe," "European," etc., I am not using the terms in a geographic or even less in a national or racial sense. I mean instead, the social-historical stream starting with ancient Greece and again, in the modern era, with the peoples of Western Europe. It is in this social-historical region alone that we observe real political struggle, not just conflicts between rival court cliques or opposing interest groups, not just competition for power within a given institutional framework, but a struggle over the institutions, a struggle aimed at the changing of these institutions. It is this struggle that brings about an extraordinary change in institutions as well as a change in the anthropological, the sociopsychic structure of man/woman giving rise to individuals able, in principle, to question the existing institution of society (the justice of existing laws, the validity of prevailing social views of the world and of human life, etc.).

The imaginary signification of unlimited expansion of "rational" mastery is in deep crisis today. One has only to look at the hollowness of the revived "liberal" rhetoric of the free market, free enterprise, etc.; there is nothing new in it, not even new arguments—it is a plastic, cheap thing, miles below the level of discussion of the great liberals of the early nineteenth century. On the other hand, a crisis equally deep has corroded the democratic, or emancipatory, or revolutionary project. Revolution does not mean bloodshed and gun fighting. Revolution is radical change in the institutions of society. After the degeneration of the traditional working-class parties and trade unions, and the decline of the ideology of "progress," be it liberal or Marxist, there is now a stalemate. Even people who would like to work to change things look around and cannot see any direction in which they could work.

For me, that much is certain on the level, so to speak, of massive and significant facts. It is much more difficult to understand why these developments took place. As you know, Hegel thought that he understood the rise and fall of cultures. I do not think he really did. All he could say was that the spirit of a certain people (*Volksgeist*) had exhausted itself, which is, of course, a tautology. When we look at a culture on the rise, we see an amazing number of geniuses and great *oeuvres,* as well as the genius of the entire community. For instance, Pindar, Aeschylus, Sophocles, and many important philosophers existed within a short span of time, along with the buildings of the Acropolis and the Demos of the Athenians. This same sort of extraordinary string can be seen from Dante and Giotto through Shakespeare and Bach to Proust, Kafka, Joyce, and Picasso. And then, in the same places, with the same geography, under the same sun, the "same" people, practically the "same" society does not create anything new. For centuries it just goes on imitating, rather poorly, what has been done before—like the thousands of statues remaining from the third century B.C. to the victory of Christianity. Even if you know nothing about sculpture, it is impossible to confuse these with the products of the previous period. I think that the same phenomenon is starting to happen today. This is what has been called postmodernism: eclecticism and imitation. In fact, it is a rather cheap version of Alexandrianism. The only really significant contribution of postmodernism is that is has shown how great and creative modernism was.

Certainly one could say that all of my judgments are subjective and depend upon my personal values. In a sense, this is trivially true, and uninteresting. Is there anybody around asserting that the (living) composer X is "worth" Johann Sebastian Bach, or the (living) painter Y is "worth" Rembrandt? Worth : value. This brings me to another dimension, or aspect, of the crisis: that of values. Of course, nobody could say that in the present society there no longer are values, that this society is a society without values. A society without values is impossible. Values are always there (and not a discovery of Nietzsche's or the neo-Kantians', as Heidegger would have us believe) because they are there, and must be there, in any society as poles which orient the making and doing of individuals, their social action and their life. There are always finalities to which the functioning of instituted society is subordinated. Therefore, in a transhistorical, descriptive, neutral sense, all societies establish or institute values. I insist on the neutrality of the term. In a tribe of headhunters, the more skulls you have in your hut, the more worthy you are. In *this* sense, there are certainly also values in our present society, but what are they? They tend more and more to be the antagonistic maximization of consumption, of power, of status, and of prestige—these are becoming the only actual translations of the imaginary signification of the unlimited expansion of "rational" mastery. And thus the latter appears increasingly futile, hollow, and internally contradictory. This effect has been, of course, reinforced by the energy crisis and the ecological crisis. If human beings are to serve the existing institutions solely because egoistic motives and desires are pushing them to do so, and, furthermore, if the modes of socialization and cooperation or commonality exist only as instrumental and utilitarian, the result can only be a critical state. Again, this is not in the sense of momentary crisis, but rather in the sense of a protracted agony for the existing institution of society.

My thesis is that this is the case to a significant and important degree, and that the process accompanies the waning of present creation, that is, cultural creation. Of course every month we find a new genius or a new revolution in this or that domain which has been invented by journalists and the merchants in the cultural field. But the revolutions get mixed up. One talks about revolution in painting or sculpture in the same way one talks about a revolution in refrigerators and toilet paper. This vocabulary, and all that goes with it, is part of the general industry, not just the cultural industry. Recently, I was in New York and I was told that there are—I do not remember exactly now—2,000 to 4,000 art galleries in Manhattan. I do not think that in Da Vinci's time there were 2,000 galleries in Milan; in fact, I do not think there was even a single one. The comparison is, of course, unfair, but one may ask, what do these 2,000 galleries in Manhattan sell? It could be said that when an epoch does not have great men, or great works, it invents them. This is true of the present period and most certainly was of the Alexandrian. As an illustration of this, there is a wonderful short story by Kafka, "Josephine the Singer," in which a tribe has a singer, a soprano, who unfortunately has no voice at all. Nonetheless, the tribe has to pretend that they have a singer with a very beautiful voice. So every time Josephine says, "Oh, I feel it coming on, here it comes, I've got my inspiration, I will sing," wherever she may be, everyone stops. People gather around her, and they all mimic the faces of people who are listening to very beautiful music, while there is no sound at all. So, in this same manner the president of the United States, or of France, or the prime minister has to be a great politician; otherwise we are lost. The painters, sculptors, other artists, and the philosophers must also be great painters, sculptors, or philosophers, etc. If they are not capable of creating new philosophical ideas, they prove their greatness by "destroying," "deconstructing," "subverting" whatever philosophies have been formulated before, thus "proving" that we have a new philosophy, even superior to the previous ones.

What has been called modernity is something which reached its climax between 1900 and 1930, and which ended after World War II. This was a really great period. People did not realize it at the time. In fact, they did not realize it until the word *postmodernity* was coined. Grand, creative, modern art was essentially finished by 1930—of course, with some exceptions. In music, Schönberg, Webern, and Berg had invented atonal and serial music before 1914. Until recently, few people who admired abstract painting knew that Kandinsky and Mondrian were born long before the turn of the century, 1862 and 1872, respectively. Dada and surrealism were in existence by 1920. And if I were to begin the following list, Proust, Kafka, Joyce . . . would you please tell me how you would continue? Certainly Faulkner was a great novelist—and today there are still some very good novelists—but if we consider the culmination of Western creation, we cannot kid ourselves that it is possible to compare what has been produced over the last forty years with Bach, Mozart, Beethoven, Wagner or Van Eyck, Velasquez, Rembrandt or Brunelleschi, Michelangelo or Picasso, Frank Lloyd Wright, Rimbaud or Rilke. And as this fact cannot be accepted, not only are fictitious geniuses invented, but the critical function has been destroyed as well.

The critical function in the contemporary world is, mostly, a part of the promotional industry even when the critics themselves are acting in a bona fide manner, innocent of any malice in the juridical sense. While we have consumers' associations which, for example, force the automobile industry to recall its defective products at times, how could there be a Ralph Nader for contemporary literature or painting, or for that matter the products of French ideology? Thus, one is left with this promotional attitude of critics who, I think, were massively scared by what happened between 1870 and 1930 and are determined not to be caught again. The "scare" probably began in 1873 with the *Salon des Indépendants* and the scandal surrounding Manet's *Olympia* (Rimbaud is writing at about the same time). Between that time and 1930 the critics were persistently, as they might have put it, "left behind"—as were individuals, museums, and governments who went on buying academic paintings, known in France as *pompier* paintings.

The result was that finally it was discovered that during all this time some curious, semibarbarian people, mostly Russians and Americans, had been buying Impressionist paintings (which is why you find so many of these today in the Hermitage Museum in Leningrad or in New York and other American cities). The conclusion which the corporation of critics has drawn from all of this is that either one should not talk about new productions, because one risks going down in history as silly, or one should applaud wholeheartedly whatever appears, acclaiming it, however nonsensical, as the beginning of a revolution, etc.

The substance of these considerations does not refer only to art. It also concerns intellectual creation; here, more than for the rest, I can only scratch the surface of the subject. For instance, technical and scientific development continues, one could even say that it has accelerated considerably. But one could also say that this technical-scientific development does not really go beyond what might be called drawing conclusions and elaborating the ramifications of the great ideas which were already there. These are in fact the ideas formulated during the great period of modern physics, between 1900 and 1930, by Planck, Einstein, De Broglie, Schrödinger, Heisenberg, and Dirac. After this period, I do not think one finds truly new, important ideas in physics. I mean germinal ideas. For instance Newton was proven "wrong" in the end, but he created a fantastically powerful imaginary scheme by means of which almost everything was brought together and which made it possible to represent, calculate, and predict accurately even today. The same was true of the great physicists of the 1900–1930 period. And if one takes the trouble to go through the present literature of physics relative to problems of the boundaries of knowledge, one sees both a chaotic situation, from the theoretical point of view, and the absence of really important, grand new ideas. I would say the same is true in pure thinking as such after Heidegger, and in a sense, already with Heidegger himself. When Heidegger proclaims the end of philosophy, he is writing, or attempting to write, his own obituary. Already with Heidegger, and certainly after his *Sein und Zeit,* philosophy is becoming more and more *interpretive:* the extraordinary vogue of hermeneutics in the present period, to the point that hermeneutics becomes a substitute for original thinking, is fully significant in this respect.

I am certain that history does not repeat itself, that it does not even stutter, as Churchill said. History creates new languages all the time, languages which are not "higher" or "lower" than the previous ones, but in some cases they may be the languages of decay. We know of at least one other period when interpretation was the predominant activity of intellectuals: the Alexandrian period. At that time, when people were no longer able to create, they began collecting the works of the past, trying to decipher their true meaning, attempting to ensure that their manuscripts were properly edited and "correct," etc.

What is happening today? It is not just that people talk interminably about Marx, Nietzsche, and Freud; they talk about interpretations of Marx, Nietzsche, and Freud; they write about what X wrote in refuting Y's interpretation of Nietzsche, or they go on trying to demonstrate or to prove the death of Western philosophy. As the French say, there are some dead whom you must go on killing forever. So philosophy is killed again and again, and deconstructed, and denounced for its logocentrism, phallocentrism, and "Platonocentrism," and it seems that the job is never properly done. One may wonder if this is not simply due to the incapacity of all these writers to find something more substantive or creative to bring forth.

Now let us consider the relation, the enigmatic relation, between a crisis of society and a crisis of culture. Hegel thinks he understands why, when a historical form is on the ascent, great works appear, and perhaps we all would like to think that we understand this. But he does not say much as to why, when the Greek *polis* starts to decline, further Greek poetry becomes impossible. The *polis,* and democracy, break down and so the Hellenistic monarchs first, then the Romans, become masters. What has this to do with poetry? Why should there not be great poets anymore? Now the dire fact is that there are not. What is the reason? I do not know. But I would tentatively suggest that the creation of great works, *oeuvres,* in a society presupposes that there are meanings in this society which are very positively and strongly cathected, invested by the people living in the society in question. I think all the great works we do have, including the modern ones, those of 1870–1930—give or take five or ten years, five or ten novels, five or ten compositions—have been created in a sort of positive relation to positive values. I know, of course, that I am using obscene terms; I must be somebody coming out of the woods to speak about positive relations to positive values. Or perhaps I am a Daughter of the American Revolution.

What I mean is not an edifying function of the work, not a moralizing function, not what the Germans would call *Erbaulichkeit*—the results of which have been ghastly, as in commercial catholic "art" (what in France is called *l'art saint-sulpicien*), or "socialist realism." This type of art was intended to school "the New Man," but resulted only in the most derisory kitsch. What I mean is not even Aristotelian catharsis. Rather, I refer to the strange relation existing between the work and values or imaginary significations of a society, relations consisting in the fact that the great work of art simultaneously reaffirms these values and calls them into question. I think this is true from the *Iliad* to *The Castle* by Kafka, going through *Macbeth,* Mozart's *Requiem,* and *Tristan und Isolde.*

I would like to explain more clearly what I have in mind. What happens in the *Iliad* from this point of view? Achilles freely chooses virtue and glory instead of a quiet life, and thereby is led to death. He knows that, and we know what death is for the Greeks. Achilles reveals it to Ulysses in the *Odyssey,* in the *Nekyia,* the chant which refers to the Nether-Netherland, the Land of the Dead. He says to Ulysses that he would rather be the miserable slave of a poor peasant on Earth than the king of all the shadows. This was death for the Greeks. The afterlife was much more dreadful than what was lived on Earth. The poems which were the basis of education for all Greeks told them that they must die eventually, and that they ought to die for *arete* and *kudos* and *kleos:* for virtue and fame and glory. They told them also that there was nothing after death, or that whatever might be after death, in any case, was more miserable than anything on Earth.

Macbeth appears at a time when there is once again a liberation of man, a time of seemingly unlimited possibilities for action. It is through this unlimited possibility for action rediscovered by modern man that Macbeth and the spectators along with him discover that we are all but poor actors strutting about on stage. That's all our lives are, Shakespeare tells the Elizabethan public, and that is what the Elizabethan public understands and sees through the work, with the famous *tua res agitur,* it is your own business which is acted out. It is not only

Macbeth, we all are poor actors strutting about the stage and yet we still go on living. The Elizabethans go on living; like the Greeks, they go on living as they do because they know that.

The same is true with *Tristan und Isolde:* if you are really to live a full love, the outcome is death. In a century when everybody is obsessed with the idea of love, this is what *Tristan* conveys. We do not stop loving after *Tristan,* but we know that, and perhaps we measure our actual loves against that.

So the great work of art creates a shock—a shock which is an awakening. The intensity and greatness of the work of art are absolutely inseparable from this shaking up, this vacillation of the established, instituted meaning of things and of life. But this vacillation can only take place if there is a positive sense in the lives of the artist and the public as well, a positive meaning not of life in general, but in what they are doing in life. That is why while *Oedipus Rex* or *Hamlet* present for all to see the ultimate meaninglessness of our destiny and of all our efforts, as well as the blindness of our clairvoyance, they still manage to stir up and even uplift their public. Those among us who in a sense continue to belong to this public continue to be uplifted insofar as we are living a life in which we cathect/invest certain values positively.

But this very same absurdity of life, which is the preferred theme of the best of present literature or theater, does not have the same meaning anymore, the same value of revealing or discovering something. Absurdity really is not possible any longer, because for us there is no strong and strongly invested pole of nonabsurdity in relation to which absurdity could become real absurdity and be lived as such. Death, as the end of life, is only pitiable today in an atmosphere of self-commiseration, because a poor, miserable being is clinging to some additional days—not because death knells the end of a relation to things which matter for all. Hegel said that philosophy, when it comes at the end of the day, can only paint gray over gray. Perhaps the best of contemporary literature paints gray over gray, or black over black. From its most common to its finest forms, from *Death of a Salesman* to Beckett's *Endgame,* contemporary literature only says in a better form and with greater intensity what we constantly live.

Another important element of art is in crisis, namely, the essential relation of the work to its public. The genius of Aeschylus or Sophocles is inseparable from the genius of the Athenian *demos,* just as the genius of Shakespeare is inseparable from the genius of the Elizabethan public. This relation has nothing to do with geographic or genetic factors. These communities instituted themselves in this creative type of relation with creative workers in various fields. I am not speaking in a nostalgic mood nor am I implying that there was an idyllic relationship between the artist and his public. It is well known that the *burghers* of Leipzig wanted to have Telemann as *Kapellmeister.* But Telemann was not available, so they hired Johann Sebastian Bach as the second best. History has decided otherwise. But the fact is that they did hire Bach, and also that, after all, Telemann was a very good musician. I am not implying either that the public in question was the whole society. It would be very easy, and not very interesting, to undertake a cheap Marxist critique of all I have said. I know that the tenants in Lancashire were not patrons of the Globe Theatre, where Shakespeare's plays were performed. The public of these plays was a certain portion of the population of London—but it was, to an important extent, the popular public, comprising artisans, merchants, etc. Similarly, Bach was not performing for the serfs of Pomerania; he was playing for the bourgeois public of Leipzig. But these bourgeois formed a community. And this community had both internally and with "its" artists a peculiar relationship for which it is impossible to find a word, and for which the word "organic" would certainly be misleading—through perhaps the only available one. This relationship is destroyed gradually during the nineteenth century, with the triumph of capitalism *stricto sensu* and the break up of the cultural scene. "Learned" art, *art savant,* becomes separated by an unbridgeable gap from popular art—and whatever existed before as popular culture is slowly or rapidly destroyed. The populace is henceforth nourished, if at all, with the crumbs falling from the dinner table of the well-to-do classes.

Up to a point the bourgeois public maintains a relation with the creator which subsequently breaks down. Why, I do not know. I surmise this is because the values and significations of the capitalistic bourgeoisie already show up as shallow and/or inhuman. The fact is that the phenomenon of the misunderstood genius, of the *artiste maudit* is very recent. It appears after the Romantics, in the last third of the nineteenth century. It is as if, at about this time, the artist suddenly is confronted with a choice. Either he decides to "go with" his public—such is the case with Paul Bourget, Georges Ohnet, Edouard Detaille, melodramatic novels and *pompier* painting of battles, etc.—or he chooses to go his own way, as did Rimbaud, Lautréamont, Edouard Manet, and the Viennese atonal musicians, Edgard Varèse, etc. What I am asserting is that this type of situation was new, historically speaking, trivial objections to the contrary notwithstanding. Johann Sebastian Bach is not the Schönberg to a Saint-Saëns of his epoch. Furthermore, there is no Saint-Saëns in the Bach epoch. There is no cheap, plastic "art," there is no kitsch. There is Bach, and there is Telemann, and there are myriads of lesser artists; there is popular music, but there is no Saint-Saëns, there is no *pompier* art. And then not only the art critics, but the bourgeoisie themselves discover that they have to jump on the bandwagon, and that the "ununderstandable" character of a work of art does not prove anything; it rather proves that the one who cannot understand it is stupid. Therefore, people who would otherwise "object," henceforth shut up, and a new pseudopublic is created, a *public d'avant-garde,* avant-garde audiences and avant-garde artists, and they are all linked together by a sort of pseudomodernistic reference.

To this we must add some considerations about the crisis or the death of forms. These things have already been said, but nobody seems to reflect on the fact that painting, epic poetry, and the novel, are creations of certain historical epochs, certainly corresponding to deep traits of these epochs and not necessarily viable in each and any period. In one of his less inspired moments, Marx asked if the *Iliad,* and more generally, ancient Greek mythology, would be possible in the modern period—a very good question. He answered in a rather silly way that it would not be possible because the feats of the ancient Gods and heroes have been made derisory by modern technique. This does not explain why we have not invented a mythology about the forces which have not been made derisory by our technique. It is true that epic poetry is impossible in modern society, but the "reasons" are both deeper and more general. Some of these "reasons" (the term is utterly inadequate) we can understand, some we cannot.

Painting also has experienced a succession of forms, "material" forms, so to speak. For most of history, painting has been mural painting. The detached painting (the painting in a frame) is something rather recent historically. We know it existed in classical antiquity, but to a great extent it belongs to the Christian period (in the form of icons), and later. However, in another sense, Christian painting is not "painting"—that is, it is not "art," because sacred objects ("icons" or the equivalent) are painted specifically to be put in the Church. Perhaps the first nonsacred "objects," or rather persons, represented in painting are the small figures of the donators standing in a corner of the painting. It is not until the beginning of the Renaissance that real lay painting begins with private patronage by kings or great dignitaries, rich people and finally museums, a very recent phenomenon. Nobody seems to notice that the very idea of painting for museums raises a host of questions. Furthermore, nobody seems to envisage for a moment the possibility that perhaps, as in the case of epic poetry, the novel is a form of artistic creation which would not fit in any and every historical period. Could a really "modern" individual read *The Idiot?* I would be inclined to answer no. The subjective posture, intellectual as well as affective, required for a reading of Dostoyevsky, or Proust, or Joyce seems to me absolutely incompatible with watching television thirty hours per week. As a psychoanalyst, a sociologist, and a historian I am confident that the same individual who spends more than half of his leisure time watching television cannot become fully immersed in a great novel. Some of the people who read Dostoyevsky certainly look at television from time to time, but they are not the audience that forms the economic basis of the television industry. This would be a strong internal antinomy.

Now I come to the problem of the relationship of the State to culture. Plato and Aristotle were, as you know, the first ones to have posed explicitly the question of the relation of culture and the political community. That is, they were the first in our tradition; the issue was probably also raised by non-Western thinkers, such as the Chinese. Plato and Aristotle, however, did not use the term "State" because the Greek *polis* was not a State, it was not an apparatus of domination separated from the body of citizens. Power, political power, was vested in the citizens, in the political community. We know that the empowered citizenry was restricted, in that women had no share in this power and that there were slaves, and we rightly and strongly disapprove of all this—but this is beside the point. The 30,000 Athenian, male, adult citizens were the political community, the sovereign body and they actually and effectively exercised power. There was a technical-administrative apparatus, but this was made up of slaves, working under the supervision of a citizen magistrate. This was the democratic *polis* exemplified by Athens.

Plato faced the problem which we also are facing: Is any and every sort of culture compatible with the desired, sought for political constitution? The question can be easily generalized, and indeed Plato himself in *The Republic* generalizes it: What is the relationship of a given institution of society with the art it creates? He is the first to have explicitly posed this fundamental question, showing, once more, the greatness of his genius. This makes it clear why, in a sense, all philosophy since him has been in one way or another Platonic, and why people today still think along his lines without even knowing it. But at the same time Plato was monstrously wicked. He hated democracy, and to discredit democracy and whatever went with it he invented a world of lies. He created a universe of falsities and illusions which still have currency today. The Sophists were great thinkers; but one who hears the word *Sophist* thinks immediately of a person who distorts the truth by means of a fallacious argumentation. This is a feat of Plato. In the same way, the word *demagogue*, although not coined by Plato, took the semantic charge it has today from Plato because he used it to describe the greatest democratic politicians of all times, Themistocles and Pericles. If all we had to go by concerning the history of Athens was the summary of it that he gives in *The Laws*, we would have a picture of this history almost as distorted as the history of post-1917 Russia according to the *History of the Communist Party of the USSR* written under the guidance of Stalin. Whatever he does not like is omitted. The battle of Salamis, the decisive battle for the Greek world, is omitted, because it is the battle and the victory of the *demos*, the populace, the rabble rowing in the ships who beat the Persians. On the other hand, the battle of Marathon, the battle of the *hoplites*, of the well-to-do and propertied citizens, is, of course, given all due praise. Such is the objectivity of Plato and his love of truth.

Despite all this, because Plato was a genius we are still grappling with the questions he raised, and in the present instance with the question of *The Republic:* What sort of art would be appropriate to the (his) ideal *polis?* What sort of art, and with what content, ought to be encouraged and promoted by the political community? Of course, Plato's answer is dependent both upon his general philosophy and upon his political philosophy and project. Plato considers art as mimesis, imitation, a conception not only consistent with but practically imposed by his ontology; this conception, Aristotle will inherit. But art, of course, is not imitation. Imitation is one of the possible external vehicles of art. Art is fundamentally creation. Art, *qua* creation, is the opening up of a window toward the Abyss, the Groundless, the Chaos which is the ultimate essence of Being. This is what *Oedipus Rex, Hamlet,* and the *Requiem* do. They open up, they tear away the veil of day-to-day life, of the familiar and domesticated, and show the Chaos to everyone. This is also what philosophy attempts to do. Religion, in various ways, tries both to make present and cover up the Chaos. An obvious example is the Christian mass of the dead where we are told at the same time that we are *pulvis, cinis, et nihil,* dust, ash, and nothing—and that we are to go to the bosom of the Father. Presenting *and* covering up, this is what all religions do all the time. But art, great art, does not cover up, it uncovers—unlike kitsch such as socialist realism with its positive heroes and happy endings. And in this also Plato appears as a forerunner, he dismisses classical Greek art (and mythology) because it is not morally edifying, presenting as it does gods with human passions and defects, etc. That this position should have been inherited by the Christian Church as well as by Leninism-Stalinism-Maoism is another instance of the ironic vengeance of history. Great art is not edifying and uplifting, it does not present "positive heroes" (and not "negative" ones either) nor does it have happy endings.

But this was not the actual position of the city, of the *polis,* with regard to culture. I will not discuss this attitude fully now; instead I will ask you, if you are interested, to take a look at a paper I have written about the Greek *polis*.[1] The attitude of the classical Greek *polis* in relation to culture is best expressed in an extraordinary text, the "Funeral Speech of Pericles" in the Second Book of Thucydides' History. The sentence which most interests us in this present context is the famous *Philokaloumen met'euteleias kai philosophoumen aneu malakias:* "We love the beautiful and we live the beautiful, we love wisdom and we live wisdom." The Greek verbs in this sentence cannot be translated simply into a transitive mode, they are verbs of state, like the verbs *to be, to live, to sleep,* etc. What Pericles says in this sentence is that we are practicing and loving beauty and wisdom, we are doing so in the act of philosophizing, that we *philokalize,* meaning "love the beautiful." And that is of course the real work of the *polis*. In the *polis par excellence,* Athens, there is extraordinary creation: in tragedy, in architecture, in sculpture, and so on. This Athenian flowering is the result of a positive public attitude toward what we call "cultural creation." Tragedy, for instance, is at the same time a public feast, a religious feast, and an essential political institution. Tragedy cannot be reduced to politics, but tragedy has a fundamental political significance.

Plato's conception of *mimesis,* his rejection of Greek mythology and poetry on grounds of their *content,* could lead one to believe that, in today's parlance, for him the value of a work of art lies essentially in its "content," that is, its theme or subject matter. This would not be quite true, and an indirect indication of this is Plato's remark in *The Republic* that the citizens in the ideal city (his city) while growing up should absorb, should inhale beauty and goodness by seeing what is around them, which obviously refers as well to "formal" properties of what is seen. I mention this in order to point out the ingratitude of this man. Because the idea I just summed up is nothing but a very fitting description of the effect that growing up in fifth-century Athens, among the public buildings, the feasts and the other events, must have had on the Athenian children. Plato, here again, exploits the reality of Athens while criticizing it. But Plato and Aristotle come after the crisis and the shattering of Athenian democracy, during years of decadence,

1. "The Greek *Polis* and the Creation of Democracy," ch. 5 of this book.

and their positions are well situated within this decadence (though, paradoxically, much less so for Aristotle).

I will not linger on the intermediate period. There is the very long Hellenistic-Roman interlude, and then the Dark Ages. Disregard the periodic revival of "revisionist" views about the Dark Ages. From the fourth century A.D. on, things are really dark for centuries save for a small ripple during the so-called Carolingian Renaissance, though there is no possible comparison with what was going on during the previous era. Massive illiteracy swept over the whole Western world. However, this does not mean that nothing was happening, or that nothing beautiful was produced. Romanesque art, in fact, is born and draws to a close during this period.

But real change comes only with the protobourgeoisie creating the first new cities (or giving a different character to the existing ones). The bourgeois invent anew, without knowing it, something quite similar to the ancient *polis,* a political community aspiring to self-government, to some sort of autonomy. This community is, or wants to be, responsible for its own fate. It is no accident that Gothic art starts in this period; Gothic art is really the work of this protobourgeoisie. Subsequently, and very quickly, there arises in the new cities a differentiation, and the development of a sort of a bourgeois aristocracy, a patriciate opposed to the new *plebs,* to the *popolo minuto*. During this period, the centuries from the eleventh or twelth to the nineteenth, the powers that be, the Church, the ruling bourgeois strata in the cities, the princely rulers like the Medici in Italy, or the kings elsewhere—France, Spain, England—support art and culture, and support them apparently in the best possible way. We should remember that we owe to this period some of the best work ever done in the arts. The situation is not identical in the case of writing—poetry or the novel—where it is difficult to trace relations between the creators and the authorities (consider, for example, the case of the creator of the modern novel, Cervantes). One of the exceptions is seventeenth-century France, where Louis XIV and his court at Versailles attract and, to some extent, attempt to control the output of some of the great writers of the period, such as Racine. But in the case of the visual arts and even of music, the authorities act as patrons, and this is more or less necessary due to the nature of the thing. The budgets involved are enormous—palaces, churches, municipal buildings, etc., and the paintings and sculptures that go with them are weighty items and require weighty decisions. For a long time there is precious little "market" about them; they depend upon the decisions and orders of the existing authorities.

The point I want to stress is that, for all we know, the choices of these authorities were practically perfect. We may like or we may dislike French kings, popes, or Italian tyrants, but nobody, I think, would object to what they did in support of these arts. So it is in the case of King François I, who brought the Italian painters to France, giving thus a new dimension to the French Renaissance and inducing the creation of the *École de Fontainebleau,* or in the case of Pope Julius II, the patron of Raphael, Michelangelo, and Bramante, or the Medicis in Florence. One may ask oneself, why is it so? The beginning of an answer, I think, is that there was no split between the avant-garde and the rest of cultivated society at that time. These people—the popes, the princes, the rulers—were part and parcel of the cultured society of their time, and this stratum, even when it was represented or personified by Henry VIII or Pope Alexander VI (Borgia), was attuned to what was happening in society. These people were certain that they were doing the right things; they were also sure of their judgment when something new and strong appeared. This situation continued up to, perhaps, the middle of the nineteenth century.

Earlier I mentioned the *Olympia* by Manet. In a similar vein I would like to relate a very beautiful story concerning Wagner and Paris which also happens to be true. It concerns the relationship of Wagner to the cultivated and chic Parisian aristocracy of the Second Empire and his first and last attempt to become known and accepted in Paris. Princess Metternich, an important person in the Court of Napoleon III, acted as a mediator and finally succeeded in organizing for Wagner a performance, the first performance, of *Tannhäuser* at the Paris Opera. *Tannhäuser* is a harmless affair, in contrast to the *Tetralogy* or *Tristan*. One cannot say it is an "Italian" opera, but it is not very far from the work of Karl Maria von Weber. It is very melodic, not very deep from the point of view of harmony or orchestration; there are beautiful, melodious arias sung by the tenor, the soprano, the baritone, and gently accompanied by the orchestra. There is nothing of the magnetic chaos of truly Wagnerian music. Now, the Paris of the time was one of the most civilized places of all times, and yet its public was one of the most philistine that ever existed. They adored Offenbach, *La Belle Hélène,* etc. And these people had the Parisian jewelers make for them special silver whistles with the following inscription: *Pour la première de Tannhäuser.* They packed the opera house, started whistling at the end of the Introduction, and the performance had to be stopped immediately after the beginning of the second act because of the constant whistling.

One can see in this story the split I was talking about earlier between the creation of the new and the existing, established, instituted culture. Also very revealing are the orders and purchases of paintings by the French government from about that time on. The government did not order the painters to paint in this or that way, and neither were important painters lacking—Courbet, then Manet and the Impressionists lived in this period. But the French government would have nothing of what they were doing. It preferred to go on buying *pompier* painting. Neither was the situation different in the other European states. Some difference appeared with the construction of the *Palais de Chaillot* around 1936, but this was just an isolated incident.

One could raise the question of what happened to taste during this whole period; however, we cannot discuss it as such. But the examples just mentioned reaffirm that what Kant says in the *Critique of Judgment* about taste has a historical grounding (which of course does not, in and of itself, decide the value of what Kant says). What Kant reflects upon in the *Third Critique* is the commonality of judgment about beauty, which is reflctive commonality and not determining universality. And this is the translation of what had been created in Western Europe during the previous centuries: a common taste, transcending local and national boundaries and linguistic frontiers, corresponding to the emergence of a civilized and cultured society equally able to recognize beauty in Spanish novels, English drama, and Italian poetry, in Flemish painting and French cathedrals—and, of course, in Greek and Roman art and culture. In this society people would either agree about what is and what is not beautiful or would respect each other's judgment enough for this judgment to become not an ultimate criterion but a necessary ingredient of one's own judgment—something which, in principle, is totally superfluous in the field of cognitive judgment.

It is this effective commonality which, as I tried to indicate before, started breaking up in the nineteenth century. This break-up was the manifestation of a crisis which is continuing under different guises. In particular, at present, neither governments nor critics nor rich collectors dare say that they do not like a particular painting, that it is not good. So governments, or in the United States the various foundations, museums, etc., which are equally manned and dominated by the bureaucracy, partake of the same attitude as public opinion.

It would be totally inept to say that governments today misbehave in this respect because they do not listen to public opinion. On the contrary, they are in full agreement with the public, rather, they follow it. The public today "freely" chooses the products representative of today's "culture"—how could it be otherwise? To be sure, this "freedom" of choice is, in a very strong sense, a fiction. The public's taste is strongly shaped by whatever is supplied, and supplied in the most pervasive way. But it is impossible to separate along this continuum an initially "innocent" public and "powers of corruption" which deform its pure native taste.

Four months ago [February 1986] in France there was a great stir of public opinion about a fifth channel on television. Two months before the general elections, President Mitterrand, in the name of the newly discovered freedom of enterprise in television and information media, pulled out of his sleeve a contract between the government and a Signore Berlusconi to establish this fifth television station. The president had chosen Signore Berlusconi and the station came alive. This Signore Berlusconi was already famous for having practically killed official Italian television through the establishment of his own channels. When he first began operations in Italy, the law forbade private television stations other than local ones. In order to get around this law, Berlusconi set up numerous local stations, and these showed the same programs in sixty or more Italian towns. In a short time Berlusconi became master of Italian television, and official television was virtually out as far as big audiences were concerned. His success was due to advertising revenues, on the one hand (you are used to this, but in Europe there has been a long struggle to attempt to limit advertising time on television), and on the other, to the very vulgarity of the programming with, naturally, a heavy porno component. Of course, the "socialist" president knew all of this perfectly well. Almost certainly, Berlusconi had made an implicit political commitment to the "socialists." Anyhow, this fifth station is established, and the whole of France is waiting to see what it's like; the first evening arrives, and the success of the new station is not at all negligible. A patient of mine, on the couch, says incidentally the following day: "I watched the fifth station last night. In comparison with that, *Dallas* is pure Shakespeare." But, I should say, this is what the French public, as it is, wants, and there is no point in blaming only Mitterrand or the "socialists" for manipulating and/or corrupting the public. Of course they are doing what they can to that effect, but the public is not outside the game either. Perhaps the best one could offer on its behalf is the old saying: "when rape is inevitable, relax and enjoy it." So they relax and enjoy the corruption.

If all of this is even only 49 percent correct, sociologically, overcoming the crisis would certainly entail something quite different from the creation of new laws or other decisions by the State. It would entail radically new attitudes on the part of the people. And if, as I hope, such new attitudes in the people emerge some day, this would mean that the present state of apathy, cynicism, indifference, and privatization would be overcome. This, in turn, would entail deep political changes, changes in the structure of political institutions and in the relation of the people to them. The type of relation of people to political institutions would have to change in order to make possible the participation of the people in power and in decision making. If the historical motto of the bourgeoisie has been, "no taxation without representation," our motto should be, "no implementation of decisions without sharing in the making of the decisions." In my opinion these two things, the overcoming of the crisis of culture and the overcoming of the political crisis are absolutely inseparable.

Meanwhile, what we have to do, is to work to preserve as much as we can of authenticity, of genuine work in the fields in which we find ourselves; and we must watch for the possible signs or germs of new creation, without letting ourselves be blackmailed by traditionalism, pseudomodernism, postmodernism, or what have you.

Afterword

In view of some misunderstandings which arose during the discussion following the seminar some explanatory remarks may prove of use to the reader.

I am not speaking nostalgically of a "classical" period, neither am I supporting an "elitist" art against a "popular" one. For me, there is no opposition of value between popular (or folk) art and "artful" art, neither do I think that great art is folk art written properly, so to speak. The relation between the two is *sui generis*. The links, for instance, between musical folklore (songs and dances) and great "artful" European music are extraordinarily strong. But at some point in time—say, during the nineteenth century—the almost complete separation of the two species of art takes place simultaneously with the virtual destruction of popular art. It is known that there are two exceptions, jazz and cinema, the two great creations of the first quarter of the twentieth century. But, what happened to these two as the century proceeded? What have we to say about jazz after the death of Thelonius Monk, for instance? Of course, everyone is entitled to his/her opinion and taste, but as far as I am concerned up to the 1960s jazz developed as a very high form of art. While the period after the 1960s is too short to allow a definitive judgment, it is clear that present-day disco and rock music simply cannot enter into comparison.

The relation between popular and "artful" art has always existed, from the time the latter appeared; it was broken, for the first time, during the nineteenth century. And for a long period, perhaps for its entire existence, avant-garde or modern art was disliked by the bourgeoisie—and artists in general hated the bourgeoisie. Nonetheless, the creation of great art went on for a long time (seventy years or more) in the form of true modern art. Atonal and serial music was created around 1906, and now Luciano Berio is inserting long quotations from *La Traviata* or Beethoven's symphonies into his pieces. Where is the musical creation of today? When Lenin said to Klara

Zetkin, "I cannot understand why these painters paint a sort of broomstick with two long forks attached, and call this 'Portrait of Mrs. X,' " he was, of course, expressing the philistine part of his nature, and he was talking exactly as a cultivated bourgeois of his time would talk. But the truth of the matter is that the workers and peasants of that time (and of today) would certainly not like cubist painting any more than the petty bourgeois public did. Cubist painting is great painting, nevertheless. And this is the tragedy of great modern art: it was the first great art which was inaccessible to the largest segment of society (something from which the eclectic pauper-soup of postmodernism escapes the easy way). And this fact stands against all "populist" theories of art, and, for that matter, traditionalist theories, or "class" theories. And that is how we entered the present dismal period of emptiness. Of course, in this huge world of ours it is almost inevitable that important figures will emerge—Samuel Beckett or Claude Simon, René Char or Paul Célan, to mention but a few. But here I am talking about the social-historical trend.

New York and Minneapolis, April 1986–Paris, May 1987.

10

Dead End?

Everything has already been said.[1] Everything remains to be said. This massive fact might, by itself, bring us to despair. Humanity would seem deaf; it is so, for the most part. This is what is most at issue when basic political questions are raised. And such is, for modern humanity, the question of the relationship it maintains between its knowledge

1. Reasons of space and time have led me on several occasions simply to state in the text ideas which I have advocated elsewhere for a long time. Permit me to refer the reader to the following articles: "Modern Science and Philosophical Interrogation" (1973) and "Technique" (1973), in *Crossroads in the Labyrinth,* tr. Martin H. Ryle and Kate Soper (Brighton: Harvester, and Cambridge, Mass.: M.I.T., 1984); "Reflections on 'Rationality' and 'Development" (1975), ch. 8 of this book; "La Logique des magmas et la question de l'autonomie" (1981), pp. 385–418, and "Portée ontologique de l'histoire de la science," pp. 419–55, in *Domaines de l'homme. Les Carrefours du labyrinthe II* (Paris: Seuil, 1986); and, finally, "From Ecology to Autonomy," tr. Alastair Davidson, *Thesis Eleven,* 3 (1981), pp. 8–22. [Translator's Note: The latter article consists of Castoriadis's remarks to a 1980 conference on ecology in Louvain-La-Neuve, Belgium. The other main invited speaker was the former French student leader (and now Greens party Frankfurt city councilor), Daniel Cohn-Bendit. Their remarks, and the public's responses, were originally published in *De l'écologie à l'autonomie* (Paris: Seuil, 1981).]

Originally published as "Voie sans issue?", in *Les Scientifiques parlent,* ed. Albert Jacquard (Paris: Hachette, 1987), pp. 261–98. Reprinted in *Le Monde morcelé. Les Carrefours du labyrinthe III* (Paris: Seuil, 1990), pp. 71–100. Translation by David Ames Curtis.

and its power, or, more precisely, between the constantly growing potential of technoscience and the manifest powerlessness of contemporary human communities.

The word "relationship" here is already a bad choice. There is no relationship. This *power* is *powerlessness* in the face of the basics of contemporary technoscience; it is a power that is anonymous in all respects, irresponsible and uncontrollable (because unattributable) which, for the moment—a very long moment, indeed—goes with a complete passivity of human beings today (including scientists and technicians themselves in their capacity as citizens). This passivity is not only total, it exhibits a complacency toward a rush of events which people still want to believe is beneficial for them without their being fully convinced any longer that it will be so in the long run.[2]

Every term used in this debate will have to be reexamined, reinterrogated, reelucidated. In this essay I will try to do so for some of them. But before going any further, and to justify my argument, let me pose a few very specific questions: *Who* decided about in vitro fertilization and embryo transplants? *Who* decided that the path was open for gene manipulation and genetic "engineering"? And *who* decided about those "*anti*"-pollution devices (which retain the carbon dioxide) that have produced acid rain?

For a long time now we have not been able and we do not want—we *should* not want—to give up rational questioning, this unearthing of the world, of our being, of the very mystery which drives us tirelessly to seek out answers and to ask questions. We can allow ourselves—and society should exist in such a way that anyone who would want to should be able—to become engrossed in the proof of a mathematical theorem, in the enigmas of basic physics and cosmology, in the intricate and inextricable meanderings of nervous systems, and to do so with a joy that differs qualitatively from, but whose intensity yields nothing to, what we might feel when listening to Bach's *Musical Offering*, looking at Van Eyck's *The Marriage of Giovanni Arnolfini and Giovanna Cenami* or reading Lautréamont's *Les Chants de Maldoror*. The author of the present essay, in his joy as a humble

2. There are certainly exceptions to this passivity, as in the case of the ecology movements—not to mention, of course, a few isolated individuals.

amateur (i.e., a lover; the Greek *erastes* is the true word) gazing from afar on these vast fields of endeavor, can bear witness to this experience. So too can he testify to the fact that he owes his very survival as well as that of those who are dear to him to the technical effectiveness of modern medicine—and this many times over. And he has, on countless occasions, criticized the inconsistencies so widespread among the members of certain ecology groups, whereby one verbally rejects modern industry upon a background of electronically recorded music and expects miracles from technomedicine just as everybody else does when one is sick.[3] It is therefore not some antiscientific or antitechnical prejudice that is being voiced here; the prejudice frankly pushes me in the opposite direction.

No real question would be raised, but instead just a "practical"—though certainly immense—problem, if we could really say (as some actually do when they examine the apocalyptic potential of technoscience): "Let's prohibit science, let's stop technical advancements," or: "Let's set precise limits on them." When all is said and done, we cannot—at least so long as we do not want to surrender our freedom. We cannot, not because we would be imposing legal restrictions on a form of activity (after all, killing is outlawed), but because, in Greco-Western history, the creation of freedom is indissociable from the emergence of questioning and rational research. And it is because we cannot do so that the question leads toward an antinomy, one which cannot be surpassed on the strictly theoretical level but which cannot be settled [practically] either, *except* through the political action and judgment of human communities acting collectively. I will return later to this point.

It also must be emphasized, however, that we remain unaware of this question when we claim that the "good" and "bad" sides of science and technique are today perfectly separable, and that all we would need to do, in order to separate them, would be to exercise greater care, devise a few technoscientific ethical rules, eliminate capitalist profiteering, or abolish the managerial bureaucracy. Let the following point be understood as clearly as possible: It is not at the level

---

3. See "Reflections on 'Rationality' and 'Development' " and "From Ecology to Autonomy."

of inventing this or that device or even of altering formal institutions that reflection can be brought to bear upon this question; a truly democratic society, rid of all economic, political, and other sorts of oligarchies, would still collide into this question just as hard. What is at issue here is one of the core significations of the modern Western imaginary, the imaginary of "rational" mastery and of an artificialized rationality that has become not only impersonal (nonindividual) but also inhuman ("objective"). Before going any further, however, we need to start excavating some of the outer layers of this question.

The Actual Reality of Technoscience

Everyone knows about the tremendous achievements of modern technique. Behind them, obviously, lies scientific knowledge. These achievements imply an equally tremendous capacity for *doing* things. Why then talk about powerlessnes? Why say that this enormous scientific potential goes hand in hand with increasing impotence?

What do we mean by "power," or even "potential"? Do we really have to change now the meaning of these words, by referendum or by some other means? Have we not always intended by "power" the possibility for someone, given the appropriate means and devices, to do what s/he wants when s/he wants? But listen carefully: for *someone* who *wants*. Where and who is this someone today—be it an individual, group, institution, or community acting collectively? In what sense does this someone *want* something and *what* does s/he want? Or again: *Who* decides, and *for what purpose?*

Take the biologists who discovered/invented the facts and methods upon which genetic engineering is based. Undoubtedly, they *wanted* (?) to do *what* they did. But to what extent did they truly want these *results?* How could they want them when they did not know what these results were and when no one to this day knows what they are—no more than anyone knew about Hiroshima and Chernobyl when Hahn, Strassman, and Joliot-Curie, at the end of the year 1938, succeeded in producing the first fissions of uranium atoms? Five years earlier Lord Rutherford had described the possibility of atomic power as the "merest moonshine."[4] And Rutherford was not only one of the greatest physicists of the century, he was also the one who initiated some of the most important experiments in the new physics.

This illusion of power also conceals an illusion relating to our knowledge: that we might be able to know all the results of what we do (or at least those results which matter to us). Such is obviously not the case. The results of our acts do not cease to trail behind us and—most importantly and much more concretely—we are aware even of the most immediate results only within the tiny vicinity of the moment of the act, a vicinity which itself is divided and fragmented. No agnosticism or sense of ethical and practical indifference follows from this. In daily life, in our familiar world, we know enough—we can and *should* know enough—about the humanly foreseeable results of our actions so that they are, for most intents and purposes, dependent upon what we do; therefore, it is both possible for us to undertake reasonable action and to require a sense of responsibility vis-à-vis our acts and their consequences. That does not mean we can draw a geometrical line at the frontiers of the foreseeable. Computers will never replace juries. What we do is sketch a boundary at the limit of what may be required in terms of foresight—a boundary which itself is in some way tacitly instituted by each society—and it is within this boundary that we raise the question of responsibility.

That already is an achievement of civilization. There are cultures in which the fact that someone is placed, really or imaginarily, at some point in the chain of occurrences leading to a injurious event was enough to mark this person as guilty. As the Biblical saying goes, "Woe unto the man by whom the offence cometh" (*Matt.* 18:7): not necessarily the actual author of the offense, but all those who have, even blindly, allowed it to occur.

It should be granted that, in daily life and in our familiar world, in those regions that have been explored from time immemorial, we can act in full knowledge of the relevant facts—first and foremost because, for the most part, this is really the case. The difference between the

4. *Nature,* 132 (16 September 1933), pp. 432–33. Cited by Pringle and Spigelman, *Les Barons de l'atome* (Paris: Seuil, 1982), p. 14.

work of a good and bad artisan is almost always recognizable; failing that, we would have no social life. But this is also so because the contrary hypothesis would lead to a conclusion that is directly opposed to all communication and living: "anything goes." But it is more than problematical that crossing over to a state in which the very phrase, "in full knowledge of the relevant facts," has lost all meaning, is legitimate.

This, humanity has always known. From the fruit of the Tree of Knowledge to the Sorcerer's Apprentice, myths dealing with what is—without any "reasonable" reason—to be forbidden, and especially with the "secrets" that a hero or heroine *must* not try to uncover, are to be found in the imaginary of all peoples. True, such ideas as "there is something that *must* not be known unless we want to court catastrophe or commit radical sin" or "there is something upon which human eyes should never gaze"—these ideas must be placed among the pillars of a heteronomous (as opposed to an autonomous) institution of society.

There is in our tradition, however, another myth, one which cannot play this role. It is a Greek myth, a beautiful image of the truth. Ulysses—whom some people recently have tried naively and stupidly to make into a hero heralding the rise of capitalism—succeeds in outwitting the Cyclops, folling the Sirenes, foiling Circe, and descending into Hell where he learns the ultimate secret: that life after death is infinitely worse than life on Earth. It is after having learned this that he rejects Calypso's offers of immortality, choosing instead to return to Ithaca to die like a man without equal and yet mortal.

But do we need myths? Do we not have before our very eyes the great atomic scientists who produced the bomb for Hiroshima and later repented at length (with the exceptions of Edward Teller and a few others)? Do we not still witness the obliviousness of their successors and of those who today venture into other fields (such as genetic engineering) whose risks are potentially much more dangerous? What need have we for myths when the environment, and Earth's biosphere, are being destroyed at as fast a rate as we are now destroying them? "We don't want that! We don't know the consequences!", it is said. Why then do you continue to do things now whose consequences no one can foresee and which are profoundly analogous to others whose horrible results we already know?

> "Would you tell me, please," said Alice to the Cheshire Cat, "which way I ought to go from here?"
> "That depends a good deal on where you want to get to," said the Cat.
> "I don't care much where—," said Alice.
> "Then it doesn't matter which way you go," said the Cat.
> "—so long as I get *somewhere,*" Alice added as an explanation.
> "Oh, you're sure to do that," said the Cat, "if you only walk long enough."
>
> Lewis Carroll, *Alice in Wonderland*

If you do not know where you want to go, how could you choose one road rather than another, and for what reason would you do so? Who among the proponents of technoscience today really knows where they want to go—not from the standpoint of "pure knowledge" but with regard both to the kind of society they would wish to live in and to the paths that will take them there? And under such conditions, how could you refuse to take a broad path which apparently is right there for the taking, and upon what grounds would you refuse to do so?

This path—quite paradoxically, considering the amount of money and effort being expended—is less and less that of the *desirable* in any sense, and more and more that of the simply *doable.* We do not try to do what "would be necessary" or what we judge "desirable." More and more, we do what we can, we work on what is deemed doable in the approximate short term. To put it more pointedly: we go after what we think we can achieve technically, and then we see what "applications" we can invent. No one asked if there truly was a real "need" for family computers; they could be made at an affordable price for people in certain income brackets, they were then manufactured, the corresponding "need" was manufactured along with them—and now they are even being *imposed* upon the populace, as in France where the State phone company's *Minitel* system is replacing other means of obtaining information.[5] What is technically feasible will be done regardless. Likewise, embryo transplants, in vitro fertilization, fetal sur-

5. "Family computers" (which should not be confused with minicomputers as such) may well prove to have some usefulness. The point I want to emphasize is that amazing sums of money have been invested in something that is, for the moment, no more than a gadget.

gery, and so on, have been put into practice as soon as the respective techniques were mastered. At present, many years later, questions about these techniques are not even really discussed, despite the courageous and commendable efforts of Professor Testard;[6] and in France, a book which insanely advocates, with its dime store ideas, things like male "pregnancy," has long been on the best-seller list.

The best image is that of a World-War-I-style trench warfare against Mother Nature. Machine guns are constantly being fired across the entire front, but huge battalions are sent into action wherever and whenever a breach seems to open up; one takes advantage of any breakthroughs that may result, but does so without any overall strategy.

Here again, logic leads to the illogical. It is perfectly reasonable to concentrate one's efforts where it seems most profitable to do so. When the mathematician Hilbert was asked why he did not attack Fermat's last theorem, he responded that it would take him three or four years of preparatory work without there being any guarantee of success. Indeed, we often see this: some great physicist has been able to advance scientific knowledge and to make an important discovery by concentrating not on problems that are great in absolute terms but rather on those which the scientist in question had the flair to see were "ripe" for the taking. How can we criticize this attitude? But how too can we remain blind to the overall unexpected result, when it embraces nearly everything?

The results would have to be known. We would also have to want them. To want them, goals would have to be laid out and *choices* made. Besides the issue of feasibility and certain instances of "pressing social demand" (e.g., medical research, notably concerning cancer—but here too the problem is less simple than it at first appears, as we shall see later), genuine choice would require the establishment of

6. See his interview in *Le Monde,* 10 September 1986. Also, he said a year before in *Libération,* apropos of male "pregnancy": "Don't worry; it if is technically feasible, someone will do it someday in the United States." See also the statments of Dr. F. Frigoletto of Harvard on fetal surgery: "The effectiveness and the innocuousness of fetal surgery have not been established" (*Le Monde,* 10 October 1986, p. 12). In fact, such operations are already being performed.

criteria and *priorities*. What criteria, what priorities, and upon what basis? Not only is it impossible in the last analysis to provide an indisputable foundation for criteria in these matters, but even if we possessed them, a somewhat consistent (I am not even saying rigorous) application of such criteria would itself raise tremendous problems. They could be applied only in a highly uncertain and multiply-varying situation.

Let us take a highly topical example. The United States National Institute of Health (NIH) has promulgated a set of scientific laboratory guidelines aimed at eliminating (or just limiting?) the risks inherent in genetic engineering. If you believe that such regulations settle the issue, then you are granting NIH a kind of omniscience.

Let us also note that governments certainly are not "subject to the rules" of NIH. For example, Field Marshal Sergei Akhromeyev, head of the General Staff of the Soviet armed forces, does not seem overly concerned about the rules promulgated by NIH. In his January 18, 1986, speech[7]—during which he clarified Mr. Gorbachev's allusion, a few days earlier, to "nonnuclear arms based upon new principles in physics"—he indicated that, among other things, these arms included "genetic weapons." Dominique Dhombres, *Le Monde*'s Moscow correspondent, comments: this area "did not seem of interest to the military before now." As far as I am concerned, I would gladly bet a few bucks that as soon as the possibilities of genetic engineering became apparent, at least the two superpowers (and why not others?) began earmarking some money and a few experts for research work in this field. Moreover, we know that research on what not so long ago used to be called the ABC weapons (atomic, bacteriological, and chemical) has never omitted the second term of this triad. And in Russia at least, we know that an explosion occurred at the Sverdlovsk plant in April 1979 and that, in June of that same year, another accident took place in a plant on the southern outskirts of Novosibirsk; in both cases, these factories were manufacturing or processing bacteriological weapons. At Novosibirsk, anthrax was involved; at Sverdlovsk, a "V-21" or "U-21" virus. In both cases, the dead could be counted in the

7. As reported in *Le Monde,* 21 January 1986, p. 3.

thousands.[8] More recently, when speaking of chemical arms the president of the French Republic, François Mitterrand, declared that he saw no reason why France should be deprived of the full panoply of defensive weapons. Why then should France be deprived of biological arms?

As things stand right now with the potentialities of genetic engineering, "bacteriological" weapons take on a quaint nostalgic hue. Anthrax is to genetic engineering as gunpowder is to the H-bomb. If research and storage facilities remain limited in this area (we have no hard data, except in the case of Russia, where we can assume the opposite), it is because of our existing overkill capacity in nuclear weapons; and perhaps also because, as in the case of nuclear arms, biological weapons can have a boomerang effect, creating once again the same two-scorpions-in-a-bottle situation.[9]

The chemical weapons the French president would like to have (and probably already has) will not be manufactured by plumbers; they will be manufactured by chemical scientists. When physicists and mathematicians were needed to manufacture nuclear weapons (without von Neumann and Ulam, there probably would not have been an American A-bomb) they were easily found—in the United States, in Russia, in Great Britain, in France, in China, in India, and perhaps elsewhere. When the KGB needs psychiatrists, it finds them as easily as the Argentine police found doctors willing to keep torture victims alive so that

8. Marie Samatan, *Droits de l'homme et répression en URSS* (Paris: Seuil, 1980), p. 143; Boris Komarov, *Le Rouge et le Vert, La destruction de la nature en URSS* (Paris: Seuil, 1981), cf. Leonid Plioutchtch's postscript, p. 207. [The English translation of Komarov's book, *The Destruction of Nature in the Soviet Union,* tr. Michel Vale and Joe Hollander (Armonk, N.Y.: M.E. Sharpe, 1980), does not include the postscript found in the French edition.]

9. As in the case of nuclear weapons, dissuasion here is not an absolute; and it seems even more unilateral than in the former case. Russia does not have interests in the New World in any way comparable to those of the United States in the Old. It would therefore be less affected if the New World were to be placed under quarantine. The relatively small cost of such weapons and the unsettling ease with which they could be delivered to their targets must also be taken into account. Let us note that in this case too there are, in theory, the equivalent of a surgical first strike and a "defensive strategy": the pathogenic agent is to be delivered once one has made sure that one possesses enough of the antidote to protect one's friendly populations.

their torture could continue. Experience shows, if there was any need, that scientists as a group are not better and no worse than other human beings—and, one might add, no wiser or less wise (I did not say any more "knowledgeable" or full of "expertise").

Many considerations are at work here, and they cannot easily be disentangled. We may leave aside simple greed—against which training in the principles of science provides no more protection than the training in any other discipline; nor does it shield scientists against political and national (not necessarily even "chauvinistic") motivations—as has been proved on a grand scale during two world wars. Everything else being equal, a career in military research is much easier than a career in "civilian" research. I am speaking here of a "career" not from a financial standpoint but from the point of view of being able to "do more interesting things," to do them "in one's own way," to direct a lab instead of just working in one as a subordinate. And above all, there is the "research virus," which in itself is neutral or even praiseworthy. In the last analysis, this was the "virus" that infected Stalin's prisoners in Solzhenitsyn's *The First Circle* and which led them to collaborate enthusiastically in a project aimed at helping the KGB locate and identify suspects. All of them thought that Stalin was a monster, that the KGB was his most monstrous tool. But the desire to solve a scientific problem—identification of an individual by use of a voice spectrogram—went beyond all other considerations. There is nothing to criticize in that. From the scientific point of view, the question of how to destroy humanity is as valid as the question of how to save it.[10]

---

10. The argument that, in destroying humanity, the scientist "acts in contradiction with himself" because without humanity there would be no science, does not hold. I have yet to see a scientific proof to the effect that science itself *should* exist. A scientist who would destroy humanity would act in contradiction, perhaps, with him/herself as a person—or with ethical values, if s/he has some—but not with any scientific proposition that would place a value on science.

To value science is in no way obligatory; cf. Ayatollah Khomeini and his supporters, to take the example closest to hand. Likewise, one could maintain that the proof of Goldbach's conjecture would have, *scientifically speaking*, more interest than the discovery of a treatment for cancer: it would have bearing upon a class of objects whose universality is much vaster. The strictly scientific point of view *may* lead to this conclusion—and in any case it has no means, *as such*, to evaluate the relative worth of two types of research.

We could also show quite easily that—like its best buddy, arms policy—military research itself, which is supposed to be based on straightforward criteria, is, in fact, in no way ruled, trivialities apart, by any sort of instrumental rationality (Max Weber's famed *Zweckrationalität* notwithstanding). But military applications are, even in the worst of cases, only a tiny aspect of the problem, if I may dare say so. Permit me two quotations:

> The worst thing that can happen—will happen—in the 1980's [they are now over—C.C.] is not energy depletion, economic collapse, limited nuclear war, or conquest by a totalitarian government. As terrible as these catastrophes would be for us, they can be repaired within a few generations. The one process ongoing in the 1980's that will take millions of years to correct is the loss of genetic and species diversity by the destruction of natural habitats. This is the folly our descendants are least likely to forgive us.
>
> Few problems are less recognized but more important than the accelerating disappearance of Earth's biological resources. In pushing other species to extinction, humanity is busily sawing off the limb on which it is perched.[11]

Such environmental destruction is not for the most part the result of hunting, DDT spraying, or even the horrible practice of whaling which has monopolized the energies of "environmentalists." It has a name: the near-certain disappearance of the tropical forests within the next thirty years. It is the result of the intensive deforestation and agricultural exploitation to which countries in the tropical and equatorial zones of the world have become, by necessity, committed (something has to be done in order to make it look like something is being done to feed the starving, and the developed-lending nations are driving them to do it). The catastrophic results of this chain of events will make themselves felt not only in the form of the certain extinction of dozens, perhaps hundreds and thousands, of species, but also in the form of a very serious disturbance in the Earth's thermal balance, in its hydrological and meteorological systems, and in the great cycles of its

---

11. The quotations are from E. O. Wilson of Harvard and Paul Ehrlich of Stanford in *Scientific American*, February 1986, p. 97.

biochemical metabolism. An Earth whose land surface is covered by forests and an Earth whose land surface is covered with grain crops are two completely different planets.

Chernobyl, which impressed people so much, is obviously in this scheme of things a very tiny affair. People shouted so much about it because it allowed them to stir up the population, exploiting its immediate fears in order to direct it toward an apparently achievable political objective: the closing of nuclear power plants (which is both impossible under present circumstances and woefully inadequate as a solution). But how can we mobilize the population against the destruction of the tropical forests? Those people need to eat. If you reply that we could begin by giving them the industrialized countries' surpluses (which are, as is known, principally agricultural surpluses) and then stop penalizing farmers who could produce much more if given the opportunity, you will be accused of wanting to maintain Third World countries in a state of neocolonial dependence. If you then reply that, obviously, you are well aware that this could not be accomplished except through radical changes in the political and social structure of the "developed" countries, that will be the end of the conversation: you will be called an incorrigible "utopian"—whereas those who are incapable of seeing anything two years down the road are obviously the "realists."

Who will maintain that this whole chain of events and changes corresponds in any degree to actual *choices?* And these choices, were they to exist, would be choices by *whom?* As such, scientists do not decide; *as such,* scientists would have no qualifications to decide (it is not *as* a laser specialist that a physicist can decide whether or not laser research has some priority over immunological research.) Inasmuch as they participate in decision-making processes, scientists can have an influence only by allying themselves with some clan or by winning the confidence of one politico-bureaucratic clique or another during power struggles in which these cliques use scientific or technical issues as emblems or rallying points, or—as happens much more frequently—in which they need "experts" to dress up in scientific clothing options that have already been decided upon for other reasons. (The well-documented history of Churchill and Frederick A. Lindemann [later Viscount Cherwell], on one side, and Tizard, on the other,[12] belongs to the simple, epic, and "honest" era of these kinds of disputes.) Let us add to what has been said earlier about motivations relating to the funding of own's own projects when they are placed in competition with those of others, that it is not only a question of career advancement and personal prestige; for each scientist, his/her idea is his/her "brain-child," and "objectivity" here is, on the subjective level, almost impossible.

As for the politicians who have final control over research budgets, charity requires one not to scrutinize the issue too closely. When they are not downright ignorant, they have their personal whims; and this is perhaps the worst of cases. We recently heard a former president of the French Republic angrily defending the funding of "sniffing airplanes" which supposedly could detect oil underground by invoking Galileo's condemnation by the Church. Moreover, this affair involved recognized experts and specialists. And when the politicians are ignorant and know it (not at all the same thing), they are coached by advisors who as a general rule went into careers in management and politics because their personal scientific performance was neligeable; they are to scientific truth what critics are to literary and philosophical creation. To a great extent their motivations are tied to the survival of the clan into which they have managed to insinuate themselves.

It will be said that we are in a democracy and that the public or public opinion can, or should, control what is going on. A pale abstraction. It is no longer sufficient merely to repeat what was, not so long ago, quite well known but which now seems strangely and overwhelmingly forgotten these past years with the rediscovery of "free-market values": namely that public opinion accepts the information it is given, that it is manipulated in all sorts of ways, that it must make enormous efforts—and then it does so only after the fact and in small part—just to stand up to what State, political, and economic bureaucratic apparatuses perpetrate twenty-four hours a day. The question goes much deeper: it concerns the formation of modern man's representations and will.

12. For example, by C. P. Snow in *Science and Government* (Oxford: Oxford University Press, 1961) and *A Postscript to Science and Government* (Oxford: Oxford University Press, 1962).

It can be said, at a first level, that these representations and this will are constantly being formed by the entirety of the contemporary instituted world, including its weighty component of technoscience. In turn, the latter has endowed the world out of which it arises with an instrument that is intrinsically adaptable not only to the scope but also to the very substance of the manipulation to be carried out, that is, the mass media. This is quite true, but it does not exhaust the question. Let us also ask: Who has willed modern technoscience in its present state, and who wills its indefinite continuation and proliferation? No one and everyone. We must stop doing to humanity as a whole what Marxism did to the proletariat: making of it an all-powerful subject, and yet totally innocent of anything that might happen to it, as if it were beyond all influence. If ever a nuclear winter comes to pass, if ever the polar icecaps melt, if ever a quick-spreading lethal virus escapes from a genetic-engineering laboratory—and if ever the shaggy, starving survivors haul the remaining physicists or biologists into court, the resulting paradoxes and aporias will be as acute and as intense as when one recalls the Nuremberg trials, the presence of Soviet prosecutors at these trials, and the recent election of Mr. Waldheim to the Austrian presidency. For, just as no totalitarian regime could do what it has done without millions of Eichmanns and Waldheims (I accept, in the latter's case, the most recent official version of his conduct, namely, that he had served as an interpreter for an armed unit charged with exterminating Yugoslavian and Greek partisans)—and they would be nothing without the tolerance of their respective peoples—so, even more clearly, the avalanche of contemporary technoscience is fed not by mere tolerance but by people's active support. Can we haul entire peoples into court? What kind of tribunal would that be, and who would bring them there? But perhaps they are in the process of bringing themselves to trial, taking with them the thirty-nine righteous ones of the Jewish parable.

Everyone—liberals, free-marketeers, Marxists, the rich, the poor, the educated, the illiterate—has believed, has wanted to believe, still believes, and still wants to believe that technoscience is quasiomniscient, quasiomnipotent, that it would also be almost entirely beneficial were it not for some bad people who divert it from its true ends. The question therefore goes far beyond any idea of "particular interests" or underhanded "manipulation." It concerns the core imaginary of modern man, of the society and institutions which he creates and which create him. I will return to this point at the end of the present essay. Let us recall now simply that, if this is truly the case, the transformations we will have to undertake are infintiely vaster and more profound than what, until now, we might have imagined they would be. Human beings' creation of a sedentary life-style or their domestication of living species offer merely pale analogies.

This last statement will seem excessive only to those who have little understanding both of how vast the stakes are and, above all, of the agonizing character of the virtual choices, rooted as they are in basic, antinomic questions.

From an abstract point of view, we may state: no one wants—no one should want—a return to the stone age (though it seems that we have already made this choice without knowing it or wanting it); and no one should continue to harbor any illusions about technoscience being "a good tool that has fallen into bad hands."

More concretely speaking, let us ask: *From the standpoint of humanity as a whole,* who has made and who could make a cost/benefit analysis between the money spent on cancer research and the amount that would be needed to come to the aid of the starving people of the Third World? What "rational" option can there be between the admirable results of the Centre Européen de Recherche Nucleaire (CERN) experiments (along with the millions of dollars spent on them) and the living corpses on the streets of Bombay and Calcutta? I will not say anything about the debate—which, indeed, has not even begun—over the "right of sterile individuals to have children of their own" and the research time and money spent on it, as this question seems to me a sinister farce when the living skeletons of Ethiopian and Eritrean children are being shown on television at the same time. The choice has already been made: Mr. and Mrs. Smith will have *their own* child—at a cost in dollars and labor time that could have kept perhaps fifty African children alive.

I am not even saying that all these choices, and the thousands of others that could be mentioned, are "wrong." They are, as a first approximation, completely "arbitrary," and, as a second approximation, not arbitrary at all. They are determined by something altogether different from "rational" or human priorities. When it is claimed that this or that option serves the ongoing and universal interests of humanity (every human being might one day be stricken with cancer, for example), this universal turns out to be empty (a good proportion of humanity does not even have the opportunity to reach the age where there is a significant incidence of cancer). The choices are "determined" by a process—"random" in its details, but moving overall in a clear-cut direction—through which technoscience develops and grows; a hammer without a hand guiding it, its mass constantly increasing, its pace ever swifter.

On the Social Representations of Science

As has been said a thousand times, the situation of contemporary man is supremely paradoxical. The more he is "powerful," the more he is impotent. The more he knows, the less he knows. And, despite the fantastically arrogant claims of a few men of science, the more he knows, the less he knows what knowing might be.

The more one knows, the less one knows. It is not difficult to illustrate this idea both within knowledge itself, considered "intrinsically" (I will speak briefly about this aspect in the third part of my essay), and in the relationship between knowledge and the subject of knowledge.

First, the individual subject. S/he knows ever more about ever less; less, not only in scope—each particular field is continually shrinking—but also and especially with regard to the meaning and the conditions of his/her knowledge. As for the collective subject—that is, as regards scientific communities, for whom three decades of talk about multi- or transdisciplinary studies have not been enough to counterbalance either the reality of an acceleration of specialization or its consequences, but also as regards the human community itself—let us note that, long before anyone spoke of "two cultures" and of their mutual separation within contemporary society, the German sociologist Max Weber noted that a savage knew infinitely more about the practical world around her than someone today knows about his. As for the "theoretical" world, the religious faith of yesteryear has given way to a vague belief in science and technique. This is an abstract belief, a container which most often includes only a few stale crumbs fallen from the table of the vulgar popularizers of science (who often are scientists themselves). As this belief is itself only a weak and watery filtrate of representations issuing from scientists themselves, it would be better to talk directly about these representations.

I have neither the intention nor the opportunity to do so here: that would fill up a book. Rather, I am going to speak of two fallacies which seem to me extremely widespread, highly representative (in themselves and in their various, more or less incoherent combinations), and worthwhile noting—even when those who hold such views are not in the majority—for they serve to reveal the underlying problems.

The first, the least plausible, and certainly one that is almost never defended openly, denies that science has any truth value at all, or—what amounts to the same thing—assigns to the term "truth" only the most narrowly pragmatic sense of "it works." *What* works? As it should, pragmatism gives birth to the skepticism contained in it: everything works, anything works, or as the philosopher of science, P. K. Feyerabend says, "anything goes." This outcome is inevitable. The pragmatist's thesis is this: we accept as true those theories that "work." But a question arises: How do we know when a theory works? My argument here is not designed to recapitulate the philosophical "refutation" of skepticism, but to note that this borderline idea of "epistemological anarchism" starts from a statement of fact that it neither understands nor expresses correctly: *the history of science does not constitute a system that unfolds over time.* And it forgets another, equally massive fact: far from our being able to say "anything goes," the theories capable of providing competing explanations of "the accepted facts" at a given moment are rather small in number.

The second fallacy, by far the most widespread—and which I believe to be held by the large majority of scientists—is a version of nineteenth-century progressivism. In this view, it is claimed that our knowledge, as it evolves over time, approaches truth asymptotically; that our successive scientific theories constitute less and less inexact expressions of reality; and that, if there be a succession of these theories, it is because previous theories represent "particular cases" of subsequent theories, which, in turn, are "generalizations" of the earlier ones. This untenable view unconsciously carries with it a weighty metaphysics which implies, among other things, that there is a preestablished harmony between a sequencing of strata of Being and a process of development in our thought, or that what is most "profound" and the least immediately accessible in terms of phenomena is necessarily universal. In order to give some basis to this belief, people obstinately go on invoking the case of the Einsteinian succession of Newtonian theory (which is in no way typical of the history of science), thereby obliterating the upheaval of changes in categories, axioms, and representations separating the two theories. And it leads quite naturally to a triumphal dogmatism—a dogmatism in which the almost-last-word is always promised for tomorrow, and the promise is reiterated every day. Examples of this dogmatism abound. Already in 1898, at the opening of a conference of physicists, Lord Kelvin stated that the edifice of physics was almost complete, except for two tiny problems whose solutions would be found during the next few years. One wonders what is most amazing, the megalomaniacal arrogance or the unfailing instincts of the brilliant physicist who pointed precisely to what was going to topple the edifice whose near completion he was then celebrating (i.e., the Michelson experiment and black-body radiation) among so many of the questions that were then and sometimes still today open to scientific inquiry. Since then, similar proclamations have often been heard, and they have been immediately rebroadcast by vulgarizers and journalists who keep on repeating every few weeks that the ultimate enigma of the Universe has finally been solved.

These two fallacies have political implications: that we scientists know, that we know everything, and that therefore we should be left alone to do what we will [*laissez-nous faire*]. Or, that we know nothing and that no one knows anything, that coherent discourse is impossible (or that an infinite variety of discourses concerning the same object can exist, which boils down to the same thing), that, therefore, the existing order of things is as good or bad as any other.

The resulting two conclusions have one thing in common: they both want to bar philosophical interrogation, which not only lies at the origin of Western science but is, today more than ever, needed by science, faced as it is with unprecedented theoretical difficulties.

Sociologically and historically speaking, what is perhaps most interesting is that there clearly is a group of scientists (I am not speaking here of their statistical weight, which I believe to be great) who think with divided minds and who live on two different levels of "self-consciousness" or "self-representation" at once without being able to say that one of these two levels is paramount, or more profound than the other.

At one of these levels, a scientist representative of this group will think and will state that we possess the truth or that we are going to possess the humanly most feasible approximation thereof. At another level, this scientist will say: it is stupid ("metaphysical") to ask questions about the truth, this question has no meaning, science examines not the *what* but the *how;* it does not interrogate the object, it simply manipulates it and predicts its behavior. There are computations and experiments that work, others that do not, these results are to be polished to perfection or else rejected in favor of other hypotheses. If this scientist is epistemologically more sophisticated, s/he will gladly accept a view that manages to effect a strange synthesis between the two preceding ones and will state that a theory is never true but only "falsifiable," that it is provisionally accepted so long as it has not been refuted. Of course, this clever scientist will never pose the question of what makes the refutation of a theory "true" or valid; and still less will s/he examine all that is presupposed, both on the side of the subject as well as on that of the object of science, for procedures like the positing of hypotheses and then their "falsification" or "refutation" to be possible.

But even more serious is that, for this type of scientist, the two levels described are completely concealed by his/her real attitude, which is, in a sense, the most authentic one. In this attitude, the question of truth is not posed; it is not even asked to the extent that one could reply, "This question has no meaning." Of course, a question of *correctness* or *exactitude* is raised: Are the results correct? Are the observations accurate? And, most especially: Are these observations consistent with, and do they correspond to, what one was looking for? Do they meet and advance "the accepted body of beliefs," the body of scientific beliefs considered in each instance as established (whether provisionally or not). At this real, effective level, scientific activity becomes a techno-pragmatic activity designed to manipulate objects, instruments, algorithms, and concepts and to assure itself that all this "works" somehow or other as it forbids any kind of self-interrogation or any questions about the conditions for its success, *even its pragmatic success*.

In order for this technopragmatic activity to be sociologically possible and for technoknowledge to develop; in order for the scientific enterprise, with its generally huge but not rationally justified costs (which does not mean that they are positively *un*justified), to be funded adequately; in order for it to attract gifted young people and to build up its authority and prestige; and, in order to ensure that the many and varied risks it creates will remain outside the public eye, a certain image of modern science must be presented to the public—exactly the same image, as it turns out, that the public, in the grip of the imaginary signification of the unlimited expansion of "rational" mastery, expects of science and demands of it. This image is that of a triumphal march during which theoretical uncertainties within science itself as well as basic questions relating to its object and to its relation to society must at all costs be evacuated. In addition, science must give assurances, against what scientific evidence itself tells us, that no problem or major risk is involved in the utilization or application of scientific discoveries—or that a few rules of good behavior on the part of the laboratories concerned are all that are needed in order to counter any such risk.

Thus, of all human activities, science would be the sole one simply to resolve questions without raising any, it would be released from the need for questioning as well as from any burden of responsibility. A divine innocence it would possess, a marvelous form of extraterritoriality.

At the same time, all communication between science and philosophy—or more simply put, all thought, reflection, and interrogation—would also have to be abolished. The questions raised by the successive crises of science as well as by its very history, but also by the conditions and the foundations of scientific activity and, last and most especially, by what it says or does not say about *what is* and its mode of being as well as about *the one who knows* and about his/her mode of being—these questions too must all be forgotten. This happens to such a degree that I have to ask myself whether what I am saying here (and have said elsewhere for a long time), the language I employ, these concerns (which have been, in their time, if I am permitted to quote these names, those of such feeble-minded people as Democritus, Plato, Aristotle, Descartes, Leibniz, Newton, Kant, Maxwell, Einstein, Poincaré, Bohr, Weyl, Eddington, Hilbert, Broglie, Heisenberg, etc.), this very sense of wonder—what Aristotle called *thaumazein*—which cannot but immensely grow in scope and intensity with the very success, itself in a sense *unreasonable,* of modern science, will have any meaning at all, even as something considered ridiculous, for the scientist thirty years from now, or whether these words will apear to him/her simply unintelligible.

Contemporary Science as Theory: Some Aspects

As I said, the more one knows, the less one knows. This certainly may seem like just a clever way of playing on the difference between the reality of knowledge and the idea one has of it, between what one knows and what one thinks one knows. But in truth, that is not the case. The "classical" scientific worlds were, so to speak, complete (in a "topological" sense). For Newton (or Laplace) there were no gaping holes in his (or Laplace's) system of the world, nor were there any in Euclid's mathematics *for* Euclid. In both cases, there obviously were problems—which is something entirely different. The Euclidian world (with Hilbert's reform of it) is complete—once you "exile" therefrom the question of whether it is valid to postulate the existence of parallel lines; it is complete with the indisputable validity of this proposition taken as a point at infinity. The Newtonian world is complete so long as we leave aside one or two apparently "peripheral" questions (e.g.: What does it mean for two distant observers to make simultaneous observations? Or, How can this simultaneity be verified?). And the miraculous dovetailing between Euclidian geometry and Newtonian physics was "complete," too. In other words, the "gaps" were at the edges of the system, and there was only one or there were only a very few; it was therefore possible to cover them up or, in any case, to "isolate" them. Today such isolation and covering up are no longer possible, they *should* no longer be possible.

In order to show their importance both for science and for philosophy, I wish I had the space here to sketch out more clearly those aporias that seem to me to spring from within contemporary science itself.[13] Lacking this opportunity, and in order to shake up what seems to me a certain epistemological torpidity that has taken hold of our age, I will attempt simply to provide a series of key examples, ones which seem to me to justify scientists taking some interest in the foundations of their activity and renewing their ties with the process of philosophical interrogation.

First things first. Let us begin with a few examples relating to mathematics. After Gödel proved his two incompleteness theorems (1931), other theorems were established (notably, Church's 1936; and Turing's 1936). Taken together, these theorems imply that, except for trivial (finite) cases, undecidable propositions exist in mathematics, that the consistency of formal systems is never provable within these same systems, and that we can never devise a machine (or algorithm) that will tell us in advance whether a proposition is or is not provable.

Since the time they were first published, discussion about these theorems seems to have become confined more and more within a narrow circle of specialists in mathematical logic. This was, in a sense, natural: these theorems did not affect the current work of mathematicians, whatever the "depth" of the subject matter. Their importance instead lies elsewhere. They destroy the idea that we can have rigorous hypothetico-deductive knowledge in the sole nontrivial domain wherein it seemed as if we were approaching that goal. Not only am I unaware of any genuine philosophical elaboration of these theorems but, to my knowledge, no one has tried to examine their implications for *real physics* (which, of course, is supposed to relate only to finite quantities but which constantly makes use of infinite sets in the procedures it employs).

On the other hand, mathematics since Cantor has been progressively reconstructed from the bottom up on the basis of set theory—and, in any case (apart from all "foundational" questions), it contains this theory as one of its essential parts. Now, in set theory an (apparently secondary) question necessarily arises which bears upon the sequence of cardinal numbers of infinite sets. Roughly speaking, the question is the following: Between the infinity of natural numbers (1,

13. I did it fifteen years ago in "Modern Science and Philosophical Interrogation," *op. cit.*

2, 3 . . .) and the infinity of real numbers (those that correspond to the points of a line), is there or is there not an infinity of another "type of multiplicity" (of another cardinal)? Cantor's hypothesis, called the continuum hypothesis, answers in the negative: to the infinity of natural numbers the infinity of real numbers follows immediately (from the standpoint of cardinality). Now, Gödel first demonstrated in 1940 that the continuum hypothesis (and even a stronger hypothesis, called the generalized continuum hypothesis) is compatible with the habitual axioms of set theory, notably the Zermelo-Fraenkel system of axioms. Then, in 1963, Paul J. Cohen demonstrated that the *negation* of the continuum hypothesis is equally compatible with set theory. It follows, first of all, that set theory is incomplete; second and above all, that it could be completed by the addition of a supplementary axiom—which would lead to a situation comparable to that of Euclidean and non-Euclidean geometries. It appears that the, probably considerable, implications of a plurality of set theories have not yet been worked out.

In the third place, an enormous portion of the conclusions of twentieth-century mathematics relies upon the axiom of choice as formulated by Zermelo, which is tantamount to saying: every set can be well ordered. Now, it can be shown that this axiom—which appeared entirely counterintuitive to great mathematicians like Emile Borel and Hermann Weyl and the entire intuitionist school—is both equivalent to propositions that seem intuitively obvious (e.g., that the Cartesian product of a family of nonempty sets is not empty) and incompatible with other propositions which seem just as intuitively obvious, like J. Mycielsky's axiom of determinacy (1964; this axiom states that infinite games with perfect information are determined, in the sense that there is always a winning strategy for one or the other player). Here the question concerns not only the possible fragility of a large portion of the results of modern mathematics (which had led the collective author Nicolas Bourbaki to mark with an asterisk those theorems whose proof depends upon acceptance of the axiom of choice), but the vacillations of mathematical intuition in its attempts to come to terms with its more outlandish creations.

At the intersection of mathematics and physics, and as we pass now from one to the other, let us recall that the question of the extraordinary effectiveness of mathematics when applied to the physical world remains as open today as it was when the first who raised it, Pythagoras, was at work. And let it not be said that the issue of applied mathematics' extraordinary effectiveness has been resolved by Kant's *Critique of Pure Reason.* For, on the one hand, most of these applications presuppose the mathematical theory of measure of the set of real numbers, which remains obscure even from the strictly mathematical point of view. On the other hand and above all, what is to be explained is the applicability to a physical world, that *is not* that of our current experience, of "tools" (or forms, if you prefer) coming from parts of mathematics as complex and distant as, for example, absolute differential calculus and the theory of distributions—whose relation to Kant's "Transcendental Aesthetic" is highly improbable, to say the least.

In physics, properly speaking, the work, the great work, is constantly being taken back to the shop for further elaboration. Thus, for example—and despite the relentless, one-sided publicity given to one theory during at least the past thirty-five years—it would be wrong to say that we can at the present hour decide between the various extant cosmological models, and in particular between those of an "open" and those of a "closed" Universe. If, in the present state of our knowledge, an "explosive" singularity in the history of the Universe fifteen or twenty billion years ago cannot seriously be challenged, the model of an "open" Universe (in indefinite expansion, starting from a *unique* event marking an absolute origin) is being put into question more and more by scientists' constantly rising, revised estimates of the average density of the Universe. (This situation was not, a priori, so hard to foresee!) If these estimations of average density should one day exceed a certain critical level (and present estimations appear to be rather close already) we would be obliged to accept a "cyclical" model of the Universe, one which is alternatively in expansion and in contraction and during whose history the Big Bang would have been simply one important event in a perhaps indefinite series of events of the same type. But in this last model, energy-matter is not conserved (it would "increase" with each cycle, during the contraction phase). Let us simply note here that, beyond the basic intrinsic importance of cosmology and of making a choice between these models (or others), the mere existence of a coherent model (as derived from the theory of general relativity and Friedmann's equations)—that is compatible, in principle, with possible observations and within which the basic laws of conservation of present-day physics do not hold—suffices to show how extravagant it would be to think that our physics is really standing on solid theoretical grounds.

At the other end of physics (and intimately connected with the first) the "zoology" of elementary particles, about which Heisenberg complained, has changed form but perhaps not substance. Though some order has been established among the hundreds of "elementary" particles, there remain a good thirty "really basic" particles—which themselves "result" from the combination of a more limited number of [subatomic] characteristics. This leads us to think that the genuine question concerns less the multiplicity of particles than the plurality of basic characteristics; why charge, spin, "up," "down," "bottom," "top," and all the rest? Moreover, the attempts to construct a really unified theory still collide with the problem of the incompatibility between the structure of general relativity and that of quantum theory—both of which are constantly being "confirmed" by observation and experimentation. But if, as seems to be the case, the quantum position is unshakeable (cf. again recently the fate of the "Einstein-Podalsky-Rozen [EPR] paradox" and the question of inseparability), a unification [of general relativity and quantum theory] would require a quantification of space-time—an expression to which it seems impossible to attach any meaning at all. The situaiton of basic physics is still in flux and new basic concepts are periodically being introduced, such as "supersymmetry" recently, or "strings" and "superstrings" which would take the place of particles in a "real" underlying Universe of ten dimensions.

In biology, a large misunderstanding has dominated thinking practically ever since we have gone beyond Darwin's original insights. People are talking all the time about *evolutionary* theory. Both in common parlance and in Darwin's mind (cf., to mention only two examples, the terms "selection" and "survival of the fittest"), the word "evolution" has undeniably had the sense of an unfolding of possibilities, of a progression or, at least, of an increasing complexity. Now, if the *fact* of evolution is incontestable, no *genuine theory* of evolution really exists. Clearly, neo-Darwinian theory (the "modern synthesis") is a theory of species *differentiation,* not one of the *evolution* of species. For, not only would the same theory "explain" just as well an Earth history which would have led to the existence of a completely different set of species than now exists, but nothing in this alleged "theory" would make intelligible to us why evolution would proceed in a "direction" that goes from a few primitive organisms to hominids; nothing in it tells us why differentiation occurs in the direction of increasing complexity and not, so to speak, "laterally." Why these millions of present-day species, and not, to take one example, just a few million single-celled species?

After a torrent of exaggerated claims lasting twenty years, it has finally been admitted, it seems, that DNA and the genetic code—fundamental discoveries though they were, as no one would deny—are far from providing us with everything we would need to render intelligible the self-production and even the reproduction of living beings. We need only recall that the majority of neurologists as well as immunologists reject the idea of complete genetic predetermination (as coded in the DNA molecules) for the specialized development of nerve cells and cells of the immune system. They prefer "epigenetic" hypotheses (which make this process of specialization the result of the "history" of each cell, to a large extent codetermined by the "surroundings" in which it finds itself: namely, its "neighborhood"). More likely than not, these hypotheses contain a great deal of truth (in any case, the predetermination hypothesis is untenable for the types of cells mentioned). But we may also ask whether the epigenetic view does not bring us back, at another level, to the same problem it was supposed to have addressed at the outset: one would still have to hypothesize a genetic predetermination that makes such cells capable of a particular sort of epigenetic development and not another, a particular sort of reaction to its "history" and not another, etc. And, on the other hand, it leads us to reexamine the most basic abilities and properties of living beings; of these, scientists still show no signs of theoretical comprehension. It is one thing to say that a gene determines a specific characteristic. It is something else again to say that a gene determines the capacity to produce an indefinite number of characteristics (about whose existence, moreover, we are certain, given the example of the language abilities of human beings).

What does all this mean if not that science is, rather fortunately, more open than ever, more questioning than ever, less comforting to the inquiring mind than ever? What does all this mean, for genuine scientists and for those who cannot remain indifferent to their vast work, if not an appeal for the renewal of human thought?

In Lieu of a Conclusion

Contrary to what has happened since Hegel, science is, and ought to be, an object of passion for philosophy. Not as a set of certainties, but as an inexhaustible well of enigmas, an inextricable mixture of light and darkness, the evident testimony to an incomprehensible meeting, ever assured and ever fugitive, between our imaginary creations and what exists, and also as an outstanding affirmation of our autonomy, of the rejection of simply inherited or instituted beliefs, of our capacity constantly to weave the new into a tradition, to transform ourselves by using our past transformations as supports.

But we should distinguish the philosophical import and the abstract practical possibilities of science from its social-historical reality, from the actual role it plays in the contemporary world, and in the massive drift our world is experiencing. Considered as a whole, this role is far from univocally positive. The destruction of the environment, with its incalculable and largely unknown consequences, perhaps already began with the end of the neolithic era (the beginning of the elimination of a variety of living species, deforestation). It has taken qualitatively different dimensions since then: not so much in the industrial revolution but in the scientific revolution of industry, what Marx called "the conscious (!) technical application of science"[14]; in short, ever since we ceased living with a "naive" (!) technology and instead began living with a scientific technology. What worth (for those who may enjoy them) would the comforts of modern life have when weighed against the prospect of the polar icecaps melting? And how many pennies would all the conquests of modern medicine be worth if World War III were to explode?

These accounts cannot be added up in any particular field—the

14. Translator's Note: This quotation comes from "The Historical Tendency of Capitalist Accumulation," of Karl Marx's *Capital,* vol. 1, ch. 32.

pluses and the minuses are inextricably bound together. Even less can a balance sheet be drawn up in all fields at once—unless reality does it for us one day. To add things up you need separate elements, which do not exist in this case. The fallacy of separation—for instance, let's keep modern medicine and reject (the military consequences of) nuclear physics—contains an illogical premise identical to that of the young ecologists who were fleeing from an industrial world by establishing rural communes—within which they could not do without industrial products. Modern medicine and (theoretical and applied) nuclear physics are not different plants but two branches of the same tree, if not to say two substances in the same fruit. The existence and development of the one like the other presuppose the same anthropological type, the same attitudes toward the world and human existence, the same modes of thought, technical activity, and usages of tools and instruments.

All this does not mean that scientific research is "bad" in itself—far from it—nor that we would have to stop it (in any case, we could not and should not). It simply reminds us of a few obvious points, some banal, others less so.

Let us recap first with the obvious and banal: beyond the doors of their laboratories, scientists are men and women like any others, as vulnerable to ambition, desire for power, flattery, vanity, influence, prejudices, greed, errors of judgment, and unreflective stands as anyone else. In addition, and as could have been predicted, the immense progress in the attainment of positive knowledge and in its applications has not been accompanied by an inch of moral progress, either among the protagonists of science or among their fellow citizens.

Obvious, but less banal: the fantastic autonomization of technoscience, which Jacques Ellul has the imprescriptible merit of having formulated as early as 1947 and which scientists and nonscientists alike mask under the illusion of the separability of "means" and "ends," thereby purveying the false idea that another "master" might be able to direct technoscientific evolution in another direction. But this set of practices, potentialities, and forms of knowledge which fabricates laboratories and lab assistants, inventors, imitators and researchers, apocalyptic weapons, test-tube babies, and real-live monsters, poisons and medicines—this supermegamachine is dominated by no one. No one controls it, and, in the present state of things, the question whether someone would be able to control it is not even raised. With technoscience, modern man believes he has been granted mastery. In reality, if he "masters" a growing number of limited areas of interst, he is less powerful than ever over the totality of the effects of his actions, precisely because these actions have multiplied to such a great extent and because they affect strata of physical and biological Being about which he knows nothing—which does not prevent him from poking around with an ever-growing stick into an ant hill that is also without doubt a hornet's nest.

We must be done with the idea that science and technique confer upon humanity a power that might at present simply be "badly utilized." On the one hand, technoscience constantly produces "power" in the limited sense of an actual ability to do things; on the other hand, with the way contemporary society is evolving (cf. *infra*), this power could not be "utilized" in any other fashion than the way in which it now is, and by no one else than the one who now utilizes it, that is to say, Nobody. There is no "technocracy" or "scientocracy." Far from forming a dominant ruling group, scientists and technicians serve the existing Power Apparatuses (strictly speaking, they are part of it); and these Apparatuses exploit, certainly, and also oppress almost the entire world, but they do not really direct anything.

At the heart of the modern era, and ever since the end of the "Dark Ages," two intrinsically antinomic but connected social imaginary significations have arisen. (We will not dwell on this connection here.) On the one hand, *autonomy* has animated the emancipatory and democractic movements which traverse the history of the West as well as the rebirth of questioning and rational inquiry. The *unlimited expansion of "rational" mastery,* on the other hand, is at the basis of the institution of capitalism through its various phases (including, by a monstrous inversion: totalitarianism). It undoubtedly culminates in the unfurling of technoscience.

For reasons I have developed at length elsewhere, rational "mastery," when indefinitely expanded, can in reality be only a *pseudorational* mastery. But another dimension also is of importance here. As soon as "rationality" was seen to be perfectly "objectifiable" (which quickly came to mean: capable of being put in the form of an algorithm and susceptible to impersonal mastery), "rational mastery" came to imply, and in truth requires, impersonal mastery. But impersonal mastery, when extended to everything, obviously becomes the mastery of Nobody, of *outis*—and it becomes, thereby, complete non-mastery, impotence. (In a democracy, there is of course an impersonal rational rule, the law—thought without desire, as Aristotle would say—but there are also flesh and blood governors and judges.)

Completely symptomatic in this regard is the present-day tendency toward the "automatization of decisions." This goal is already being implemented in a large number of secondary cases, but it is beginning to take on a new appearance with the introduction of "expert systems." And still more illustrative is the idea, which is in some way its realization, of a "Doomsday" machine, an expert system that would automatically send missiles from one camp to the other as soon as those from the other side have been computed or assumed to have been fired, thereby eliminating from deterrence policy all "subjective" (and therefore fallible as well as influenceable) politico-psychological factors. Are we really so far away from that point now?

In the societies preceding our own, human mortality could be negated by religion in the broadest sense of the term. This negation has always taken the form of denial, in the Freudian sense of the term: a negation which, in the very act of being formulated, demonstrates the contrary of what it explicitly affirms. (If man was immortal, he would not need all these proofs of immortality and all these articles of faith.) This role is today played, as much as it can be, by technoscience. It is not enough for us to go on repeating that, in the modern world, science has taken the place of religion. What must be understood are both the limits of this substitution (which do not concern us here) and the element of truth that it contains. Science offers a substitute for religion inasmuch as it now embodies the illusion of omniscience and omnipotence—the illusion of mastery. This illusion is minted in an infinite variety of ways—from the hope for a "miracle" drug, passing through the belief that society's "experts" and governors know what is good, to the voicing of the ultimate consolation: "I am weak and mortal, but Power exists." Modern man's difficulty in admitting the potential harmfulness of technoscience is analogous to the sense of absurdity a believer would experience when hearing someone say: "God is bad."

From valuing the power of doing as such to the adoration of naked force there is just a single tiny step.

The phantasy of being all-powerful has undoubtedly existed ever since man became man. It has been coined into some power and it took refuge in magic, or military conquest. With its fecondation by its own offspring—rationality—it has, for the first time, been able to become actual historical power, the social imaginary signification dominating an entire world. If this has been possible, it is not only that the human imaginary has taken this turn and has provided itself with means other than magic or elementary military technology. It is also that the world—the "prehuman" world—lends itself to this happenstance and that this world is knowable and even manipulable.

The world is knowable to an apparently unlimited degree. It unveils to us, through our work, one after another of its connected yet heterogeneous strata. And yet, it clearly is not limitlessly manipulable—and this, not simply from the standpoint of "extent" (we cannot change the direction in which our galaxy rotates, for example), but also from a qualitative standpoint. We have clearly attained this limit, and we are in the process of crossing it at several points at once. Moreover, as I have tried to show, the most intimate sort of connection exists between the limitless unfolding of our knowledge and the limits we ought to impose upon our manipulations [of the world].

Now, at the same time that the rage for "power," the fetishism for "rational mastery," waxes triumphant, the other great imaginary signification of Greco-Western history—that of autonomy, notably in its political manifestations—seems to be suffering an eclipse. The present crisis of humanity is a crisis of politics in the grand sense, a crisis of creativity and of our political imagination as well as of political participation by individuals. The reigning conditions of privatization and "individualsim" give free rein, in the first place, to the arbitrariness of the Apparatuses and, at a deeper level, to the autonomized march of technoscience.

This is the ultimate point of the question at hand. The enormous dangers, the very absurdity contained in the all-out, directionless development of technoscience, cannot be avoided simply by promulgating a few "rules" set forth once and for all, or by installing a "panel of wise men" who would become merely a tool, if not themselves the actual subject, of a tyranny. What is required is more than a "reform of the human understanding"; it is a reform of the human being as social-historical being, an ethos of mortality, a self-surpassing of Reason. We have no need for a few "wise men." What we need is for the greatest number of people to acquire and exercise wisdom—which in its turn requires a radical transformation of society *qua* political society, thereby instaurating not simply formal participation but also actual passion on the part of all for the common affairs of humanity. Wise human beings, however, are the very last thing that present-day culture produces.

"What is it that you want, then? To change humanity?"

"No, something infinitely more modest: simply that humanity change, as it has already done two or three times."

Bibliography

Other Works by Cornelius Castoriadis in English

Crossroads in the Labyrinth (1984)
The Imaginary Institution of Society (1987)
Political and Social Writings, 2 vols. (1988)

And in French

La Société bureaucratique, 2 vols. (1973)
L'Expérience du mouvement ouvrier, 2 vols. (1974)
L'Institution imaginaire de la société (1975)
Les Carrefours du labyrinthe (1978)
Capitalisme moderne et révolution, 2 vols. (1979)
Le Contenu du socialisme (1979)
La Sociéte française (1979)
Devant la guerre (1980)
De l'écologie à l'autonomie, with Daniel Cohn-Bendit (1981)
Domaines de l'homme: Les Carrefours du labyrinthe II (1986)
Mai 68: La Brèche suivi de Vingt ans après, with Edgar Morin and Claude Lefort (1988)
Le Monde Morcelé: Les Carrefours du labyrinthe III (1990)
La Société bureaucratique, 2d ed. revised (1990)

Index